Logic

The Library of Liberal Arts

IMMANUEL KANT

Translated,
with an introduction,
by ROBERT S. HARTMAN
and WOLFGANG SCHWARZ

Logic

THE LIBRARY OF LIBERAL ARTS
published by
The Bobbs-Merrill Company, Inc.
Indianapolis and New York

IMMANUEL KANT
1724-1804

His *Logic* was first published in 1800
in an edition by Gottlob Benjamin Jäsche

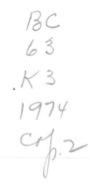
Copyright © 1974 by The Bobbs-Merrill Company, Inc.
Printed in the United States of America
First Printing
Design: Starr Atkinson

Library of Congress Cataloging in Publication Data
Kant, Immanuel, 1724–1804.
Logic.
(The library of liberal arts)
Includes bibliographical references.
1. Logic—Early works to 1800. I. Title.
BC63.K3 1973   160   72–10560
ISBN 0–672–51434–6
ISBN 0–672–61228–3 (pbk.)

Contents

Immanuel Kant's Logic

Note on the Translation

This is the first complete English translation of Jäsche's edition of Kant's *Logic*, published in 1800 by Friedrich Nicolovius in Königsberg (Kaliningrad today). Three other prints appeared during Kant's lifetime. For our translation we used a copy of the first edition of 1800 (Warda's bibliography No. 207), and to this edition we refer in the notes when quoting a German word or phrase. We did not find it necessary to refer to other editions. The sectional and paragraph structure of the work makes the locating of references an easy task. Max Heinze, the editor of the *Logic* in the Academy edition,[1] reports that some copies of the first edition have a glued-in extra leaf listing printer's errors. Our copy did not have this extra leaf. Three of the "errata" as reported by the Academy edition relate to passages of some roughness of style rather than to errors (one an anacoluthon). These passages, the meaning of which is never doubtful, become naturally smoothed out in a translation. The fourth instance gives a very minor and inconsequential variation of meaning which we have adopted, footnoting the original version. Two other really doubtful passages, which one would hope to have cleared up perhaps as printer's errors, are not included in the list mentioned by Heinze. We are commenting on them in our notes. On the whole, the small number and the nature of the aforementioned "printer's errors" indicate that the text of

1. *Kants gesammelte Schriften,* edited by the Königliche Preussische Akademie der Wissenschaften (Berlin and Leipzig: Walter de Gruyter and Co., 1923), Vol. IX, pp. 1–150. Also see *Kants Werke,* Akademie-Textausgabe (Berlin: Walter de Gruyter and Co., 1968).

the original is of good quality. The Academy edition, in the main, lists variants of other editions that followed the first.

In his text of the *Logic*, Jäsche surely wanted to show how far the Kantian notions of co-division and subdivision were applicable. In the Introduction, he does not number paragraphs, but often separates them by a straight line. Within these paragraphs, specific determinations introduced under a governing statement are often numbered. The text of the one hundred and twenty paragraphs of the *Logic* itself abounds with Notes. Many words, particularly the terms of dichotomies, are emphasized in the original by spacing. In these arrangements our translation follows the edition we had before us, except that italics have been used for the spaced words of the original and that the straight lines between paragraphs of the Introduction have been dropped. They do not always conform to the various subjects of the sectional headings. In a few instances, emphasis by spacing of the key words in comparisons or oppositions is incomplete in the original. We have added it (italics) where parallelism or symmetry clearly required it for a particular word, without footnoting the addition of such an emphasis, since the text itself points to it.

All example sentences have been italicized in the translation, to distinguish them from the argument of the Introduction or the formal determinations of the *Logic* itself. The original edition does not distinguish the examples by different type. The sentence-by-sentence structure of the original text has been retained, following quite literally Kant-Jäsche's excellent German. (This, however, does not apply to Jäsche's own somewhat wordy preface.)

We have omitted the Latin translation of technical terms—which, in the original, follows the German term in parentheses—whenever, in an English translation, it would be a mere repetition of the English word except for a Latin ending, e.g. universal (*universalis*), pure (*purus*).

As to punctuation, we have changed many semicolons into commas, but otherwise—subject to English rules, of course—have retained whatever could be incorporated into a modern

English text. In the case of colons, rather freely used by Jäsche, we have adhered more closely to modern habits and changed many into commas. Jäsche carries his flair for divisions deep into the development of the Introduction by frequent use of dashes between sentences. In agreement with the usage of his time, the dashes often designate the introduction of a causal clause or simply the separation of different coordinated thoughts under a general topic. We believed that a more continuous text would be more adequate for modern readers and have therefore not reproduced the great majority of these dashes. Nevertheless these punctuations are further evidence that Jäsche—contrary to common judgment—applied great care to his text.

No attempt has been made to dress up the linguistic appearance of Kant-Jäsche's *Logic* in modern logical terminology. Which one should we have chosen? Any such attempt would quickly have led to insoluble incongruencies. In our opinion, the work represents a historical formulation of general logic which has its lasting value beyond the service it provided in its time in the clarification of the logical underpinnings of the *Critique of Pure Reason,* as will be explained in our Introduction. If it were not able to stand up in its original form, it would not deserve our attention at all.

The introduction of the work has previously been translated into English by T. K. Abbott (reprinted by the Philosophical Library, New York, 1963). Apart from it being an introduction without the introduced and without Jäsche's own preface, Abbott takes liberties with the original such as have earned Kant in some discerning quarters the reputation of being subtle without always being consistent. Abbott, for example, translates *Erkenntnis* and *Kenntnisse* by "knowledge." When he comes to *Wissen,* he must again use "knowledge," which blurs important distinctions. On page 4 of his translation he switches for once to "cognition" for *Erkenntnis* when rendering *Selbsterkenntnis:* "self cognition of the understanding and the reason." He should always have stayed with "cognition" for *Erkenntnis.* Even Abbott, generally a man of a fairly good understanding of what he translates, occasionally succumbs to the confusion between

Erscheinung, "appearance," and *Schein,* "semblance," or "illusion." On page 19 he says, in reference to the Eleatic school: "In the senses is delusion and appearance," where the original runs: *in den Sinnen ist Täuschung und Schein,* "in the senses is deception and illusion." "Appearance" in this context is quite misleading and should be retained, in Kantian texts, for *Erscheinung.* (The meaning of "phenomenon," Kant's *Phänomen,* is not the same as that of "appearance"—cf. A 248). Another serious shortcoming of Abbott's translation is his vacillation between "concept" and "conception"—in a book on logic!

For all recurring key expressions in the original we have retained identical words in the translation. This rule, which unfortunately requires mentioning in view of the practices of some existing translations, has been followed even for systematically less important terms and, wherever possible, even down to particles. In this respect we may say that we have translated like a computer would translate while avoiding the pitfalls, we hope, of mechanization. The word *Schein,* for example, seems rendered best in most passages by "semblance," and yet "illusion" appears indicated in two or three places as above. On the other hand, when the reader sees "in respect of," "in respect to," and "in regard to," he looks at variations, minor though they are, that follow corresponding differences in the original.

While careless use of one English word such as "knowledge" for several German expressions and meanings blurs clarity and distinction and creates difficulties where there are none in the original, the opposite is true when a German word has no English counterpart covering all its applications. Available English words are specific, the German word is more general. The most troublesome case in point is undoubtedly the German word *allgemein,* for which an English translation has always to choose between "universal" and "general." Others are *wenn* ("if" or "when"), *Grund* ("reason" or "ground"). A helpful rule in deciding a good many cases of this kind may be that the first word in the pairs of words mentioned (and definitely "if") is preferable in a formal logical context, while the second is applicable to a context relating to real conditions. In the paragraphs of the *Logic* itself that deal with concepts, we have rendered their property of *Allgemeinheit* or being *allgemein* by "generality" and "general," respectively. In the paragraphs on judgments, we have used "universality" or "universal." Otherwise we have adopted the aforementioned rule whenever possible, without claiming to offer more than approximations to the original. The reader can always try, in the above-mentioned three instances, whether substitution of the alternative will yield a better sense than our choice.

Several decisions affecting the text throughout had to be made. Obviously we translate *Satz* by "proposition" rather than "sentence" except when there is a reference to grammar rather than logic. The "extension," the *Umfang* of concepts, in many paragraphs, is called their *Sphäre*. We saw no reason for shunning "sphere," for, though metaphorical, in the context the word is usually an explicative device rather than a technical term. Once *Umfang* is translated as "extension," it is only consistent to translate *Inhalt* by "intension" (rather than "content") where the correlative of extension is meant.

Speaking of concepts, we have given preference to "characteristic" for *Merkmal* over "attribute" or "property." We have reserved "attribute" for cases where Kant-Jäsche speak of *Attribut*. "Presentation" is preferable, in Kantian contexts, to "representation," *repraesentatio* notwithstanding. As is common in English translations, we have rendered Kant's *Anschauung* by "intuition," short of knowing a better word that would be generally acceptable. In a logic, the term cannot play a key role, but it is nevertheless frequently used in contrast to concepts, e.g. § 1 of the actual logic defines *Anschauung* as a "singular presentation" (*repraesentatio singularis*) compared with the general presentation of a concept. "By means of sensibility objects are given to us, and it alone furnishes us intuitions [*Anschauungen*]," says Kant in the *Critique of Pure Reason* (B 33) in an epistemological context. [Cf. the *Shorter Oxford English Dictionary* (1934): "5.Mod.Philos. . . . . c. Immediate apprehension by sense."]

We have resisted translating *gemeiner Verstand* by "common

sense" and rather said "common understanding." The English expression "common sense" is freighted with so many associations, popular or scholarly, that "common understanding" seemed preferable, all the more so since it retains the specific meaning of *gemeiner Verstand*.

Every translator of Kantian writings is confronted with the difficulty of rendering his frequently used particle *überhaupt* (also *überall*) by an adequate English word. There is no single one serving the purpose. The closest English paraphrase may be "at all," which has the disadvantage of being restricted to negative or conditional clauses. Other expressions that may serve to cover the meaning of Kant's *überhaupt* (literally "over head") would be "in general," "unrestrictedly," "in greatest abstractness," "absolutely," "over-all," "regardless of specifics," "as such," "in themselves," etc. Any English paraphrase of *überhaupt* often solves one translating problem only by creating another. We have sometimes rendered *überhaupt* by the Latin word "generatim"—analogous to "verbatim," "seriatim," "literatim"—which has the advantage of expressing, depending on the context, the primary meaning of *überhaupt,* i.e. "in general," as well as other secondary developments of this meaning, and of permitting easy assimilation into an English text. As always, it seemed advisable not to be more specific in the translation than the author himself, since greater specificness would amount to interpretation rather than translation, if not deviation from the text. As to interpretation, the reader's judgment may be as good as, or better than, ours.

The foregoing rules have also been applied by us in translating passages from Kant's other writings (including the *Reflections*) to which we refer in our Introduction or in the notes to the translation. In view of the very uneven quality of existing English translations of Kant's works, these translations were necessary in order to retain consistency of terminology in Kantian formulations.

All in all, the following text of Jäsche's edition of Kant's *Logic* is to our knowledge the closest English translation of any Kantian text. In retaining the sentence-by-sentence structure it goes beyond the translation of the *Prolegomena* by Lucas, with whom we agree in our translating principles.

> *Robert S. Hartman*
> *Wolfgang Schwarz*

February 1972
Cuernavaca, Mexico
Hamilton, Canada

Abbreviations

A   with page number   first (1781)   edition of the
B   refers to   second (1786)   *Critique of Pure Reason.*

[ ]   marks insertion by the translators.

*   marks the only two footnotes in the original text, appended to Section IX of the Introduction. All numbered footnotes are by the present editors.

Four-digit Arabic numbers in footnotes   refer to the numbers of "Reflections," Kant's annotations in his copy of G. Fr. Meier's *Auszug aus der Vernunftlehre* (Halle: J. J. Gebauer, 1752), as published in *Kants Gesammelte Schriften,* the Akademie edition (see below), Vol. XVI (1924).

Akad.   followed by volume and page numbers, refers to the standard edition of Kant's works: *Kants gesammelte Schriften,* edited by the Königliche Preussische Akademie der Wissenschaften, 23 vols. (Berlin and Leipzig: Walter de Gruyter and Co., 1900–1956).

Translators' Introduction

I. The Significance of Kant's Logic

The importance of Kant's *Logic* has never been fully appreciated. This is one of the reasons why this work, published in 1800, is only now appearing in a complete English translation. Its importance lies not only in its significance for the *Critique of Pure Reason,* the second part of which is a restatement of fundamental tenets of the *Logic,* but in its position within the whole of Kant's work.

The second part of the *Critique,* the Transcendental Doctrine of Method, is the framework within which the *Critique* must be understood. It defines the distinction between philosophy and science which, in metaphysics, is "the business" of the *Critique.*[1] Kant himself underlined the importance of the Methodology by the division of the *Critique* into two parts, the Doctrine of Elements and the Doctrine of Method. Few scholars have bothered to take Part Two seriously, even though it presents the methodology within which the elements of pure reason have their place. It is, so to speak, the meta-critique explaining the purpose of the *Critique* and the terms it uses. As a result, if one does not take into consideration the meanings of fundamental terms as found in the Methodology and in greater detail in the *Logic,* one flounders in his understanding of the *Critique.*

Consider, for example, the various meanings of "analytic" and "synthetic" in Kant's distinction of analytic and synthetic

1. *Critique of Pure Reason,* B xxii.

concept as against analytic and synthetic *judgment*. From the
Methodology and the *Logic* it becomes clear that both analytic
and synthetic judgments contain primarily analytic concepts;
and synthetic a priori judgments, synthetic concepts only. Each
kind of judgment belongs to its own kind of method, the analytic and the synthetic method, respectively. Once this is understood and the basic difference between analytic judgment and
synthetic a priori judgment comprehended, it is impossible to
identify mathematical judgments, such as "5 + 7 = 12," with
analytic ones, such as "All bachelors are unmarried," and to do
so in the Kantian sense of "analytic." The many sins against Kant
committed in this respect, in particular by Anglo-Saxon philosophers, arise in part from ignorance of the texts mentioned.[2] Kant
was a *systematic* philosopher who abhorred "rhapsodies" and
"false subtleties" in philosophy and would not honor these by
the name of "analytic." He regarded as the true method of metaphysics the one "Newton introduced into the natural sciences"[3]
and never wavered in his determination to transform philosophies—metaphysics, ethics—into sciences. His use of terms was
strict and consistent, and thoroughly explained. Misunderstand-
ings in this respect are excusable only by the unavailability of
sources—a shortcoming we hope to have partly relieved by this
translation.

That the Transcendental Doctrine of Method is so short, de-
spite its fundamental significance both for Kant's work as a
whole and for the *Critique of Pure Reason,* is explained precisely in the fact that it is a distillation of the *Logic,* and as such
was common knowledge to the philosophical profession in
Kant's time. Kant read the *Logic,* often twice a year, for over forty
years, from 1755 to 1796, and based it on a well-known textbook, G. Fr. Meier's *Auszug aus der Vernunftlehre* (though at
the end of Kant's course, not much survived of this text). Kant's

2. There is, however, no excuse for the caricatures of Kant found in German positivists, e.g. Hans Reichenbach's *The Rise of Scientific Philosophy*
(Berkeley and Los Angeles: University of California Press, 1951).

3. *Inquiry on the Distinctness of the Principles of Natural Theology and
Morality,* Second Consideration; *Critique* A xi, B x ff., xxii, 741.

own *Logic*, Jäsche tells us, set the trend for textbook writers of his age. Jäsche's text of Kant's *Logic* is of 1782 and thus belongs to the critical period, even though some fundamental tenets, such as the a priori character of aesthetic judgment, are not yet recognized. But the *Critique of Pure Reason* had already been published, and in Kant's mind the whole of what we call Critique was no more than equal to the methodology, that is the *Logic*. Kant's *Logic* may thus be seen as the matrix of which the methodology of the *Critique* is an excerpt and without which the *Critique* itself, that is the Doctrine of Elements, consisting of Transcendental Aesthetic and Transcendental Logic, the latter in turn of Transcendental Analytic and Transcendental Dialectic, would lack its terminological and material framework. Most of the subjects discussed in the *Critique* can be found in the *Logic*.

But there is even more to the *Logic*. Because Kant read it for so many years during which he developed his system, it gives us many insights into his work aside from the *Critique of Pure Reason*. In this respect, the *Logic* is an introduction to Kant's system. Nowhere does Kant specifically set down the fundamentals of both his critical and practical philosophy; but his Logic lectures developed into such an introduction. One will find in this book a transcendental critique, a moral philosophy, a rational theology, a history of philosophy, even an anthropology, all rolled into one—beside, of course, a masterful introduction into the logic of his time. The *Logic*, thus, is like the hub of a wheel, with the spokes going in all directions, showing us the structure of the total system. It is a unique and amazingly rich presentation not only of Kant's theoretical and practical but even of his aesthetic philosophy, with many details of the Critiques put into a new and illuminating light. In order to make these connections clear, we have given references to the Critiques and others of Kant's works, as elicited by the text.

The emphasis, of course, is on the *Critique of Pure Reason*; for what we have is an introduction to logic based on the objective unity of consciousness of the manifold in cognition—a logic, that is, based on the transcendental apperception. We thus have a general logic embedded in a transcendental matrix;

but we also have a transcendental logic embedded in a matrix of general logic.

Its relevance for the *Critique of Pure Reason* is the most important feature of this logic—or, to be more exact, its relevance for the distinction between philosophy and science which, as was mentioned, is Kant's basic concern in the *Critique*. "In that attempt to alter the old procedure of metaphysics, and that is to say, by revolutionizing it after the example of the geometers and natural scientists, consists the business of this critique of pure speculative reason."[4] The *Critique*, for Kant, is a treatise on scientific method.[5] The metaphysics of natural science stands, in Kant's mind, above natural science, just as the metaphysics of morals stands above moral science. The logic of scientific discovery, indeed, of discovering science, is that of the analytic-synthetic method; and it is this logic which Kant condenses in the Methodology of the *Critique* and elaborates in the *Logic*. The *Logic*, thus, is the indispensable background of the *Critique*.

In dealing with the difference between science and philosophy in a precise and detailed manner, the *Logic* is useful beyond the limits of the *Critique of Pure Reason*. To all those who are interested in the foundations of science, or those few who are themselves endeavoring to transform an intellectual discipline that is still in its philosophical stage (such as some of the humanities and social disciplines) into an exact science, a thorough knowledge of the Kantian difference between philosophy and science is indispensable. Indeed, without Kant's logic it is impossible to discover *that* these disciplines are still philosophies rather than sciences—and hence, from the scientific point of view, are no more developed than was alchemy in relation to chemistry or astrology in relation to astronomy—comparisons Kant himself was fond of. It is impossible to discover the unscientific stage of a discipline as long as one stands within the discipline and does not move into the corresponding metaphysics or critique, and, indeed, beyond the latter, into the meta-

4. B xxii.
5. *Ibid.*

critique, which is the critique of philosophy and science themselves. Which sociologist, psychologist, or political scientist
today would *deny* the scientific character of his discipline? But
which Kantian scholar of philosophy and science would possibly
assert this character? These disciplines are not sciences, they
are philosophies.

Philosophy, according to Kant, makes concepts given in everyday discourse analytically distinct and articulates the notes or
predicates of conceptual intensions or contents. Science, on the
other hand, interrelates synthetically concepts not given but
made, *the definitions of which are at the same time the constructions of the corresponding objects.* The latter process is expressed in symbols or signs, arrived at in formal intuition; the
former takes place in words of everyday language, whose meanings are arrived at in abstraction from empirical intuition. Science is schematic, philosophy categorial; schemata are constructed, categories abstracted. The logic ruling philosophy is
general or formal logic, that ruling science is transcendental
logic. Formal logic shows how to clarify concepts, transcendental logic how to construct objects.[6]

These Kantian distinctions are perfectly clear, yet they are
not found in either the transcendental analytic or dialectic but
in the *Logic* and the Transcendental Doctrine of Method. The
neglect of the logical distinction between philosophy and science is the reason for most of the confusions today in the dis-
cussions on the nature of science, especially the confusion between its empirical content and its synthetic a priori form. The
true method of metaphysics, we remember, is "at bottom the
one Newton introduced into the natural sciences"; and this is
the method of analysis and synthesis.

In this respect, Kant's *Logic* may actually be more relevant for
today's science and philosophy than the *Critique* itself is. For,
whereas it is incorrect to state that the details of the method of
analysis and synthesis as found in the deductions of the *Critique*
are still applicable today, it is correct to state a weaker thesis,

6. Below, p. 69.

"the thesis, namely, that categories and synthetic principles a priori are indispensable for science."[7] The *Logic* gives, precisely, the synthetic a priori without the categories of the *Critique*, that is, it presents the pure method of which the *Critique* is a specific case. Thus all the objections directed against the details of the *Critique* are irrelevant for the *Logic*; what counts is the nature of science as based on categories and synthetic principles a priori. Kant, in the *Logic*, shows what science is as against philosophy, rather than what natural science is as against natural philosophy. In the solution of this general problem he is, and will forever be, correct; and

> from this correctness follows the incorrectness both of the posi-
> tivistic as of the rationalistic philosophy of mathematics and natural
> sciences, since both deny the possibility of synthetic principles a
> priori. The axioms of mathematics are not, as Hume and Leibniz
> believed, analytical, and natural science cannot do without theo-
> retical concepts, that is concepts a priori, nor without theoretical
> propositions, that is synthetic principles a priori—as even most
> modern positivists concede.[8]

Beside this methodological meaning within the Kantian system, Kant's logic has a historical significance, being an intermediary between the logic of Port Royal and the logic of the sciences, or between general logic and transcendental logic. It stands at the end of a development that began with Descartes, was continued by Leibniz, and culminated in the Methodology of the *Critique of Pure Reason*, being applied to natural science in the first part of the *Critique*.

We can still learn a great deal from the *Logic*. The time will certainly come in philosophy when the one-sided emphasis on symbolic manipulations will be overcome and logic will be seen in its totality. Compared to a textbook in symbolic logic the Kantian *Logic* shows a marvellous philosophical richness. In par-

---

7. Stephan Körner, "Zur kantischen Begründung der Mathematik und der Naturwissenschaften," *Kant-Studien,* LVI (1966) Heft 3–4, p. 473. Also see Ernst Cassirer, *The Problem of Knowledge* (New Haven: Yale University Press, 1950), pp. 74 ff.

8. Körner, *ibid.*

ticular, we find fully treated here the fundamental concept of any logic, the concept of concept, which cannot be found in a modern text on symbolic logic—just as one cannot find the concept of psyche in a modern psychology text. But just as a renaissance has set in in psychology, and new and relevant psychologies—humanistic, existential, transpersonal—have recovered the old meaning of that term, so will there be a philosophical renaissance in logic recovering the old meaning of that discipline. A fresh and yet classical logic text such as this may help this development. Logic here is neither mutilated nor overextended. The pretensions of modern logic, such as its simplification of existence into a sign or the extension of a sign into metaphysics,[9] are foreign to it. Kant is not a positivist; he will not tailor philosophical outlook to one of consonance with logic. He will enrich logic if it is to be made relevant to an enlarged field; and this is the opposite of the positivistic procedure.[10]

In his *Nachricht von der Einrichtung seiner Vorlesungen in dem Winterhalbenjahre von 1765–1766* Kant says that there are two kinds of logic, the first being "a critique of, and prescription for, common understanding, which on the one hand borders on crude concepts and ignorance and on the other hand borders on science and erudition. A logic of this kind must precede all academic instruction of philosophy. It is, if I may say so, the quarantine to be observed by the apprentice who intends to proceed from the land of prejudice and error to the domain of a more enlightened reason and the sciences." The second kind of logic is an organon of sciences; its presentation follows attainments in particular sciences. Thus, at the end of the Metaphysics course he adds a consideration of the peculiar method of metaphysics as an organon of that science. In the Logic course "I shall present

9. See pp. lxxxvi, 24, 38. Cf. Paul Weingartner, "Der Begriff der Existenz in Russells Theorie der Deskription," *Deskription, Analyzität und Existenz* (Salzburg-München: Anton Pustet, 1966), pp. 84–85.

10. Cf. Henry S. Leonard, "The Logic of Existence," *Philosophical Studies*, VII, 4, p. 64; Robert S. Hartman, *The Structure of Value* (Carbondale: So. Illinois University Press, 1969), pp. 64–65.

the logic of the first kind, following the manual of Professor Meier, because he well observes the limits of the said intentions." When the *Critique of Reason* is treated, "the close relationship of the subject matter provides an occasion to pay some attention to the *Critique of Taste,* that is, *aesthetics,* the rules of one always serving to explain those of the other and their contrast being a means of a better comprehension of both." The complete logic is a critique and prescription of "the total of world wisdom," that is, of philosophy as a whole, and this, says Kant, "can have its place in education only at the end of all philosophy. For only when we have acquired knowledge of it and of the history of human opinions will we be able to reflect on the origin of both insights and errors and to design the exact plan on which such an edifice of reason can be constructed with durable regularity."[11] There is in logic itself an architectonic— and this architectonic is that of Kant's own system. Our text is a small part of this grand design but a part that, like a Cartesian simple, contains the whole within it.

II. Analysis and Synthesis in General Logic

Analysis and synthesis play a double role in Kant's work, one in general logic and one in transcendental logic. In general logic they serve as stages in the process of intensional clarification, in transcendental logic as mechanisms for constructing objects. We shall examine the first role in this section and the second role in the next.

The subject of general logic, according to Kant, is "to make clear concepts distinct." The concepts here meant are analytic concepts, those of everyday discourse. They are clear when their meanings are unmistakable, and distinct when the details of these meanings, the notes of the conceptual contents, are fully

11. *Inquiry,* Akad. II, 310 f.

determined. The subject of logic, in other words, is to clarify intensions.[12]

Analysis and synthesis play a fundamental role in this process of intensional clarification. It is, in the *Logic,* a definite and precise process of thought, leading from the description of a state of affairs to the definition of a concept. The distinction between the analytic and the synthetic judgment is the means by which this process is carried out.

1. Analytic of Concepts

It is imperative for our understanding of the subject of logic to distinguish between Kant's doctrine of the analytic and synthetic *judgment* on the one hand, and his doctrine of the analytic and synthetic *method* and the analytic and synthetic *concept* on the other. Historically, his distinction of the judgments arose from his distinctions of the methods.[13] Once he had found the former he abandoned the latter, except for occasional references in his critical writings. For his critical philosophy the methods were of relatively small importance, and it may be held that for this reason he failed to develop them in detail. On the other hand, it is equally true that throughout his teaching career, from 1755 to 1796, he taught the methods in his Logic course. They were, thus, constantly before his mind.

The main business of logic, to repeat, is *"to make clear concepts distinct."*[14] Accordingly, he establishes what may be called a hierarchy of clarities. "The first level . . . of a perfection of our cognition as to quality is its clarity. A second level, or a higher degree of clarity, is *distinctness*. This consists in the *clarity* of *characteristics*."[15] The first stage in the "perfection of our cognition" consists in the clarity of the concept, the second stage in

12. Below, p. 69.
13. Vaihinger, *Commentar zu Kants Kritik der reinen Vernunft* (Stuttgart, 1881), I, 272 ff., 412 ff.
14. Below, p. 69.
15. Below, pp. 67 f.

the clarity of the attributes contained in it.[16] The first stage, the clarity of the concept, is, at the same time, clarity about the thing conceived in the concept. All cognition of things is by means of concepts, that is, by means of attributes or characteristics.

> Human cognition on the side of the understanding is *discursive*, that is, it takes place through presentations that make what is common to several things the ground of cognition, thus through *characteristics* as such. We thus cognize things only *through characteristics;* and this means precisely *cognizing,* . . . which comes from . . . being cognizant.
> A *characteristic is that in a thing which makes up part of its cognition,* or—which is the same—a *partial presentation so far as it is considered as cognitive ground of the whole presentation.* All our *concepts* therefore are characteristics and all *thinking* is nothing but a presenting through characteristics.[17]

The first conception of a thing is *relatively* clear; unless it were at least to some degree clear it would not be the conception of one thing rather than another. But it is not clear enough to give all the characteristics of the thing. The ultimate clearness of the characteristics, at first only vaguely conceived, is the *distinctness* of the concept. To bring this about, is, precisely, "the business of logic." Clarity, we may say, is an extensional, distinctness an intensional characteristic of concepts.

"The question, then, is: in what manner does it [logic] make them [the concepts] distinct?" Kant states two alternative methods of clarifying concepts. There is synthetic and analytic distinctness, characterized by the two alternatives: "*to make a distinct concept,* and *to make a concept distinct.*"[18]

> When I make a distinct concept, I begin with the parts and proceed from these to the whole. There are no characteristics present here; I obtain them first by synthesis. From this synthetic procedure then results synthetic distinctness, which actually expands my concept as to content by what is added as a characteristic *over and above* the

---

16. Cf. Konrad Marc-Wogau, "Kants Lehre vom analytischen Urteil," *Theoria*, XVII (1951), 148. English summary in *Philosophical Quarterly*, III, No. 12 (July 1953), p. 263.

17. Below, pp. 63 f.

18. Below, p. 69.

concept in intuition (pure or empirical). This synthetic procedure in making distinct concepts is employed by the mathematician and also by the philosopher of nature. For all distinctness of mathematical as well as of experiential cognition rests on expansion through synthesis of characteristics.

But when I make a concept distinct, then my cognition does not in the least increase in its content by this mere analysis. The content remains the same, only the form is changed, in that I learn to distinguish better or with greater clarity of consciousness what already was lying in the given concept. Just as by the mere illumination of a map nothing is added to it, so by the mere elucidation of a given concept by means of analysis of its characteristics no augmentation is made to this concept itself in the least.[19]

Yet, it is the analytic procedure which is the sole business of logic. "The analytic method to produce distinctness, with which alone logic can concern itself, is the first and principal requirement in making our cognition distinct. For the more distinct our cognition of a thing is, the stronger and more effective it can be."[20] The process of clarification, therefore, is the essential process of logic, both as a method of elementary and of systematic thought.

Just as the doctrine of elements in logic has the elements and conditions of the perfection of a cognition as its content, so on the other hand the general doctrine of method, as the second part of logic, has to deal with the form of a science as such, or with the manner of connecting the manifold of cognition into a science.

The doctrine of method is to put forward the manner of attaining perfection of cognition. Now, one of the most essential logical perfections of cognition consists in distinctness, in thoroughness, and in its systematic arrangement into the whole of a science. Accordingly, the doctrine of method will primarily have to state the means of furthering these perfections of cognition.[21]

These means are *exposition* and *definition*—as means of the clarification of concepts.

19. Below, p. 70.
20. *Ibid.*
21. Below, §§ 96, 97.

> Distinctness of cognitions and joining them into a systematic whole depends on distinctness of concepts both in respect of what is contained *in* them and in regard to what is contained *under* them.
>
> The distinct consciousness of the *content* of concepts is furthered by their *exposition* and *definition;* the distinct consciousness, however, of their *extension,* by their *logical division.*[22]

Kant turns first to definition. Definition is the result of the process of clarifying the concept. "A definition is a sufficiently distinct and delimited [precise] concept (*conceptus rei adaequatus in minimis terminis, complete determinatus*)."[23] It is, in other words, the concept spelled out and completely determined in a minimum of terms. The definition alone is the logically complete concept.

Definitions are either synthetic or analytic. The former are the definitions of "made" or invented concepts, the latter are those of given concepts. Both, made and given concepts, may be made or given either *a priori* or *a posteriori*. The synthesis of made concepts is either *exposition of intuitions* or *construction*. The former is the synthesis of empirical concepts, which adds to a simple empirical concept more and more of its properties given through intuition; the latter is the synthesis of arbitrarily invented concepts, such as those of mathematics. The former can never lead to definition; the latter is identical with synthetic definition. "Since the synthesis of empirical concepts is not arbitrary but empirical and as such can never be complete (for in experience ever new characteristics of the concept can be discovered), empirical concepts cannot be defined."[24] Empirical synthetic definitions are, thus, impossible. Arbitrarily invented concepts, on the other hand, not only *can* be defined, their declaration *is* definition. These concepts do not precede the definition, and the definition, therefore, is not their clarification, but they rise *together with the definition*. "Such definitions . . . could also be called *declarations,* since in them one declares

22. Below, § 98.
23. Below, § 99.
24. Below, § 103.

one's thoughts or renders account of what one understands by a word. This is the case with mathematicians."[25]

Given concepts, on the other hand, whether given a priori, such as the concept of substance, or a posteriori, such as the concept of water, "can only be defined through *analysis*. For given concepts can only be made distinct *by making their characteristics successively clear.*"[26] In other words, the procedure by which a given concept can be made distinct is to attend successively to all the characteristics contained in the concept and at first only vaguely conceived in it, arranging them one by one —as predicates of judgments—and finally to select those which are most essential, for admission into the definition.

> If *all* characteristics of a given concept are made clear, the concept becomes *completely* distinct; and if it does not contain too many characteristics, it is at the same time precise, and from this springs a definition of the concept. . . . [But] since one cannot become certain by any proof whether all characteristics of a given concept have been exhausted by complete analysis, all analytic definitions must be held to be uncertain.[27]

Thus, synthetic empirical definitions are impossible and analytic definitions are uncertain. The only kind of definitions that are logically both definite and certain are constructive, synthetic definitions. Analytic definitions can only be approximate, and these approximations to definitions Kant calls *expositions* and *descriptions*. "Not all concepts can, but also not all need to be defined. There are [however] approximations to the definition of certain concepts; these are partly *expositions* . . . , partly *descriptions*."[28] The exposition of a concept—as against the exposition of intuitions—consists in the successive representation of its characteristics insofar as these have been found through analysis. Exposition, as approximation to the definition of a given concept, may be regarded as part of the definition of

---

25. *Ibid.*, Mathematicians explain in words what they mean by a sign.
26. Below, § 104. Last italics added.
27. *Ibid.*
28. Below, § 105.

such a concept, or as a phase of it, if definition means the process toward complete clarification of the concept.

As it is not always possible to make an analysis complete, and as, in general, an analysis must be incomplete before it becomes complete, an incomplete exposition as part of a definition is a true and useful exhibition of a concept. Here the definition remains the idea only of a logical perfection we must seek to attain.[29] Definition, then, for given concepts, is a goal which we asymptotically approach.

So far we have dealt with concept, exposition, and definition. There remains description. "Description can take place only with empirically given concepts. It has no definite rules and contains only materials for definition."[30] It is, then, a more or less helter-skelter assembly of the various characteristics of a thing, arranged in no particular order, which precedes exposition. It is exposition, but not yet precise, that is, "measured."[31] The concept has not yet, as it were, staked out the realm of characteristics of the thing which it wants to claim as its own. But this means that the concept either is not yet, or has only just been, applied. Description corresponds to primary cognitional representations of the thing. It gathers, without any rule, the raw material out of which first exposition and then definition are to be produced.

The hierarchy of clarification, then, for empirically given concepts, that is, for concepts of empirically given things, is Description, Exposition, and Definition. Kant does not tell us how, in detail, description arises out of the first impression of the thing, and how exposition arises out of description, and definition out of exposition. He does, however, give us "Rules for Preparing Definitions."[32] They are (1) to seek true propositions, that is, propositions that are true of the thing to be defined, (2) to look for propositions whose predicates do not already presuppose the concept of the thing, (3) to assemble a number of these propositions and compare them with the concept of the thing to see

29. Cf. *ibid.*
30. *Ibid.*
31. Below, p. 69.
32. Below, § 109.

whether they are adequate to it, that is, make the concept complete and precise, and (4) to see that no predicate is contained in, or subordinate to, any other.

These are rules for the selection of those predicates of expositions which are ultimately to be admitted into the definition. The most important rule is (3), which requires that from the totality of all analytic judgments to which the exposition gives rise, some be assembled and compared with the concept of the thing. If the predicates of these judgments fit the concept—which by that time must be sufficiently clarified to be compared with a subset of the total set of all its analytic predicates—then these predicates, supposing that the other three conditions are fulfilled, may be admitted into the definition.

But the rules do not tell us anything about the role of the concept in the description. On the contrary, description, Kant tells us, has no rules at all. This raises a number of questions. How is description possible without any rule at all when it is description at least of something? This, it seems, presupposes at least so much of a rule that a *certain* set of impressions, a *certain* thing is to be described. Again, how can it be an "exposition," namely, of a concept, even if ever so imprecise, if there is no rule at all? This would mean no concept either. It seems that we must say that description has at least one rule, namely, to describe at least a certain, if ever so vague, experience. The experience, if ever so vague, must be the rule of the description. The question then is only whether or not to call this experience, as rule, an incipient concept. If it is called a concept, then the judgments making up the description would all be analytic, for their predicates would all be contained in this vague concept; however, its content is yet entirely undetermined, and hence anything that is experienced would be contained in it. If, on the other hand, we do *not* call this first rule a concept, for the reason that this rule of description refers merely to a general appearance but gives no rule whatsoever for its properties—since it refers without any rule to the set of *all* the properties of something that appears in intuition—then all descriptive judgments would be synthetic.

It is indeed questionable whether there can be a concept at

all as long as nothing whatsoever is determined about its content. Judgments about a thing thus conceived, it may be held,
must all be synthetic. For if no rule has as yet been established
as to what is to be contained in a concept, or none is at all
establishable, then judgments about it cannot possibly be analytic. On the other hand, as we have just seen, they may be
called analytic for this very reason, if the vague rule is called a
concept. And even if it is not, the *descriptive judgments may yet
be called analytic,* not with respect to the concept but with respect to the vague rule, *even though it is experience itself.* In
Kant's logic, the distinction between an experience and a concept at the beginning of inquiry is that between the exposition
of an experience and the exposition of a concept. The former
proceeds by synthesis, the latter by analysis.[33] The result of empirical synthesis, we must assume, is empirically given concepts,
and with these begins the exposition of concepts. The exposition
of experience overlaps largely with description, the latter being
"the exposition of a concept so far as it is not precise."[34] Its rule
proceeds from experience to concept through the intermediary
stage of the name of the thing, which "is meant to be a *designation* only and not a concept of the matter."[35] This concept appears as a result of "experiments," *Versuche,*[36] that is, of synthetic exposition. With the appearance of the concept of the
thing, that is, a given empirical concept, analytic exposition can
begin and the difficulties are resolved: it now becomes clear
which predicates are contained in the concept and which are
not. Those predicates that are analytic are lined up by the exposition in successive judgments for inspection as to their fitting-
ness to serve in the definition. From them the final set is selected
which makes up the definition, as the minimum set of predicates
which make the concept both *complete* and *precise.* The definition combines these predicates with the concept of the thing,
not like a judgment, as predicates of a subject, but in its own

33. Cf. below, § 105.
34. *Ibid.*
35. B 756.
36. *Ibid.*

manner, as definiens of a definiendum. Whatever the process may be in detail—and it is our task to find this out—Kant's account makes clear that it is a *movement of thought* from experience of a thing to its definition.

So much for the process of *clarification,* as determination of the *content* of concepts. Kant then turns to the process of *classification,* as determination of the *extension* of concepts—their *Einteilung* rather than their *Teilung* (or analysis.)[37] This classification may be of concepts individually or of concepts collectively, that is, combined in methods. In the classification of methods we find one kind especially, the analytic and synthetic method, which refers to classification of concepts as complex or simple. The analytic method begins with the undefined concepts of given complexities and breaks them down into simple principles "(*a principiatis ad principia*)"; the synthetic method begins with simple principles and builds up their complex consequences. The analytic method proceeds from the complex to the simple, the synthetic method from the simple to the complex. The former could therefore also be called *regressive,* the latter *progressive.*[38]

These methods are not examined any further in the *Logic,* but they are discussed at various places in those of Kant's pre-critical and critical writings which refer to the distinction between mathematics and philosophy, a subject treated in the same sense in our text.[39] Let us, then, first follow his treatment of the method in some of his other writings, mainly the *Critique,* and then see how the doctrine of the analytic *judgment* fits into that of the analytic *method.* In this way we shall be able to answer some of our questions.

2. Analytic of Methods

In the pre-critical and critical writings the Analytic of Methods— as we may call the doctrine of the analytic and synthetic method

37. Below, § 110.
38. Below, § 117. Cf. *Prolegomena,* § 5, note.
39. Below, pp. 26 f.

—is stated not in its pure form as in the *Logic,* but is used to bring out the distinctive features of mathematics and philosophy. The distinctive feature of mathematics is its synthetic procedure. It begins with simple definitions of arbitrarily invented concepts. The distinctive feature of philosophy is its analytic procedure. It begins with complex concepts of entities given either a priori or a posteriori. Hence, the *synthetic* of method, which in the *Logic* is combined only with *construction* and *simplicity,* is in the other writings combined also with definition —as if only definitions could be starting points of the synthetic method and not also concepts which are simple, as is possible in the "exposition of intuitions" in the *Logic.* On the other hand, the *analytic* method is said to have its starting point in complex concepts—as if it could not also have it in complex definitions. We must, therefore, if we want to disentangle the synthetic and analytic methods from Kant's account of the procedures of mathematics and philosophy, separate the two interwoven strands, simplicity and complexity on the one hand, and definition and concept on the other, and compare the results with the account in the *Logic.* Let us first discuss the relationship of simplicity and complexity, then that of definition and concept.

a) Kant discusses the two methods first in the *Inquiry on the Distinctness of the Principles of Natural Theology and Morality* (1764) and later in The Transcendental Doctrine of Method in the *Critique,* which corresponds to the General Doctrine of Method in the *Logic.* The difference between the analytic and the synthetic methods is, as in the *Logic,* the fact that the analytic method begins with a complexity of data and the synthetic method with a simple datum. This datum is given by a definition in those sciences which invent their own data, such as mathematics. Kant confines the method to mathematics; but also natural science, and even its philosophy, may build itself up from simple elements—not necessarily definitions but even concepts, "simple empirical concepts" as they are called in the *Logic,* concepts of elements of nature regarded as simple—and combine them to ever higher structures. We may even start out with such elements undefined and only vaguely conceived, and develop their more distinct features in their interrelationship with other elements. There can, thus, be a *synthetic* method which does not start with definitions but with concepts. On the other hand, there can be an *analytic* method which starts out with complex definitions rather than concepts, and whose development is the analysis of these definitions. And this method, again, is applicable to both mathematics and the sciences.[40] But, no matter what synthetic or analytic method we use, the definitional or conceptual, the synthetic method builds up the simple into the complex and the analytic method develops the complex into the simple.[41]

b) Different from these "progressive" and "regressive" aspects of the two methods is that aspect which deals expressly with the relation between concept and definition. This relation, once isolated, appears in the writings mentioned in the same way as it does in the process of clarification in the *Logic.* The combination with the procedures of mathematics and philosophy obscures this fact only if we do not clearly keep in mind that by definition in mathematics Kant means synthetic definition, and by definition in philosophy he means analytic definition, and that the synthetic definition in mathematics serves as point of *departure* for mathematical procedure whereas the analytic definition in philosophy serves as point of *arrival* for philosophical procedure. In the latter, definition always means the concept analyzed into its elements. In mathematics we begin with definition, in philosophy we strive toward it.[42] Mathematics, Kant says in the first paragraph of the *Inquiry,* arrives at its definition synthetically, but philosophy, analytically. In mathematics "the concept is never given before the definition, rather, it arises from it. A cone, no matter what else it may be, arises in mathematics by the arbitrary conception of the rotation of a

40. Vaihinger, *Commentar zu Kants Kritik,* I, 417 ff.
41. Below, § 117.
42. Cf. B 758 f.

rectangular triangle around one of its sides."[43] In philosophy the matter is quite different. "Here the concept of a thing is already given, but obscurely or not sufficiently determined. I have to analyze[44] it, compare the isolated properties both with one another and the concept itself, and make this abstract thought explicit and definite."[45]

This is the same process as described in the *Logic*,[46] the process of clarification of a concept. The concept is given because the thing is given and the concept represents our first vague knowledge of the thing. In order to know the thing distinctly, I dismember the concept of it and see what is contained in it.[47] "We must look at this idea in all kinds of relations in order to discover characteristics of it through analysis, connect different abstracted properties in order to see whether they will form one consistent concept and hold together among each other, and to see whether one does not partly include the other."[48] The elements of the concept, the properties contained in it, spread, so to speak, out before me, and the most important ones I reassemble to form the definition. To speak with Ewing, who comments on this passage, "we do not know the definition to begin with, but this need not prevent us from proving with certainty many properties of the concept, and when we have done so we may quickly arrive at the definition, for the latter is the sum total of [the concept's] properties."[49] In order to determine these

43. *Inquiry,* Akad. II, 276.
44. Kant uses the term *zergliedern* ("dismember").
45. *Inquiry,* Akad. II, 276.
46. It may be held that the formulation in the *Inquiry* precedes that in the *Logic* by twenty years and its publication by forty years. On the other hand, when the *Inquiry* appeared Kant had read the *Logic* already for nine years.
47. In some cases, of course, such conceptual dismemberment goes hand in hand with the actual dismemberment of the thing, such as the dissection of an animal or a plant, the chemical analysis of a material, the dismantling of a machine. This is what Kant calls exposition of experience. He calls it synthetic because I add the concept to the experience. See below, §§ 102, 105; B 756.
48. *Inquiry,* Akad. II, 277.
49. A. C. Ewing, *Kant's Treatment of Causality* (London: Kegan Paul, 1924), p. 30.

properties I have first to assemble them, that means, to differentiate them out of the concept. Only then can I stake out the conceptual limits of the thing, that is, define it.

As Kant puts it in the *Critique,* the definition is the completeness and distinctness of the antecedent concept, it is "completeness and precision in the determination of a concept . . . complete enumeration of all those [characteristics] that make up the whole concept."[50] To define "only means the original exhibiting of the complete concept of a thing within its limits,"[51] where, as Kant tells us in the footnote,

> *Completeness* means clarity and sufficiency of characteristics; *limits* means precision, that there are no more than belong to the complete concept; *original,* however, means that this limiting determination is not somehow derivative and thus in need of further proof, which would make the supposed explanation incapable of heading all judgments about an object.

We recognize the first two requirements as those discussed in the *Logic.* Completion and precision are that which gives distinctness to the concept. By originality Kant here means the originality of an invented concept whose definition does not have to be derived from any other source but is given together with the concept itself. He means, in other words, the originality of synthetic definitions.

There is, however, also what may be called an originality of analytic definitions. The essential properties of a thing are, as Kant tells us in the *Logic,*[52] either constitutive *"(essentialia in sensu strictissimo),"* or inferred *"(rationata)."* With the definition the thing is, so to speak, transferred from the realm of experience to that of thought. Its *essence* is established, and this essence can be nothing else than its logical essence. It cannot, nor does it have to be, its real essence. The logical essence is easily accessible to thought, the real is not. The logical essence is nothing else than the cognition of all those predicates which

50   A 241.
51.   B 755.
52.   Below, pp. 66 f.

are determined by the *concept* of the object; whereas the real nature of the thing would be determined by everything which belongs to its existence. In order, for example, to determine the logical essence of a body we do not need to assemble all its data in nature. All we have to do is direct our attention to those properties which are the essential constituents of its concept. For the logical essence is nothing else than the original fundamental concept of all the necessary predicates of the thing.[53]

By analytic originality, then, we could mean logical essence. The analytic definition is the thing as subject of our thought. The transition from concept to definition can be regarded as an aspect of the relation between experience and thought—and this is "the key to the whole secret of . . . metaphysics," as Kant wrote in the famous letter to Hertz in 1772. Although he solved his problem transcendentally rather than by general logic, it may be said that this relation is represented by the process of clarification if it refers to, and links, both the a posteriori given and the a priori given. It mirrors the impossibility of a solution by their separation, in the logical impossibility of analytic definition, no matter whether of a posteriori or of a priori given data. It mirrors the possibility, and indeed, the obviousness of a solution by their combination, through the synthetic a priori, in the obviousness of synthetic definition. The impossibility of analytic definition arises from the impossibility of assembling empirical data in a conceptual frame. There is no such difficulty in synthetic definition. In mathematics the concepts and definitions do not have to accommodate themselves to a given thing, they and their objects are free creations of the mind. Thus no transition is necessary from experience to thought or vice versa. Thought is what we start out with and within thought we remain, the realm of "arbitrarily thought concepts,"[54] even though, it is true, this kind of thought is suffused with "non-empirical intuition."[55] In metaphysics it is different. Here we want to know the principles of the given reality, "we cannot make deductions from an as-

53. See *ibid.*
54. B 757 f.
55. B 741.

sumed and uncriticised basis, but [have] to discover the real; [metaphysical] definitions must describe something objective, otherwise they are fictions, not explanations."[56] In the strict sense, therefore, definitions are impossible in metaphysics. One reason is, and here Kant makes a significant addition to the reason given in the *Logic*, that we can never be sure whether we always use the empirical word to be defined in the same sense.

> . . . It is never certain whether under the word designating one and the same object one does not think sometimes more, sometimes fewer of its characteristics. Thus, in the concept *gold* one man may think beside its weight, color, malleability, also the property of resisting rust, of which another may know nothing. We avail ourselves of certain characteristics only so long as they are sufficient for distinctions; new observations remove some and add others, the concept thus never staying between secure limits. And indeed, what purpose would be served by defining such a concept, since, for example, when speaking of water and its properties, one does not linger over what one thinks by the word "water" but proceeds to experiments, and the word, with the few characteristics attaching to it, is meant to be a *designation* only and not a concept of the matter, the alleged definition thus being nothing but a verbal determination.[57]

This word belongs to experience. Only if I *invent* with the word its object do I really have a *concept*, and can I *define* the word, as in mathematics.

> In that case I can always define my concept, for certainly I must know what I wanted to think, as I have deliberately made it myself and it is given to me neither by the nature of the understanding nor by experience . . . hence only mathematics has definitions. For the object it thinks is also exhibited by it in intuition a priori, and this object surely can contain neither more nor less than the concept, because through the explanation the concept of the object had originally been given, i.e. without deriving the explanation from anything.[58]

In short, then, as in the *Logic*, only invented concepts can be defined. Given concepts, whether given a posteriori, as the con-

56. Ewing, *Kant's Treatment of Causality*, p. 30.
57. B 755 f. Cf. above, n. 47.
58. B 757.

cepts of empirical things, or a priori, as those of the categories, "cannot be defined at all but only be made explicit."[59] In the a posteriori given concept, as we have seen in the *Logic*, I can never be certain that I have examined all the characteristics of the thing; in the a priori given concepts it is the same; . . .

> For I can never be certain that the distinct presentation of a (still confusedly) given concept has been developed to completion, unless I know that it is adequate to the object. But since the concept of the object, in the way it is given, may contain many obscure presentations that we pass by in analysis, although we always use them in application, the completeness of the analysis of my concept is always doubtful and can be made, through numerous fitting examples only *supposedly*, never *apodeictically* certain.[60]

For this reason Kant prefers the term *exposition* to that of definition, "which still remains tentative and which the critic may admit up to a certain point but still with reservations as to its completeness."[61] Yet, we need not, for this reason, "be so stringent in our requirements as to deny philosophical explanations the honorable name of definition,"[62] if only we keep in mind that "philosophical definitions are brought about only as expositions of given concepts, mathematical definitions, however, as constructions of originally made concepts, the former only analytically through dissection (whose completeness is not apodeictically certain), the latter synthetically and thus *making* the concept themselves, whereas the former merely explain it."[63]

From all this it follows, and this makes clear the point with which we are concerned, that definition in philosophy always follows from, and is the elaboration of, vague and confused concepts.

> For since they [definitions in philosophy] are analyses of given concepts, these concepts, though still confused, precede, and the incomplete exposition comes before the complete; so that from

59. B 755.
60. B 756 f.
61. B 757.
62. B 758.
63. *Ibid.*

a few characteristics drawn from an incomplete analysis we can conclude several things before reaching the complete exposition, i.e. the definition; in short, [it follows] that in philosophy the definition, as precise distinctness, must end rather than begin the work. In mathematics, on the other hand, we have no concept whatever prior to the definition through which the concept itself is first given, and mathematics must therefore begin, and indeed can always begin, with the definition.[64]

Mathematics and philosophy, then, are analyzed by Kant as examples of the synthetic and the analytic methods. The latter, in turn, are specifications of the general method of clarification. We shall now from the Analytic of Methods turn to the Analytic of Judgments and examine the role which the analytic and synthetic judgments play in the process of clarification.

3. Analytic of Judgments

It is clear from Kant's account that the *definition* of an empirical thing follows the *concept* of that thing, as the result of a process of clarification. What is not so clear, or has at least not been emphasized clearly enough, is that the analytic judgment, as such, is a stage in this process. *Each analytic judgment is a step in the clarification of the concept in the direction toward the definition.* The analytic judgment is not a tautology, subject and predicate are not identical but different. Thus, there is a movement of thought[65] in the analytic judgment. Although, as Kant rightly emphasizes, the analytic judgment does not amplify or enlarge the concept of the thing and in this way does not *add*

---

64. B 758 f.

65. This movement is neither a psychological nor an epistemological, but a logical one—but logical in Kant's sense, not in that of modern logic, which knows neither concept nor intension. Quine and others, as a result, find Kant's notion of conceptual containment "metaphorical" and see no place for it in logic. See, on the whole question, Jørgen Jørgensen, *A Treatise of Formal Logic*, (Copenhagen and London: Levin & Munksgaard and Humphrey Milford, 1931), III, 109 ff. Also Marc-Wogau, "Kants Lehre vom analytischen Urteil," pp. 140 f., and Alan Gewirth, "The Distinction between Analytic and Synthetic Truth," *Journal of Philosophy*, L (1953), 397.

to our knowledge, it does *clarify* the concept and bring out what was only vaguely conceived in it. In this qualitative rather than quantitative sense, it *does* add to, or rather—since we speak of qualitative "addition"—*improve* our knowledge. There is an advance of knowledge in the analytic judgment, even though it is not one of quantity but of quality. Kant, we remember, in denying the "addition" to knowledge, uses the analogy of a light thrown upon a chart, saying that the light does not add to the chart. But he can hardly be regarded as so much of a realist that he considers the concept as equally independent from the knower as the chart from the reader. On the contrary, he held that the exposition and definition of the concept improve the concept itself, making it "a better" concept, so that it is "more of a concept" after the process than before. "In mathematics" he tells us, "definition belongs *ad esse,* in philosophy *ad melius esse.*"[66]

It is clear, thus, that the analytic judgment represents a *dynamic of thought* and not the static circle of tautology. There are two kinds of identity in the Kantian analytic judgment, "either explicit (*explicita*) or *non-explicit* (*implicita*). In the former case analytic propositions are *tautological.*"[67] They are not tautological in the second case. For "tautological propositions are *virtualiter* empty or *void of consequences,* for they are of no avail or use." Take, for example, the proposition *Man is man.* "If I know nothing else of man than that he is man, I know nothing else of him at all."[68] It is very different with implicitly identical propositions. "Implicitly identical propositions, on the contrary, are not void of consequences or fruitless." They "clarify the predicate which lay undeveloped (*implicite*) in the concept of the subject through development (*explicatio*)."[69] Thus "analytic judgments make explicit in the predicate what is only implicit in the subject concept."[70]

    66. B 759n.
    67. Below, § 37.
    68. *Ibid.*
    69. *Ibid.*
    70. Paton, *Kant's Metaphysic of Experience* (London: Allen & Unwin, 1936), I, 85.

This process or development of the concept which takes place within each analytic judgment is often overlooked when the analyticity of a judgment is discussed, and especially when the modern logical use of the word is confused with the Kantian.[71] The emphasis is put on the fact that the predicate is contained in the subject-concept, but not on the equally important fact that this containing means that the subject-concept is in this degree undeveloped and that the statement of the predicate makes the concept in this same degree more clear and distinct—that analysis refers to a definite movement of thought from vagueness to clarity. Kant never fails to mention this point when he discusses the analytic judgment. "Analytical judgments express nothing in the predicate but what has already been actually thought in the concept of the subject, though not so clearly and not with equal consciousness"[72] as I possess of the concept *after* I have made the judgment. In the analytic judgment "the predicate B belongs to the concept A, as something which is (covertly)[73] contained in this concept. . . . These judgments could also be called *explicative judgments,* because they add nothing through the predicate to the concept of the subject, but merely break it up, through analysis, into its conceptual components that had already been thought in it (*although confusedly*)."[74] And this explicativeness, although, as Kant says, "thought through identity," is yet not tautological or explicit identity but implicit identity.

71. Especially when the concept itself is disregarded. Cf. the discussion by Susan Stebbing, *A Modern Introduction to Logic* (London: Methuen, 1948), pp. 439 ff. Also, Bertrand Russell, *Principles of Mathematics* (Cambridge: Cambridge University Press, 1903), p. 63.

72. *Prolegomena,* § 2. Jørgensen, in *A Treatise of Formal Logic* (III, 109 ff., 121), calls this particular emphasis psychological. But Kant makes clear that it is logical and not psychological. Logic is "a science a priori of the necessary laws of thinking . . . not subjectively, i.e. not according to empirical (psychological) principles of how the understanding thinks, but objectively, i.e. according to a priori principles of how it ought to think" (below, p. 16). The rules of thought are those of concepts, but "something precedes . . . before a presentation becomes a concept." It is not a matter of logic to show how presentations arise, but it is a matter of logic to show how concepts arise out of presentations (below, p. 38).

73. *Versteckter Weise* (in a hidden manner).

74. B 10 f. Italics added.

Thus there is a definite direction in thought, a process by which it clarifies concepts and makes them more and more distinct. The method of this process is analysis and its tool is the analytic judgment. Analysis, as it is the main business of logic, is the main activity of our reason.

> A great, perhaps the greatest part of the business of our reason consists in *analyses* of the concepts we already have of objects. This supplies us with many cognitions which, while nothing but elucidations or explanations of what has already been thought in our concept (though still in a confused manner), are yet valued equal to new insights, at least as to their form.[75]

Thus, clarification for Kant is a matter of the form of thought, and for this reason the process of clarification is a logical, and not an epistemological or psychological one. This formal procedure of reason is dangerous since reason "surreptitiously slips in, without being aware of so doing, assertions of an entirely different kind,"[76] yet, it is indispensable for the progress of thought. Thought clarifies itself by analysis.

Analysis is possible only through judgment. Thus, in the last instance, *judgment is the tool by which thought clarifies itself.* This doctrine Kant stated as early as 1762, twenty years before the *Critique.* In *The Mistaken Subtlety of the Four Syllogistic Figures* he shows that all thinking is judgment and inference, and both are the determination of the concept by its attributes, that is, analysis. A concept can be completely determined only by determination of *all* its attributes, not by that of some of them— not merely through its species, but also through its genus. The species is the attribute of the concept, the genus is the attribute of the species. Thus, to determine a concept completely means to determine it by the attribute of its attribute. To determine a concept through its attribute is *judgment,* to determine it through the attribute of the attribute is *inference.* All inference, therefore, is mediate judgment. Its principle is the rule *Nota notae rei ipsius nota. All true thinking is of this analytic kind.* It

75. B 9.
76. B 10.

is simple natural thinking, such as "This body is, as an extended thing, divisible," rather than the artificial threefold division of this thought in a synthetic syllogism: "Everything extended is divisible, this body is extended, therefore this body is divisible." This threefold division arranges a thought as if it had movable pieces, like those on a chessboard, and produces the mistaken subtlety of the four syllogistic figures. The whole syllogistic must be discarded and "the colossus must be destroyed whose head is in the clouds of antiquity and whose feet are of clay."[77]

What is important here is the role of analytic judgment in the clarification of thought, and the difference between judgment as a power of the understanding and inference as a power of reason—even though understanding and reason are only aspects of one and the same *power of cognition*. Traditional logic, says Kant, is mistaken in treating distinct and complete concepts before judgment and rational inference, since the latter alone make the former possible. The point is not that concepts synthetically produce judgments and ratiocinations, but rather that judgments and ratiocinations analytically produce concepts. They are, in other words, means of the process of clarification, which two years later, as we have seen, he discusses, in another context, in the *Inquiry*. "I say then first, that a *distinct* concept is possible only by means of a *judgment,* a *complete* concept only by means of a *syllogism*." We have here again a sequence of clarifications. Its first step is this: "In order that a concept be distinct, I must clearly cognize something as a characteristic of a thing, and this is a judgment. In order to have a distinct concept of body, I clearly present to myself impenetrability as a characteristic of it. Now this presentation is nothing but the thought, 'a body is impenetrable.' "[78] This latter expression is the formal statement of the judgment. This judgment is a means of clarifying the concept. "Here it is to be noted that *this judgment is not the distinct concept itself, but is the act by which it becomes actual; for the presentation of the matter itself arising as*

---

77. *The Mistaken Subtlety of the Four Syllogistic Figures,* Akad. II, 57.
78. *Ibid.,* p. 58.

a result of this act, is distinct.''[79] The final step is the completion
of the concept by means of ratiocination. After the concept has
been made distinct by means of judgments it can be completed
by means of inferences. "It is easy to show that a complete concept is possible only by means of a syllogism. . . . We could
therefore call a distinct concept one that is clear by means of a
judgment and could call a complete concept one that is distinct
by means of a syllogism."[80] Although judgment and ratiocination (syllogism) are on different levels of cognition, namely
understanding and reason, these are basically the same power—
understanding the power of judging immediately, reason the
power of judging mediately.[81]

> Secondly, just as it is evident that a complete concept requires no
> different basic power of the mind than does a distinct concept
> (since the same capacity which cognizes something immediately as
> a characteristic in a thing is also used to conceive in this character-
> istic another characteristic and thus to think the matter by means of
> a more distant characteristic), so also it is evident that *understand-
> ing* and *reason,* i.e. the faculty of cognizing distinctly and the faculty
> of forming syllogisms, are not different *basic powers.* Both consist
> in the faculty of judgment; but when one judges mediately, one
> concludes.[82]

This process of exhibiting the attributes of things by means of
judgments precedes the definition of the thing. "Every definition
is preceded by several such [judgments], when in order to reach
the definition, one conceives as a characteristic anything that
one cognizes foremost and immediately in a thing."[83] Kant here
means judgments and not ratiocination, although in the *Inquiry*
it seems that the latter also precedes definition. Both, however,

79. *Ibid.* Italics added.
80. *Ibid.*
81. In our text Kant shows *Verstandesschlüsse* as those of immediate inference and *Vernunftschlüsse* as those of syllogistic inference. The latter are
based on the rule *Nota notae rei ipsius nota,* rather than on the *Dictum de
omni,* which latter is said to follow from the former (see below, §§ 44 ff., 56 ff.,
63). Cf. *The Mistaken Subtlety,* Akad. II, 49.
82. *The Mistaken Subtlety,* Akad. II, 59.
83. *Ibid.,* p. 61.

are what he later calls analytic judgments. They show the natural analytic of thought, as against the unnatural synthetic of ancient logic.[84] Thus we see here the same process of which he says twenty years later that "by means of several such analytic judgments we seek to approach the definition of the concepts."[85] At least the first, and probably both steps of thought as shown in The Mistaken Subtlety are, therefore, identical with what in the Logic is called exposition. Since it is impossible to know what at this early date Kant meant by analysis and also what exactly he meant by description, we are probably not justified in saying that the first step is description and the second exposition; although, perhaps, a case for this interpretation could be made.

In any case, Kant's work establishes the fact that the analytic judgment is part of the method of clarification, of the melius esse which is the purpose of philosophical definition. Each analysis clarifies the concept a little more, until finally all analyses have advanced the clarification of the concept so far as to make it ready to become formulated as definition. Each analytic judgment is one step in the Analytic of Methods. It is, as it were, a differential in the process of clarification. It advances the process by that infinitesimal degree that lies in the difference between implicit and explicit identity of subject and predicate. The Analytic of Judgments shows in close-up, "micrologically,"[86] what the Analytic of Methods shows in large, macrologically— the transition from the experience of a thing through its concept to its definition.

4. Logical Relativity of Analytic and Synthetic Judgment

By inserting the Analytic of Judgments into the Analytic of Methods we find the characteristic relation between analytic

84. Cf. Vaihinger, Commentar zu Kants Kritik, I, 270; Kuno Fischer, Immanuel Kant: Entwicklungsgeschichte und System der kritischen Philosophie (Mannheim, 1860), I, 160 ff.

85. Prolegomena, trans. L. W. Beck, "Library of Liberal Arts," LLA 27 (New York: Bobbs-Merrill, 1950), § 2, p. 18.

86. Below, pp. 52, 54.

judgment and, on the one hand, experience and, on the other, definition. In the former relation, that of abstraction, we find that the very act of abstraction is performed by means of judgments, by surrounding, as it were, or enclosing, the thing by judgments. "Kant appears to be saying . . . that the act of abstraction or *analysis* whereby we make a concept is a judgment; and if to conceive is essentially to think in abstraction what is common to a plurality of possible instances, his assertion seems to be true."[87] The identification of thinking and judging may be said to be the fundamental discovery which enabled Kant to write the *Critique of Pure Reason* and solve the "secret of metaphysics." As he tells us in the *Prolegomena,* after having discarded the categories of Aristotle—as "only a miserable list of names, without explanation or rule for their use," a "rhapsody which proceeded without any principle,"[88]—"in order to discover such a principle, I looked about for an act of the understanding which comprises all the rest and is distinguished only by various modifications or momenta, in reducing the multiplicity of representation to the unity of thinking in general. I found this act of the understanding to consist in judging."[89] This happened as early as 1762, twenty years before the publication of the *Critique.* In the *Critique* the principle is repeated and clarified. "We can reduce all acts of the understanding to judgments, and the *understanding* as such can therefore be conceived as the *faculty of judging.* For, according to what was said above, the understanding is the faculty of thinking. Thinking is cognition through concepts. But concepts relate as predicates of possible judgments to some presentation of a not yet determined object."[90]

---

87. Paton, *Kant's Metaphysic of Experience,* I, 250.

88. By a "rhapsody" Kant means a mere accumulation of cognitive material without plan or system, without benefit of an *Architektonik;* see below, § 116; B 106, 860.

89. *Prolegomena,* trans. L. W. Beck, § 39, pp. 70–71. We have substituted *momenta* for Beck's "phases." See note 18 of the Introduction to the *Logic* for Kant's term *momentum.*

90. B 94.

Thus, to speak with Paton,

> the obvious objection . . . that the act of conceiving is a different act from the act of judging Kant meets . . . by asserting that it is as predicates of *possible* judgments that concepts relate to some idea (ultimately to some intuition) of an object *as yet* undetermined. Indeed, he affirms that a concept is a concept only because it contains under it other ideas (ultimately intuitions), by means of which it can relate to objects. This implies that it is a concept only as the predicate of a possible judgment.[91]

For, as we have seen, all concepts are attributes, and all knowledge is knowledge of things by attributes. A concept of a thing, then, is the concept of all the other concepts which as predicates refer to that thing. The concept 'metal,' for example, refers to a thing if it comprises all the other predicates by which such a thing is known, e.g. 'body,' 'weight,' and the like, so that the concept is the predicate of a possible judgment: "Something X, which I know through the predicates that together constitute the concept 'metal' I think through the concepts 'body,' 'weight,' etc."[92] Kant states the matter in a simpler way, making use of the predicate-concept 'body' rather than the subject-concept 'metal':

> The concept body means something, e.g. metal, which can be cognized through that concept. It is thus a concept only through its containing other presentations by means of which it can relate to objects. It is thus the predicate of a possible judgment, e.g. *every metal is a body.*[93]

To say that concepts are predicates of possible judgments about a not yet determined thing can mean, then, that the object is entirely undetermined. But it can also mean that the object, originally determined, must be further determined. Suppose that the first determining judgment relates the concepts 'body' and 'metal.' Immediately the whole range of predicates is evoked which together constitute the thing which is a metallic

---

91. Paton, *Kant's Metaphysic of Experience,* I, 251.
92. Cf. Paton, *ibid.,* note.
93. B 94.

body, and a host of further judgments becomes possible which determine the thing in greater detail. This process only stops with the complete determination of the original concept, that is, its definition. Thus, in the *original* determination of the completely undetermined object we have the possibility of judgments about anything, that is, anything we choose to speak about or make the subject of our thought. We select this subject out of the matrix of experience. This original determination of the thing as subject of possible judgment is the first step from experience to thought. It is the origin of, or the original, clarification, namely "clearness."[94] The second step is the selection of predicates, in a set of judgments without any rule, Kant's "description." Thus, from the very beginning thinking is judging; "to say that concepts are essentially predicates of possible judgments is to say that conceiving is really judging."[95] The further evocation of *additional* judgments *further* determining the thing and giving it all its other predicates and, at the same time, the delimitation of the totality of predicates by the rule of concept, is the third step, exposition, which eventually leads to the fourth and final step, definition. Definition is the distillation of the essential predicates of the thing out of the "raw material" of judgments which could be made about it. It is the end result of the process which leads from the selection of the thing as subject of possible judgments through description and exposition to definition.

Definition is the result of a number of judgments the predicates of which are at first thought vaguely in the concept of a thing and which are made explicit as the process of judging proceeds. These judgments can be called analytic and synthetic only when the concept of the thing is determinate enough to be said to contain or not to contain these predicates. The first —descriptive—judgments, therefore, cannot be called either analytic or synthetic, in the conceptual sense, because there exists as yet no determinate enough concept. But as soon as

94. Cf. Marc-Wogau, "Kant's Lehre vom analytischen Urteil," p. 148.
95. Paton, *Kant's Metaphysic of Experience,* I, 251.

enough "raw material"—to use again the Kantian term—for the determination of the concept is accumulated by description, the function of the understanding may begin and bring order into the indiscriminate assembly of predicates. From this point on every judgment within, and with a predicate belonging to, this order, that is, a predicate which is contained in the ordering concept, is an analytic judgment, and every judgment not so contained is a synthetic judgment. *Analytic and synthetic judgments thus are phases of one and the same process, namely, the clarification of the empirically given concept.* These judgments are progressive determinations of the properties of the thing: at first, pre-conceptually, of the perceived qualities of the thing not yet made subject of a concept, and then, when the judgments through the conceptual order imposed on them have become elements of exposition, progressive determinations not of the disordered qualities of the actual thing but of the ordered properties of its concept—and as such either analytic or synthetic. From the conceptually analytic judgments further judgments are inferred by the function of reason. Finally, through the fourfold process of the production of definition, described by Kant, those predicates are chosen without which the concept cannot be distinctly thought, that is, the minimum set of predicates which *limit* the concept and make it *precise*. These constitute the definition. The latter contains much fewer predicates than the exposition, in which there are many more predicates without which the thing cannot be thought, simply because at that stage it is still only vaguely known. Vagueness of knowledge means, precisely, a still unlimited, an indefinite number of predicates.

From this it follows that analysis on the definitional level is different from analysis on the expositional level. Properties which on the expositional level were analytic, because they were contained in the concept, become on the definitional level synthetic, because they are *not* contained in the definition. On the definitional level the content of the concept shrinks to its minimum—the definition, as we remember, is *conceptus rei adaequatus in minimis terminis.* Thus, between the exposition and the definition many, and indeed most, predicates of the thing are shed off. Once the thing is definitely known, that is, defined and its logical essence determined, these surplus properties, which were analytic on the conceptual level of the exposition but were discarded in the process of clarification, become synthetic on the definitional level: they were contained in the explicated concept but they are not contained any more in the defined concept.[96] A thing thus rises from the empirical to the definitional level, so to speak, like a balloon, by throwing overboard the ballast of ultimately, that is definitionally, unnecessary, that is synthetic, predicates.

Thus, *analyticity and syntheticity are relative to the levels of Analytic*—a logical, not a psychological or epistemological relativity. On the definitional level the minimum number of predicates is analytic and the maximum number is synthetic. The relation between the expositional or conceptual, and the descriptional or empirical levels is similar to that between the definitional and the expositional levels. What is not conceptually analytic is conceptually synthetic, that is, empirical. But what is empirical may be called "analytic" with respect to experience, "analytic a posteriori." Description is the still non-conceptual assembly "without a rule," of qualities of a thing merely perceived but not yet conceived.[97] Yet, these qualities are part of the experience of the thing—in the merely empirical sense and not in the technical sense used by Kant in the *Critique*—and thus are not *entirely* without *any* rule whatsoever; for in that case they would not be part of the experience *of this thing*. Rather, we may call them empirically analytic: analytic in the descrip-

---

96. For this reason, for example, 'Bodies are heavy' is synthetic once the definition of 'body' as an extended thing is known. Up to that point 'Bodies are heavy' may well be regarded as analytic, 'heavy' being a predicate of the exposition. A quite definite knowledge of 'body' is necessary for deciding that extensions *is*, but heaviness is *not* an analytic predicate of 'body.' Cf. below § 6, Note 2.

97. See below, § 105, Note 2. The borderline between perception and conception is difficult to draw. A typical example of description is that of a radio commentator of, say, a football game. Here is experience in terms of judgments, all of whose predicates are "contained in" the experience.

thing, serves as the rule of description. Exposition follows the *conception* of the thing and imposes a rule on the descriptional qualities, which makes some of them conceptually analytic,[98] namely all those which fall within the rule, and makes the others conceptually synthetic. As within a mould, the former are now "contained in" the concept, which grasps them together, "conceives" them in the literal sense of this word. Those which fall outside the rule *become* conceptually synthetic or *remain* empirically analytic. As the process of clarification continues on the expositional level a characteristic relation obtains between analytic and synthetic judgments: *the number of analytic judgments is proportionate to the ignorance about the thing and the number of synthetic judgments is proportionate to the knowledge of the thing*. For the process of clarification, which has taken its start with the selection of the original content of the concept, now continues by refining and selecting the predicates for ultimate use in the definition. The earlier a judgment is in this process the vaguer is the concept of its subject and hence the more predicates there are contained in the latter; hence the more possible judgments are analytic and the fewer, synthetic. Whereas, the later a judgment is in the process the more definite the concept has become and the fewer predicates it contains; hence the fewer possible judgments are analytic and the more synthetic. Thus, on the expositional level, as soon as the process of clarification begins, the number of synthetic judgments is in direct proportion to the knowledge about the concept, just as the number of analytic judgments is in direct proportion to the ignorance about the concept. Finally, when the concept is defined, the minimum of analytic and the maximum of synthetic predicates is reached, as well as the minimum of ignorance and the maximum of knowledge.

But what is synthetic on the expositional level is not the same as what is synthetic on the definitional level. On the definitional level all of that is synthetic which is not contained in the definition, and this means all that has been contained in the concept

---

98. Cf. Marc-Wogau, "Kants Lehre vom analytischen Urteil," pp. 149 ff.

and has not been admitted to the definition, which is almost everything that had been contained in the concept. For usually only a couple of predicates are admitted to the definition. Thus, what is synthetic on the definitional level is almost everything that is analytic on the expositional level. But it is also everything that is synthetic on the expositional level. For this, of course, never having been admitted to the concept, lacks the first condition for admittance to the definition. Yet, what is synthetic on the expositional level is not the same as what is "analytic" on the descriptional level. For what is synthetic on the expositional level is only that which does not fall under the rule of the concept, the mould, so to speak, slapped onto the description. However, what *does* fall under the rule has also been descriptionally analytic before the rule was applied. Therefore, what is analytic on the descriptional level is *every* empirical quality, no matter whether or not it becomes analytic once the concept is applied.

It may seem, now, that what is descriptionally analytic, or empirical, is the same as what is definitionally synthetic, with the negligible exception of the few definitional predicates; for it seems, with the same exception, to be everything which is conceptually either analytic or synthetic. But, again, this is not the case. For between the exposition and the definition additional predicates have been created, through inference from the conceptual predicates, and these have not been part of the originally perceived qualities, and hence are not descriptionally analytic. Therefore, what is definitionally synthetic is *more* than what is empirical.

Thus, we must distinguish between definitionally analytic and synthetic predicates, expositionally analytic and synthetic predicates, and descriptionally analytic or empirical predicates. The first are those which are or are not contained in the *definition* of their subject, the second are those which are or are not contained in the *concept* or *exposition* of their subject, and the third are all those which are contained in the *description* of the perceived thing. There are an infinity of such empirical predicates, for perception can discover ever more qualities of a thing. There are an infinity of conceptually synthetic predicates, for out of

the infinity of empirical qualities a finite, though at first indefinite, number is being selected to form the content of the concept, and the subtraction of a finite number from an infinite one
does not change the infinity. There are thus very many, indeed,
indefinitely many but not infinitely many *analytic* predicates on
the expositional level. This indefiniteness is, by the rule of the
concept, progressively condensed until, for all practical purposes, though not strictly or logically speaking, the concept is
exhausted. In this sense the concept "gathers together" certain
common properties of the perceived manifold, even though
there remains a fringe of vagueness all around it. Yet, Kant did
not want to deny to exposition the honorable title of definition.
There are very few definitionally analytic predicates—only those
contained in the definiens—and an infinity of definitionally synthetic predicates, more, indeed, than there are empirical predicates. Thus the number of "analytic" predicates decreases, from
infinity in descriptional analyticity, through indefinite finiteness
in expositional analyticity, to definite finiteness in definitional
analyticity. In the definition, to repeat, there is a minimum of
analytic predicates and a maximum of synthetic predicates—
more, as we have seen, than on the empirical level. Thus, not
only does a thing rise from the plane of perception to the strato-
sphere of definition by throwing overboard the perceptional
ballast, but it also ejects what it produced during the ascent.
Some of the original load, so to speak, is fuel for the power plant
of reason. Although it is ejected as exhaust in the process, it
supplies additional thrust for the ascent.

Summarizing, we may say that the Analytic of Methods is the
science of arriving at definition: the analytic method of abstracting analytic definitions, the synthetic method of constructing
synthetic definitions. The Analytic of Judgments, that is, of the
analytic and the synthetic judgment, is a tool within the first
part of this science, that of arriving at analytic definition. This
definition is the fully differentiated concept. It is not only *definite*, in defining the limits of the concept; but also *finite*, in
possessing a certain minimum number of distinct and discrete
predicates; and also *final*, in being the end product of the ana-

lytic process. This process is a selective one: selecting first a
subject, then a set of analytic judgments out of an infinity of empirical judgments, and finally a minimum set of analytic judgments from the original maximum set of such judgments. Analytic judgments are the means of "approaching the definition of
the concept" and thus the means of clarifying thought. But they
are also, by originally determining the concept of an empirical
thing, the condition of abstractive thought in general. Thinking
in this sense *is* judging.

Although this principle was the point of departure for Kant's
solution of his problem—the relation between the thing and its
representation—he did not and could not solve it in terms of
general logic. It could only be solved by transcendental logic,
through the translation of judgment into category, and category
into schema—the synthetic method. Kant thus had to leave
philosophy behind and create the conditions for a new science.

III. Analysis and Synthesis
in Transcendental Logic

The *Critique of Pure Reason* seeks an answer to the question,
How are synthetic judgments possible a priori? The fate of metaphysics is decided by the way this question is answered. In distinguishing between analytic and synthetic judgment for the
formulation of his thematic problem, Kant relies, as far as analytic concepts are concerned, on determinations of general logic.
The pivotal point of this distinction is the subject-concept. If it
is an element of general logic, i.e. an analytic concept, the corresponding judgment may be either analytic or synthetic, depending on the fit of the predicate-concept into the subject-concept.
If, however, the subject-concept is one of transcendental logic,
i.e. a synthetic concept, then the corresponding judgment must
be synthetic a priori. These are original Kantian distinctions,
which are, however, grounded in the logical works and in the

analytic-synthetic procedure of his predecessors. An outline of the meaning of analysis and synthesis in these works, and of Kant's own critical systematization of these notions, will place in perspective the orientation of transcendental critique on both general logic and the analytic-synthetic procedure of natural science. Kant explains that in the *Critique of Pure Reason* he has exhausted the entire synthesis of concepts a priori, but that in order to call this work a system of transcendental philosophy, it would have to contain also a complete analysis of human cognition a priori. With these general statements in mind, we may turn to the role assigned to analysis and synthesis by Descartes, Leibniz, Galileo, and Newton, before determining the part these procedures play in the new science founded by Kant. The question of what exactly characterizes Kant's own method in the *Critique of Pure Reason* deserves much more attention than it has received in modern studies of his work.

1. Analysis and Synthesis in Pre-Kantian Systems

a) The Discovery of Science

General logic, we saw, analyzes concepts, transcendental logic constructs objects. The former is the procedure of philosophy, the analytic method; the latter that of science, the synthetic method. Kant, insofar as he used the synthetic method, was a scientist; Newton and others, insofar as they used the analytic method, were philosophers. The novelty of the synthetic method made scientists for two hundred years cling to philosophy as their profession. Newton's book was entitled *The Mathematical Principles of Natural Philosophy;* and as late as Faraday's time scientists disliked the newfangled term "physicist" and called themselves "philosophers."[99] It was only at the end of the nine-

---

99. "I was formerly a bookseller and binder but am now turned philosopher. . . . I, for amusement, learnt a little chemistry and other parts of philosophy . . . ," Faraday in a letter of 1813, in F. W. Westaway, *The Endless Quest* (London and Glasgow: Blackie & Son, 1934), p. 348.

teenth century when the synthetic method, the mathematical presentation of nature, came into its own that scientists threw off the label of philosophy. Mach disliked the old-fashioned term and proudly called himself "physicist."

Kant was a pioneer in this development, in his clear distinction between philosophy and science. Mathematics belongs to science, not to philosophy. He finds in the title of Newton's *opus magnum, Philosophiae naturalis principia mathematica,* the mistake of a logical metabasis:

> For just as there can be no mathematical principles of philosophy— so there can be no philosophical principles of mathematics.—One [of them] cannot serve the other as a principle (they are *disparata*), but both can be brought under the title of transcendental philosophy.—Transcendental philosophy, however, is the principle of the qualitative relations of concepts to ideas of pure reason (e.g. of God), in so far as they are thought to be united in a system of the whole.[100]

Kant attributes certain "inconveniences" in the division of Newton's work to a lack of setting up his method in advance. The proper division is given by Kant as follows:[101]

    1.) *Scientiae naturalis principia philosophica*
(not *philosophiae naturalis,* for such a sentence is tautological).

    2.) *Scientiae naturalis principia mathematica*
(not *philosophiae naturalis,* for then it would be contradictory). Accordingly, at the end of the preface to the *Metaphysical Foundations of Natural Science,* Newton's main work is called by Kant *The Mathematical Principles of Natural Science* rather than of natural philosophy.

However, what Newton did not express *in abstracto* to Kant's satisfaction, he knew very well how to apply in the execution of his work. And at the end of his *Opticks* he shows a remarkable insight into scientific methodology:

> As in Mathematicks, so in Natural Philosophy, the investigation of difficult Things by the Method of Analysis, ought ever to precede the Method of Composition. This Analysis consists in making Ex-

100. Akad. XXI, 72.
101. *Ibid.,* p. 238.

periments and Observations, and in drawing general Conclusions from them by Induction. . . . By this way of Analysis we may proceed from Compounds to Ingredients, and from Motions to the Forces producing them; and in general, from the Effects to their Causes, and from particular Causes to more General ones, till the Argument end in the most general. This is the method of Analysis: and the Synthesis consists in assuming the Causes discover'd and establish'd as Principles, and by them explaining the Phenomena proceeding from them and proving the Explanations.

This method, Newton holds, is universal. It is valid not only in natural but also in moral philosophy. "And if Natural Philosophy, in all its Parts, by pursuing this Method, shall at length be perfected, the Bounds of Moral Philosophy will also be enlarged."[102] Analysis and Synthesis, for Newton, meant Induction and Deduction, Experimentation and Systematization. These meanings persisted in the working philosophy of the scientists of the Enlightenment, from Galileo to Laplace. The Galilean terms were Resolution or Intuition, and Demonstration or Composition.

Facing the world of sensible experience, we isolate and examine as fully as possible a certain typical phenomenon, in order first to intuit those simple, absolute elements in terms of which the phenomenon can be most easily and completely translated into mathematical form; which amounts . . . to a resolution of the sensed fact into such elements in quantitative combinations. Once we have performed this properly, we need the sensible facts no more; the elements thus reached are the real constituents; and deductive demonstration from them by pure mathematics must always be true of similar instances of the phenomenon, even though at times it should be impossible to confirm them empirically. . . . That Galileo actually followed these three steps in all of his important discoveries in dynamics is easily ascertainable from his frank biographical paragraphs, especially in the *Dialogues Concerning Two New Sciences.*[103]

Galileo saw in these ultimate simple constituents, the primary qualities, the ultimate truth of physical reality. The method of

102. Newton, *Opticks* (1730 edn. reprinted, New York: Dover Publications, 1952), p. 405.
103. E. A. Burtt, *The Metaphysical Foundations of Modern Physical Science* (London: Kegan Paul, 1932), pp. 70 f.

Analysis and Synthesis was for him, as for Newton, the method of *discovering a science.*

This method was logically introduced by Descartes and Leibniz and put into its final form, that of transcendental logic, by Kant. All three of these were philosophers as well as scientific creators. Their philosophy of science was part of their creating a science—analytic geometry, calculus, theory of the Heavens, and scientific metaphysics, respectively; it was a working philosophy of science, not a theoretical one.

Today philosophy of science and science have split apart. Philosophy of science has become an abstract pursuit, a "specialty" of philosophers[104] largely divorced from scientific practice. Even if a philosopher of science is a practicing scientist, as was Philipp Frank, he is, *as* philosopher of science, detached from science; his philosophy is not a *working philosophy which he needs to do scientific work.* Most philosophers of science philosophize without doing science, and thus their philosophies are, from the point of view of the working philosophy of the originators of modern science, often incorrect. The most frequent error, largely due to Hume, is to forget Synthesis over Analysis, to emphasize the merely empirical aspect of science and, logically, to confuse axiom with hypothesis. The scientist, on the other hand, today needs no working philosophy of science to enable him to build his system. He works within the firm tracks laid by Galileo and Newton, the mathematical method. He *does* analysis and synthesis, as in chemistry, without having to ponder its meaning, as Lavoisier had to do. The reason is that science is largely routine and, even when creative, is a consequence of, and procedure within, the Galilean-Newtonian method. It is not a wild adventure, as was Galileo's. The Galilean adventure was to wrest science from philosophy, mathematical precision from phenomenal description and categorial speculation. It was the *discovery of a science,* not *scientific discovery.*

This difference is fundamental. *The method of analysis and synthesis is the method for creating sciences.* It is not a method

104. Hans Reichenbach, *The Rise of Scientific Philosophy,* p. 123.

of how to proceed in a created science. It is *epistemogenic,* not epistemological. Philosophy of science today is epistemological, not epistemogenic. It deals with scientific procedure, even scientific discovery, but not the discovery of science. This is understandable, for what goes for science today, natural science, is so set in its ways that it would be peculiar for a philosopher, as against a historian, of science to rehash the old story of the origins of natural science. Only if it were necessary today to discover a new science, to repeat the Galilean adventure in a different field, would it be important, indeed imperative, to go back to the old procedure.

Kant was both in the middle of the science of his time and engaged in the creation of a new science. He did his share in developing the Newtonian system and thus was a practical scientist. But he was, moreover, the creator of a new science, that of metaphysics; and in this task he used the scientific procedure of analysis and synthesis in the Newtonian sense.

The Newtonian method was for him a logic for creating a science.[105] Kant, at the culmination of a scientific development Descartes and Leibniz could only divine, was able to take the verbiage out of the method of discovering a science and present it in pure and exact logical terms. A philosophy, we have seen, was part of analysis; a science, part of synthesis. By philosophy Kant meant both natural and moral philosophy, and by science both natural and moral science, as had Newton, Descartes, and Leibniz. He saw the difference between philosophy and science as that between the *logical character of the concepts used in each of these two branches of knowledge*—analytic and synthetic concepts, respectively. In defining these two kinds of concepts as, respectively, verbal abstraction and schematic construction, that is spatio-temporal formations of signs and symbols, Kant brought into distinct focus what Descartes and Leibniz had seen only dimly.[106] While analytic concepts are ab-

105. This goes for the method of analysis *and* synthesis, not that of analysis alone. See below, p. xcvi; but also, § 117, Note.

106. The same subject was elaborated in our time by Ernst Cassirer in *The Philosophy of Symbolic Forms* (New Haven: Yale University Press, 1953–57).

stractions from experience, synthetic concepts are the constructions of the mind in space and time which articulate formal
intuition. Kant not only defines with precision the notion of intuition, in his concept of the schematism, but ties it to the notion
of science as a technical term. He defines the "simple natures"
in Descartes' method of discovery, at which Descartes had only
hinted, and Leibniz' "representation." He sharpens the notion of
judgment, showing that the analytic method contains judgments
with analytic concepts, and that these judgments may be either
analytic or synthetic, while the synthetic method uses judgments with synthetic concepts which are always synthetic a
priori.[107]

Analytic or philosophical concepts, then, are abstractions.
They are given either a priori, as the concept *Substance,* or a
posteriori, as the concept *Water.* The synthetic or scientific concepts, on the other hand, are constructions, as the geometrical
concept *Circle.* Since the analytic method "ought ever to precede" the synthetic, there is a transition from analysis to synthesis, from abstraction to construction, which Descartes had
captured in his notion of the "simple" and Kant defines in the
schematism and in his notion of construction in general. Descartes' "simple nature" was the identification of analysis and
synthesis, the result of analysis and the beginning of synthesis.
It contains within it, retrospectively, the whole of the phenomenon and, anticipatorily or axiomatically, the whole of its systematization. As such it must be regarded as the focal notion of science: induction and deduction, intuition and demonstration,
meet there in one pregnant formula.

b) Descartes

Descartes, as later, Newton, projected a universal frame of
reference for all phenomena whatever, both natural and moral.
As he says in Rule IV:

107. Analytic concepts were later called substantial or material; synthetic
concepts, functional or formal. The difference has been elaborated by Ernst
Cassirer, especially in *Substance and Function* (Chicago: Open Court Publishing Co., 1923).

It then follows that there must be a certain general science which explains everything which can be asked about order and measure, and which is concerned with no particular subject matter, and that this very thing is called "pure [literally, "universal"] mathematics," not by an arbitrary appellation, but by a usage which is already accepted and of long standing, because in it is contained everything on account of which other sciences are called "parts of mathematics."[108]

Mathesis universalis or *Mathesis vera* is a universal method, applicable equally to *res extensa* and *res cogitans*, to objects of sensorial and of non-sensorial knowledge. Over and above the particular sciences of mathematics there exists a pure science of order and measurement which is waiting to be discovered, a meta-mathematics, as it were, part of which today is called logic. Descartes' new science includes analytical geometry, but is concerned with order and measure in general. "It makes no difference whether such measure is sought in numbers, or figures, or stars, or sounds, or any other object whatever."[109] As a general science of order, removed from its mathematical "husk," the method would, in Descartes' metaphor, "clothe and adorn" itself in more suitable terms as a universal means of attaining true and solid knowledge, as the logical tool for the solution of all problems, whatever their subject matter.[110] Descartes actually suggests in Rule XIV, that he would prefer to have a reader who was not an expert mathematician. "This part of our method has not been devised for the sake of solving mathematical problems, but rather . . . mathematics is principally to be studied for the sake of perfecting our skill in this method"[111]—a view of mathematics similar to Plato's, in the relation of *dianoia* to *noesis,* as well as to Kant's notion of metaphysics as "that philosophy which contains the first *principles* of the use of *pure*

108. Descartes, *Rules for the Direction of the Mind,* trans. L. J. Lafleur, "Library of Liberal Arts," LLA 129 (New York: Bobbs-Merrill, 1961), p. 17.
    109. *Ibid.*
    110. Rule IV, trans. Lafleur, pp. 14–15.
    111. Rule XIV, trans. Lafleur, p. 70.

understanding" and the a priori rules of all science.[112] Descartes' *noesis,* the intuition of the "simples" of his method, leads to a body of exact meta-mathematical rules and operations. This general *science of order,* he assumed, would be applicable to both natural and moral philosophy. In both, the method must detect the absolute simple nature which contains within it the essence of the field under study.

Method in general, Descartes tells us in the *Rules,*

> consists entirely in the order and arrangement of those things upon which the power of the mind is to be concentrated in order to discover some truth. And we will follow this method exactly if we reduce complex and obscure propositions step by step to simpler ones [analysis] and then try to advance by the same gradual process from the intuitive understanding of the very simplest to the knowledge of all the rest [synthesis].
>
> In this one rule is contained the sum of all human endeavor. . . .[113]

The "secret of the entire method" is "that in all things we diligently note that which is most absolute,"[114] that is, most absolutely simple. The steps from the complex to the simple must be carefully kept in mind, noted and enumerated. This one should do by going "from first to last so quickly that by entrusting almost no parts of the process to the memory, I seem to grasp the whole series at once."[115] The reduction of the complex to the simple, or of a field of objects to a "single thing," "must reject whatever is irrelevant in the conception of [the objects] so that we can more readily retain the rest in our memory." Once the absolute simple or simples have been reached the second part of the task begins, the composition or synthesis. It consists, first of all, in distinguishing accurately the notions of the simples from those which are built up out of them. This simple or "single thing" "must be regarded in a different man-

---

112. *De mundi sensibilis atque intelligibilis forma et principiis,* par. 8, Akad. II, 395.

113. Rule V, trans. Lafleur, p. 19.

114. Rule VI, trans. Lafleur, p. 21.

115. Rule VII, trans. Lafleur, p. 25.

ner when we are concerned with its relationship to our knowledge of it, than when we speak of it in reference to its actual
existence." That is, the order of the mind which builds up the
synthesis is different from that of observation and abstraction
from which the elements of the new order were precipitated.
The compound result of synthesis is of "an order different" from
the complex which were the natural things resolved by analysis.
The compound, in other words, is the scientific subject matter.
The truth of each complex thing is the absolute simple or simples derived from it and used for the reconstruction of the compound. "We can never understand anything beyond these
simple natures and a certain mixture or composition of
them. . . ." These simples are self-evident. All knowledge is "of
the same nature and consists solely in the combination of self-
evident things."[116] The simples, which are both the result of
analysis and the beginning of synthesis, are, as the latter, the
axioms of the system. The system is applicable to reality because
the simples were analyzed out of it.

Let us now look more closely at the simples, for they are the
embryonic forms of Kant's schemata. They are, as we said, the
end result of analysis and the beginning of synthesis. The identification or fusion of the former with the latter is not as clearly
stated in Descartes as is the fusion of the categories with the
forms of space and time in Kant. Descartes says, in Rule V, that
analysis consists in reducing involved and obscure propositions
step by step to more simple ones, till we come to absolute
simples, pure intellectual intuitions, and that synthesis consists
in *starting from* these intuitions of the simplest propositions by
retracing our path through the same steps, working our way up
to the knowledge of all the others. Actually, of course, since the
synthesis proceeds in a different dimension, namely symbolization, from that of analysis, namely abstraction from observa-
tional matter, synthesis cannot proceed by the "same" steps as
did analysis. Rather, the building up of the system from the simples must follow that nature of the simples which *prescribes* the

116. Rule XII, trans. Lafleur, pp. 48–57.

course of the synthesis. This is true for any synthesis, whether in thought, in which case the simples are the axioms of a system, or in matter, in which case the simples are atoms and molecules, as in chemical synthesis.

The simple, as Descartes makes clear in Rule VI, is the *limit* of a gradually regressive movement from the more to the less relative.[117] A term is said to be *absolute* if "it contains the nature under investigation in its pure and simple form."[118] Otherwise it is called relative. The rule of analysis as *regressive* (*reductive*) process demands that we should work towards the most simple or absolute, which is also, in the words of the third precept of the *Discourse*, "the easiest to understand." This is not meant, of course, psychologically but epistemologically or, indeed, logically. The first principles of science are the most difficult to discover. But they are the easiest to understand, the most simple in the scholastic sense of the term, as Descartes uses it in the Reply to the Fifth Objection. A term is *more* known in proportion as it is required for knowledge of other terms. The *most* known of a series is that term upon which all other terms of the series in question depend in order to be known.[119] In other words, the *most* known, or the absolutely simple, is the axiom of the system. It is derived by the regressive analysis and recognized as self-evident in intuition. The *more* known are the theorems. When we know a simple nature we intuit it directly and completely. Such knowledge is not a matter of analysis, that is, of the knowledge of parts.[120] The absolute simple is the first term in the *progressive* (*deductive*) synthesis which will reconstruct, step by step but in a different order, the analytic series.

Thus, in the last analysis, knowledge depends on seeing what is simple and absolute in an analytic series, that is, the structural

117. Cf. L. J. Beck, *The Method of Descartes: A Study of the Regulae* (Oxford: Oxford University Press, 1952), p. 160.
118. Rule VI, trans. L. J. Beck, p. 163. "Absolutum voco, quidquid in se continet naturam puram et simplicens, de qua est quaestis."
119. Cf. L. J. Beck, p. 165.
120. Cf. *ibid.,* p. 166.

core of a phenomenal field. This simple nature is structured in such a way that it can be identified with a purely formal construction—an identification where *res extensa* and *res cogitans* meet. At its very core, reality is structure; and any field of inquiry contains in its core a germ of structure of which all the phenomena in question are manifestations. To discern these simple structures is a special capacity. They can only be grasped by a clear and distinct vision of intellectual intuition. We must not attempt to explain or define simple natures, we must only endeavor to see them clearly and distinctly.[121] Descartes inserts the warning that "there are only a few pure and simple natures which are not to be apprehended in dependence upon something else but are to be intuited primarily and through themselves either in experiences themselves or by light innate in us."[122] Simple natures, he repeats in Rule XII, are per se *notae,* and our main task is to elicit them from sense experience by careful analysis of the confused composite data presented to the mind. Once derived they are known *per se* as clear and distinct. They are the ultimate principles of explanation. The core of the method is the *identification of an analytic simple with a synthetic simple*. Whereas the former ends a process, the latter begins a process. Whereas analysis is a process of subtraction, synthesis is one of addition. "It is always by subtraction that the terms yielded by analysis become progressively more simple, and it is by addition in the synthesis that the successive terms become more complex."[123] In the simple, the end result of the analytic reduction, or subtraction, is used as the starting point of the synthetic addition.

This identification of analysis and synthesis was clarified by Kant, as has been mentioned, in the notion of the schema. On the other hand, the Cartesian precedent makes clear how important general logic is in the Kantian architectonic. For as analysis ought ever to precede synthesis—it prepares the point of

121. Rules VI, XII. Cf. *ibid.,* pp. 81 f.
122. Rule VI, trans. L. J. Beck, *ibid.*
123. L. J. Beck, p. 281.

departure for synthesis—so the logic of analysis ought ever to precede the logic of synthesis, that is, general logic ought ever to precede transcendental logic. Both are part of one and the same procedure, the analysis and synthesis of thought. The schematism, in the architecture of the *Critique of Pure Reason,* rather than in that of its subject matter, metaphysics, is the fusion of general with transcendental logic, the transition, that is, from metaphysical (analytic) to transcendental (synthetic) deduction.

This transition is the very core of the *Critique,* as the fusion of the result of analysis with a formula for synthesis is the very core of any science. This fusion has often been misunderstood, both in the *Critique* and in science in general. In the latter, for example, it was misunderstood as the relation of antecedent and consequent.[124] Actually, "the object of intellectual intuition is two elements linked in an immediate and necessary connection,"[125] but not as antecedent and consequent of a hypothetical judgment, but rather as two aspects of one and the same thing, like the concave and convex of one and the same curve. Every science begins with such axiomatic identification. The science of optics began, as already Lambert noted,[126] when a ray of light, the analytic simple, was identified with a geometric line, the synthetic simple.[127] The combination makes the system of geometry applicable to rays of light and this, precisely, is the science of optics. Similarly, Kant identified judgment and thought in his science of metaphysics. In the first case geometry, in the second logic, as the science of the forms of judgment, be-

124. Cf. *ibid.,* pp. 75 f.

125. *Ibid.*

126. J. H. Lambert, "On the Analytic Method, to Change Experiments into Systems," *Logische und philosophische Abhandlungen* (Berlin, 1787), § 18; reprinted in Lambert, *Philosophische Schriften* (Hildesheim: Georg Olms, 1969), VII, 70.

127. "Frequently the application of a whole science to an object depends on some trifle. Thus, almost the whole of optics is based on the fact that light propagates itself in a straight line. This is sufficient to apply the whole of geometry to it. For nothing is more natural than the corresponding premise: Where there are straight lines there elementary geometry is applicable. This is self-evident." *Ibid.*

came applicable to the field in question, light and thought, respectively, and rendered these fields scientific.

In summary, the Cartesian method is the *analysis* of the given
sense material with the aim of finding its absolutely simple constituents and, out of these, the *synthesis* of a new order which
corresponds to the given material in a new medium, usually
that of thought, but also in that of primary matter (as in chemical
synthesis) or in that of artifices (as in technology). *Synthesis is
the reconstruction in a different dimension of the subject matter of analysis.*

Descartes laid the major emphasis on the method of analysis,
which is to him the method of discovering the truth. The
method of synthesis, he thought, is chiefly a means of explica-
tion and demonstration of what is already known. Leibniz' and
Kant's emphasis is on synthesis, and in this respect represents
an important step beyond Descartes. Descartes states his view
at the end of the Reply to the Second Set of Objections. He has
been asked to state the arguments and demonstrations of the
Meditations, set forth in that work in analytical order, in "geometrical fashion." He points out that this is a synthetic procedure and adds: "It was this synthesis alone which the ancient
Geometers used in their writings not because they were entirely
ignorant of analysis but, in my opinion, because they thought
it so valuable that they wished to keep it to themselves as an
important secret." The synthetic method is akin in its process
to the syllogism, using "definitions, postulates, axioms, theorems."[128] The perfect syllogism, in the form "A = B, B = C,
therefore C = A," implies actually the first axiom of Euclid.
Here Space appears as a condition of synthetic thought; but
while this is clear in geometry, it is by no means clear in metaphysics. This subject was developed by Leibniz, in his notion of
Representation, and by Kant in the Transcendental Aesthetics.[129]

c) Leibniz

With Leibniz the vision of the *Mathesis universalis* becomes
more exact. The *scientia generalis* must not only contain the

128. Trans. L. J. Beck, in *The Method of Descartes,* p. 176.
129. Cf. H. J. Paton, *Kant's Metaphysic of Experience,* I, 157, 211.

principles and methods of all the sciences, is must be a *method of calculating with them*. These principles and methods therefore must be represented by signs and characters, in a *characteristica universalis*, whose operations are as exact as a mathematical calculus but of higher universality, including the mathematical. It would be what we call a meta-mathematical or a logical calculus. The infinite variety of the world would be reduced to simplest concepts and from these their combinations would be built up, in all possible variety, in an *ars combinatoria*. Once this universal science exists, all the sciences could be constructed from it. The *scientia generalis* is the method *omnes alias scientias ex datis sufficientibus inveniendi at demonstrandi*. It consists, beside the characteristic, of sets of axioms applicable to any particular science. From them, and from the definitions of the symbols, are derived the appropriate rules for the formulas which constitute the methodology of any particular science. From the ideal of general science, thus, follows that of ordering all the sciences in a hierarchy in which all are related, for all involve the same ultimate principles and rest upon the same harmony. Philosophy "thus becomes the most general and universal science, seeking the common principles and common structure of being which all other fields represent from a limited point of view. Its problems center in two foci, that of metaphysics and that of the methodology of knowledge."[130] Kant later combined the two.

Analysis and synthesis play the same role in this vision as in Descartes, but are more exactly defined. Analysis serves to find the simple structures which are the core of reality, and synthesis is the choice of their representative character or symbolization, as well as the operations with them. Analysis is only a means to synthesis. It leads toward the principles with which synthesis starts. Synthesis, starting from these principles in symbolic form, operates with them, leading to "tables" and "formulas" which, in turn, discover the solutions of the problems that gave rise to

130. G. W. Leibniz, *Philosophical Papers and Letters*, L. E. Loemker, trans. and ed. (Chicago: University of Chicago Press, 1956), p. 36.

analysis. It is synthesis which is the end of the method and "of permanent value." The whole method, of analysis and synthesis, is the art of discovery.[131] Representation is the function of symbols or characters to stand for objective states of things. Leibniz combined representation with analysis and synthesis in the notion of reasoning (ratiocinari) which is "the analytic-synthetic defining or 'formulating' of a structure of symbols in such a way that it can be verified as representing the structure of reality. Successful synthesis involves the choice of 'real' characters, symbols qualified by their very structure to reveal the organization of the world in their formulas."[132] Reasoning thus consists in the construction, and application to experience, of symbols according to established sets of axioms and accepted rules of operation or transformation.

Unfortunately, Leibniz believed that the ultimate "real" elements of synthesis were contained in, and could be precipitated from, common language, and by logical procedure in the Aristotelian scholastic sense. He did not see the intuitive leap that was necessary for their discovery, as had Descartes in his instructions on how to find simples or, as later had Kant, in the insight that an entirely different kind of logic would be needed. Thus, while in one sense, that of representation, Leibniz' step was one forward from Descartes, in another sense, and for that very reason, it was a step behind Descartes, to scholastic logic. Leibniz did not see that the symbols of synthesis are of an entirely different kind from those of analysis. Common language, as Kant was to show, is exclusively analytic.

Leibniz, as Mahnke has pointed out,[133] returned from the intuitive to the formal foundation of certainty, from the ars inveniendi to the ars demonstrandi. He sees the criterion of truth again in the possibility of its formally correct demonstration, and relies on the two great principles of Contradiction or Identity and

131. See Leibniz, Of Universal Analysis and Synthesis, or The Art of Discovery and Judgment, 1679.

132. Loemker, ed., Philosophical Papers, p. 36.

133. Dietrich Mahnke, Leibnizens Synthese von Universalmathematik und Individualmetaphysik (Stuttgart: Friedrich Frommann Verlag, 1964).

of Sufficient Reason. Every true proposition, according to Leibniz, is either identical or reducible to an identical one. The identical propositions are true and the contradictory ones false. If there is not an explicit or evident identity of the proposition, or an immediacy between subject and predicate, as in the proposition *homo albus est albus,* then, in order to supplement the *principium identitatis,* one has to take recourse to the *principium dandae rationis:* in order to sustain the proposition through an analysis of the subject-concept one has to show that the predicate-concept is at least virtually or in a concealed manner implied in it. In a word, Leibniz goes back from intuition to formal identity.

Yet, in the notion of "concealed implication" he foreshadows Kant's discussion of the analytic judgment in our text. In his answer to the Leibnizian Eberhard, *On a Discovery according to which any new Critique of Pure Reason has been made superfluous by an older one,* 1790, Kant uses the Leibnizian distinction between the principle of contradiction and the principle of sufficient reason as justification for his own distinction of analytic and synthetic judgment, and this time equates the principle of sufficient reason with *synthetic* judgment. This is not contradictory, since both analytic and synthetic judgment use primarily analytic concepts, and the difference between the two is relative rather than absolute, as is that of the two principles in Leibniz. Kant's interpretation of Leibniz on this point does not seem as "bold" as Martin maintains,[134] for Leibniz does speak of "contingent propositions" and discusses the nature of the "connection of subject and predicate" in them. The principle of sufficient reason is, for Leibniz, the "principle of contingency."[135]

In the end, Leibniz could find no *logical* way to recognize the final unresolvable elementary concepts that were to be the result of analysis and would be symbolized in the "alphabet of

134. Gottfried Martin, *Kant's Metaphysics and Theory of Science* (Manchester: Manchester University Press, 1955), p. 75.

135. Philip P. Wiener, trans. and ed., *Leibniz Selections* (New York: Charles Scribner's Sons, 1951), pp. 94 f.; C. I. Gerhardt, *Die philosophischen Schriften von Gottfried Wilhelm Leibniz* (Hildesheim: Georg Olms, 1960), IV, 438.

ideas." In his youth, Leibniz had hoped in a very short time to be able to find this "little alphabet of thought" from which the infinite number of more complex concepts could be constituted combinatorially. Later he recognized more and more fully the tremendous, even perhaps insuperable difficulty of this task and considered that the number of elementary concepts, as of prime factors, might be infinite. He therefore took recourse to the analysis of propositions, holding that for its completeness, analysis of the concepts was not necessary. One had to go only so far as to show that the containment of the requisite notes of the predicate in those of the subject was evident without asking further for the primitive requisites of these requisites. Thus, in spite of many difficulties, he held formal analytic demonstration of all the fundamental truths to be possible for finite intellects. In the course of these investigations, however, Leibniz was forced back—or forward—to the Cartesian position. What are the methodological criteria for recognizing elementary concepts? Leibniz had to fall back on intuition. The structures which did not possess simpler requisites were to be grasped intuitively, immediately and through themselves alone.[136] In the same way he came to hold that the identity of a formally irreducible truth could only be grasped through itself by intuition. The result was a theory of knowledge which was similar to but more explicit than Descartes', and which is the same used by Kant, in his distinction of clarity and distinctness;[137] clarity is extensional, distinctness intensional, the former concerns the cognition of the object, the latter that of its characteristic. "When every ingredient that enters into a distinct concept is itself known distinctly, or when analysis is carried through to the end, knowledge is adequate."[138] Such knowledge, in other words, begins synthesis, for analysis has been carried through to the end.

Leibniz was not sure that a perfect example of this could be given by man, but thought that our concept of numbers ap-

136. See *Meditations on Knowledge, Truth and Ideas,* 1684. Gerhardt, IV, 423; Loemker, p. 448; Wiener, p. 283.
137. Below, pp. 67 f.
138. *Meditations* . . . , Loemker, p. 450.

proached it closely. Mathematics, that is, is a synthetic system.
For the most part, however,

> especially in a longer analysis, we do not intuit the entire nature of
> the subject matter at once but make use of signs instead of things,
> though we usually omit the explanation of these signs in any actu-
> ally present thought for the sake of brevity, knowing or believing
> that we have the power to do it. Thus, when I think of a chiliogon,
> or a polygon of a thousand equal sides, I do not always consider the
> nature of a side and of equality and of a thousand (or the cube of
> ten), but I use these words, whose meaning appears obscurely and
> imperfectly to the mind, in place of the ideas which I have of them,
> because I remember that I know the meaning of the words but that
> their interpretation is not necessary for the present judgment. Such
> knowledge I usually call *blind* or *symbolic;* we use it in Algebra and
> in Arithmetic, and indeed almost everywhere. When a concept is
> very complex, we certainly cannot think simultaneously of all the
> concepts which compose it. *But when this is possible, or at least
> insofar as it is possible, I call the knowledge intuitive.* There is no
> other knowledge than intuitive of a distinct primitive concept, while
> for the most part we have only symbolic knowledge of com-
> posites.[139]

When, however, we do have intuitive knowledge of composites,
the composite appears as one whole. Intuitive knowledge deals
with single subjects. Kant later made this clear in his discussion
of space and time. Thus, complete knowledge is intuitive, and
specifically *formally* intuitive. Intuitive knowledge is the immediate noetic grasp of a symbolic argument in its total meaning;
whereas symbolic or blind knowledge is the dianoetic running
through of the argument. Kant in our text, calls this distinction
that of *axiomata and akroamata.*[140]

Intuitive knowledge, thus, is formal. It is immediate grasp of
the meaning of symbolic discourse. Both, intuitive knowledge
and symbolic knowledge, together are the method of discovery;

---

139. *Ibid.* Cf. Kant, *Critique of Pure Reason,* B744.

140. Below, §§ 33–35; B 761. Cf. Lambert's editor: "One divides mathematicians into those who calculate well and those who see well. The latter . . .
see the results which the former calculate. . . . I have convinced myself that,
in a simultaneous multitude of ideas, they so to speak *feel* important results."
J. H. Lambert, "On the Analytic Method . . . ," p. x.

for the very blindness of the symbol helps the mind to carry on the argument without understanding what it means—until it reveals itself.

The end of analysis is the primitive or primary concept. Such concepts are those "from whose combination the rest are made."[141] Insofar as a primitive concept, or set of such concepts, summarizes the total analysis preceding them, they, together with the process leading up to them, are intuited. All this can be summarized by saying that such concepts are the *limit* of analysis, in the technical sense of that term.

The distinction between analysis and synthesis appears especially clearly in Leibniz' distinction between nominal and real definition, which Kant later called analytic and synthetic definition, the former being the enumeration of the notes of a concept, the latter being a construction. For Leibniz, the real definition is the one that shows the thing to be possible—and not self-contradictory—or that actually generates the thing. "The concept of the circle set up by Euclid, that of a figure described by the motion of a straight line in a plane about a fixed end, affords a real definition, for such a figure is evidently possible. Hence it is useful to have definitions involving the generation of a thing, or, if this is impossible, at least its constitution, that is, a method by which the thing appears to be producible or at least possible."[142] Equally, a definition of any existing thing is real since its existence demonstrates its possibility.[143]

Again, Leibniz confuses two things which Kant later distinguishes, the definition of an existing thing, which is not a synthetic but an analytic definition, since all it can do is enumerate the abstracted properties of the thing, and the synthetic definition which generates the thing. Obviously, the two "things" are different, one a thing in space and time, the other a thought construction put into space and time by a schematizing construction. The latter is meant when Leibniz says that "in any case of adequate knowledge we have at the same time an *a priori*

141. On *Universal Synthesis and Analysis* (1679), Loemker, p. 354.
142. *Ibid.*, pp. 354 f.
143. See *Knowledge, Truth, and Ideas*, 1684.

knowledge of the possibility; to wit, if we have carried the
analysis through to the end and no contradiction is visible, the
possibility of an idea is demonstrated."[144] Thus, although Leibniz insists on the "distinction between *nominal definitions,*
which contain only characters enabling us to distinguish one
thing from another, and *real definition* from which the possibility of things can be shown,"[145] he has not made clear that, or
how, it is possible for the *existence* of a thing to appear in its
"real" definition. For this reason, Kant located spatio-temporal
existence in the Aesthetic rather than the Analytic of Pure Reason; and made space (and time) a form of, or formal, *intuition*
rather than thought. Yet, it may well be asked whether, and in
which way, this intuition is different from that of Leibniz. This
does not so much mean that the intuition of Space contains a
thought element (which it does), but rather that the intuition
in the Leibnizian (-Cartesian) sense contains a Space element.
It seems almost certain that it does, that, in other words, any
system of objects, in the last resort, involves Space and Time.
Space, it seems, is just one paradigm of system; and any system
involves, and is, a space.[146]

The Leibnizian possibility, or non-contradictory nature, of
definition thus seems necessary for both nominal and real definitions; though in real definitions it seems, so to speak, more
immediately necessary, since real definitions refer to things that
either exist in space and time or may be constructed. But a
"nominal" definition which contains contradictory notes can
hardly be said to be "of something." The possibility of a thing
through real definition

is known either a *priori* or a *posteriori:* the former, when we analyze
the idea into its elements, that is, into other ideas whose possibility
is known, and know that it contains nothing which is incompatible.
For example, this is the case when we perceive the manner in which
an object is produced, whence *causal definitions* are of such para-
mount significance. On the other hand, we recognize the a *pos-*

144. *Ibid.,* Wiener, p. 288.
145. *Ibid.,* Wiener, p. 287.
146. See H. J. Paton, *Kant's Metaphysic of Experience,* I, 157, 211.

teriori possibility of a thing when its actuality is known to us through experience. For whatever exists or has existed must in any case be possible.[147]

Leibniz did not recognize, as did Kant, that a posteriori possibility means analytic, and a priori possibility means synthetic definition. Yet, when he says that "usually we are content to ascertain the reality of certain concepts by means of experience in order then to synthesize them according to the model of nature,"[148] he seems clearly to mean that the former reality, that of experience, is analytic, and the latter, the construction according to nature's model, synthetic. For what precedes synthesis is analysis, and it is analysis of experience.

Leibniz summarizes the method of Analysis and Synthesis in two ways, in his essay of 1679, and in his essay, *On Wisdom,* 1693. In the former, he distinguishes Analysis and Synthesis as follows.

> Synthesis is achieved when we begin from principles and run through truths in good order, thus discovering certain progressions and setting up tables, or sometimes general formulas, in which the answers to emerging questions can later be discovered. Analysis goes back to the principles in order to solve the *given problems* only, just as if neither we nor others had discovered anything before. It is more important to establish syntheses, because this work is of permanent value.

Analysis is discussed as being of two kinds. The common type advances by leaps and is used in algebra—this is one of the Cartesian uses of the term.

> The other is special and far more elegant but less well known; I call it "reductive" analysis. Analysis is more necessary in practice, in order to solve problems that are given to us. But whoever is capable of more theoretical pursuits will be content to practice analysis only far enough to master the art but will then prefer to synthesize. . . . Combination or synthesis is the better means for discovering the use or application of something as, for example, given the magnetic needle, to think of its application in the compass. Analysis, on the

147. Wiener, p. 287.
148. *Ibid.,* p. 288.

contrary, is best suited for discovering the means when the thing to be discovered or the proposed end is given.[149]

In the 1693 essay Leibniz sets the method of discovery into a wider framework.

> Wisdom is a perfect knowledge of the principles of all the sciences and of the art of applying them. By *principles* I mean all the fundamental truths which suffice to enable us to derive any conclusions we may need, by dint of some exertion and some little application; in sum, that which serves the mind to regulate manners, to make an honest living, and everywhere (even if one were surrounded by barbarians), to preserve one's health, to perfect one's self in any sort of things we may need, and finally, to provide for the convenience of living. The art of applying these principles to situations includes in it the art of judging well or reasoning, the art of discovering unknown truths, and finally, the art of recalling what one knows on the instant and whenever needed.[150]

As is seen, this is a program for all knowledge as exact science, both of nature and of morals, both theoretical and practical. Of the three arts, reasoning, discovering, and recalling, the one that interests us is that of discovery. It consists of the following maxims, which spell out Leibniz' notion of analysis and synthesis.

> 1. In order to become acquainted with a thing we must consider all of its prerequisites, that is, everything which suffices to distinguish it from any other thing. This is what is called definition, nature, essential property.
> 2. After we have found a means of distinguishing it from every other thing, we must apply this same rule to the consideration of each condition or prerequisite entering into this means, and consider all the prerequisites of each prerequisite. And that is what I call *true analysis*, or distribution of the difficulty into several parts.
> 3. When we have pushed the analysis to the end, that is, when we have considered the prerequisites entering into the consideration of the proposed thing, and even the prerequisites of the prerequisites, and finally have come to considering a few natures understood only by themselves without prerequisites and needing nothing outside themselves to be conceived, then we have arrived at a *perfect knowledge* of the proposed thing.

149. Loemker, pp. 357 f.
150. Wiener, p. 77.

4. When the thing merits it, we must try to have this perfect knowledge present in our mind all at once, and that is done by repeating the analysis several times until it seems to us that we see it as a complete whole in a single act of the mind [intuition]. And to obtain that result we must observe some gradation in the repetition.

5. The mark of perfect knowledge is that nothing appears in the thing under consideration which cannot be accounted for, and that nothing is encountered whose occurrence cannot be predicted in advance. . . .

9. The fruit of several analyses of different particular matters will be the catalogue of simple thoughts, or those which are not very far from being simple.

10. Having the catalogue of simple thoughts, we shall be ready to begin again *a priori* to explain the origin of things starting from their source in a perfect order and from a combination or *synthesis* which is absolutely complete. And that is all our soul can do in its present state.[151]

2. Analysis and Synthesis in Kant's "Critique of Pure Reason"

The role of analysis and synthesis, as we have seen, is different in philosophy from what it is in science. In philosophy, analysis and synthesis appear in terms of abstraction, and by general logic, through the notions of entailment or implication; in science they appear in terms of construction, and by transcendental logic, as a threefold procedure of reduction (analysis), schematic (or axiomatic) identification of "simples," and deductive demonstration (synthesis).

It would be easy to discuss the role of analysis and synthesis in Kant's *Critique* if we could be sure whether to regard it as philosophy or as science. But we cannot; and the question of whether it is the one or the other, or both, is unusually complicated. This is not due to difficulties in Kant's distinction between philosophy and science—which is straightforward and precise in both the *Logic* and the Transcendental Methodology—but to different uses of these terms in the two divisions of the *Critique*,

151. *Ibid.*, pp. 78 ff.

the Transcendental Analytic and the Transcendental Dialectic; and to the additional fact that in these two divisions either of the two different notions ("philosophy" and "science" respectively) is used in its own ambiguous manner. In the Analytic, "science" is meant in terms of transcendental logic, as constructive and conceptually synthetic, but there is an ambiguity concerning two kinds of constructions, metaphysical and mathematical. In this division, it is shown how Nature in general is metaphysically constructed in the manner that natural scientists experimentally construct natural entities. In the Dialectic, "science" is meant in terms of general logic, abstractive and conceptually analytic. Here thought-experiments are conducted and their contradictions resolved by showing up the analytic-synthetic ambiguities of the terms used, in a manner similar to that of resolving fallacies in general logic.

Further, the notion of "experiment" is used differently in the two divisions: in the Analytic as literally scientific, that is, in application to objects; in the Dialectic as analogically "scientific," that is, in application to concepts and propositions of reason (the subject matter of which may be either objects of experience or things in themselves. Since objects of experience are the outcome of the science of metaphysics, this science would appear as one of the subject matters of the transcendental philosophy).

The transcendental philosophy, we remember, "is the principle of the qualitative relations of concepts to ideas of pure reason (e.g. of God), insofar as they are thought to be united in a system of the whole"[152] The science of metaphysics, on the other hand, is the relationship of concepts to objects of experience. The transcendental philosophy, we may say, deals with the relation of concepts to reason, while the science of metaphysics deals with the relation of concepts to intuition. The scientific procedure in the strict and direct sense is that shown in the Analytic, where it is examined rather than used (unless we regard the Analytic itself as a kind of meta-science, the object

152. *Opus Postumum,* Akad. XXI, 72.

of which is the science of metaphysics). The scientific procedure in the indirect and analogical sense is that of the Dialectic, where it is used rather than examined. Thus, in the Analytic we have a *science of metaphysics examined,* in the Dialectic a *transcendental philosophy realized.*

In the following we shall try, in the simplest possible terms, to unravel these strands, first by examining the relationship between transcendental philosophy and science of metaphysics, and then by discussing the role of analysis and synthesis, first in the transcendental philosophy and then in the science of metaphysics.

a) Transcendental Philosophy and Science of Metaphysics

In the *Preface* to *Metaphysical Foundations of Natural Science* Kant makes a distinction between natural philosophy and natural science. A rational doctrine of nature, he writes, deserves the name of natural *science* only when the natural laws on which it is based are recognized a priori and are not merely laws of experience. Cognition of nature of the former kind is called *pure,* and of the second kind *applied.* The word "nature" implies the notion of laws, and the latter that of *necessity* of all those determinations of a thing which belong to its existence. Hence natural science can justify its name only by a "pure section" which contains the principles a priori of all possible accounts of nature; and it is *science* only on the basis of this pure section. On it is based the apodeictic certainty reason demands in a true science. This pure part of natural cognition must show what reason can accomplish by itself and where it needs the assistance of principles of experience. Pure rational cognition based on *mere concepts* is called pure philosophy or metaphysics; whereas rational cognition based on the *construction of concepts,* through representation of an object in an intuition a priori, is called mathematics.

Natural science properly so called presupposes, first of all, metaphysics of nature; for laws, i.e. principles of the necessity of that which belongs to the *existence* of a thing, deal with a concept which cannot be constructed, namely, existence, which cannot be represented in any intuition a priori. Metaphysics of nature contains all those principles which are not empirical, and either deals exclusively with the laws which concern the possibility of the notion of nature in general, without regard to any particular object of the sense world, or it deals with such particular objects. In the first case, it is the transcendental or general part of the metaphysics of nature; in the second case, the applied or particular part.

The latter, Kant maintains, can be properly scientific only in the degree that it contains *mathematics*. For, as transcendental natural metaphysics explains, to cognize something a priori means to cognize it from its mere possibility. But the possibility of determinate natural things cannot be cognized from their mere concepts but only from the a priori *intuition* which corresponds to the concepts. This means that the concepts must be *constructed,* and this in turn means that they must be mathematical. Thus, while a transcendental pure metaphysics of nature in general, i.e. one which examines only the condition of a concept of nature in general, is possible without mathematics, a particular pure metaphysics of nature, concerning particularly determined natural things, is possible only by mathematics; and only insofar as mathematics is applicable to it is such a doctrine of nature a science. Since this is so, however, there must be contained, even in transcendental metaphysics of nature, principles of the *construction* of concepts, which belong to the possibility of matter itself. On the other hand, in mathematical cognition one cannot omit the principles of transcendental metaphysics which are derived from the essence of the cognitive capacity itself and contain the pure actions of thinking, that is, concepts and principles a priori which alone bring the manifold of *empirical representations* into that lawful connection through which alone it becomes *empirical cognition,* i.e. experience. Hence Kant concludes this part of the Preface:

> I have considered it necessary, in that part of the pure section of natural science (*physica generalis*) where *metaphysical and mathematical constructions* are usually intermingled, to present the former [i.e. metaphysical constructions] in a system, and together

with them, the *principles of the construction of these concepts,* i.e. of the possibility of a mathematical doctrine of nature itself.[153]

This passage contains the problem in question. For whereas Kant distinguishes natural philosophy from natural science by the difference between "pure philosophy or metaphysics," which does *not* contain construction of concepts, and mathematics, which *does* contain such construction, he now speaks, with reference to the pure part of natural science, of *metaphysical constructions,* which are intermingled with mathematical constructions. What then are these metaphysical constructions?

Obviously, the metaphysical constructions of the pure part of a natural science, i.e. of an *applied* transcendental metaphysics, must come from the transcendental metaphysics itself. This latter deals with the concept of nature in general; and the question is whether that notion, of nature in general, is an abstracted or a constructed one. If the former, we have in the *Critique* merely transcendental philosophy; if the latter, we also have in it a science. And the point at which the philosophy would become a science would be the point at which the pure concepts of the understanding become constructions, i.e. schemata. In other words, the deductions of the *Critique* would present the transition from transcendental philosophy to the science of metaphysics. We shall discuss this matter in greater detail in Section (b) below.

Suffice it to say, at this point, that the notion of construction, originally connected in Kant's mind only with mathematics, was gradually extended both within and beyond mathematics. In the celebrated examples in the Preface to the second edition of the *Critique,* concerning the procedures of Thales, Galileo, Torricelli and Stahl, Kant shows how in various fields of mathematics and natural science concepts construct their own objects; that is, how reason has insight only into that which it produces after a plan of its own. Here we have examples both from mathematics and from natural science, and both as prototypes of the

153. *Metaphysical Foundations of Natural Science,* Akad. IV, 473. Italics added (trans. James Ellington, Indianapolis: Bobbs-Merrill, 1970).

revolutionary scientific procedure applied in metaphysics; so that the constructive approach, as Buchdahl notes, "covers *four* domains: The constructive activity of mathematics; the constructive element among the conditions determining cognitive judgment in general; the constructive activity of the scientist . . . ; and, finally, the constructive approach of the 'metaphysics of nature'."[154] In the latter, Kant shows that the physical forces require mathematization, through the notions of "real motions" expressed quantitatively in terms of velocity; that velocity becomes *intelligible,* i.e. can be shown to be possible only through *construction in space* (in the form of what today we would call "vector quantities"); and that only through such spatio-temporal construction can a material or "mathematical" body be represented in mechanics. Moreover, and this is the point that we want to make, and here we adduce the testimony of Buchdahl,

> construction links up with intuition: "for it is in intuition" that "we construct [any] concept" of a mathematical, e.g. geometrical, nature. In this way, "construction" becomes a basic ingredient in Kant's definition of possible cognitive experience, of which intuition is an integral component. Here we can see clearly at work Kant's method of re-interpreting and re-locating the concepts of his earlier period. The truly mechanical becomes the mathematical, which in turn is further articulated in the crucial aspect of "construction". And "construction" itself, from being initially located in the realm of mathematical operations, is *generalised in the body of the "critical" argument as the process of "synthesis" of the "empirical manifold",* i.e. *of a process which operates on the material of sensation, our perceptions. In this way, "synthesis", and with this "construction", become transcendental elements.*[155]

Here, then, we have "metaphysical construction." Not only the object of natural science, but *any* object, for its cognition, requires spatio-temporal construction.

> Construction thus stands for an *a priori* formal component of cognitive experience in general. . . . Although *Metaphysische Anfangs-*

154. Gerd Buchdahl, *Metaphysics and the Philosophy of Science* (Cambridge, Mass.: The MIT Press, 1969), p. 497.

155. *Ibid.,* pp. 555 f. Italics added.

gründe der Naturwissenschaft discusses construction primarily
under the aspect of its relevance for science, what it says defines at
the same time Kant's general position in respect of cognitive experience as such, with its *implicit* employment of the categories.
It informs us that, if we want to formulate the conditions of physical
(as against purely logical) language, we cannot operate "merely
with concepts", subject only to the law of contradiction.[156]

As we have seen, the possibility of determinate natural things
cannot be cognized from their mere concepts. "From these may
be grasped, it is true, the possibility of the thought (that it does
not contradict itself) but not that of the object, as a natural thing
which can be given outside of thought (as existent)."[157] Hence,
there must be added the corresponding a priori intuition, which
means construction.

What Kant says of the scientific cognition of natural things in
the *Metaphysical Foundations* is valid, *mutatis mutandis,* of the
cognition of all natural things; and this cognition thus becomes
scientific, albeit not by mathematical but by metaphysical construction. Kant speaks a language similar to the Preface of the
Metaphysical Foundations in the Postulates of Empirical
Thought of the *Critique*—in a section written *after* the *Metaphysical Foundations*—where he shows that change, coexist-
ence, etc., require "outer intuition."[158] And in the chapter of the
Critique on the "schematism of concepts," as again Buchdahl
notes,

> the same point is made though in a different language. A category
> concept can only be "applied" when the formal conditions of sensi-
> bility (space and time) are given. Thus, the concept of the triangle
> must be regarded as a "rule of synthesis", as "the representation of
> a method", of drawing "in thought", in conformity with the rule
> implicit in the concept. The reader should note the peculiar equiv-
> alences, implied in the passage from *Metaphysische Anfangsgründe,*
> between "constructing a concept" and "giving the concept in an
> *a priori* intuition". There is always an easy traffic in Kant between

156. *Ibid.,* pp. 561 f. Cf. pp. 673 f.
157. *Metaphysical Foundations of Natural Science,* Akad. IV, 470 (trans.
James Ellington, Indianapolis: Bobbs-Merrill, 1970).
158. B 291 f.

possibility, a *priori*, intuition, and construction, and of course, space and time, as forms of intuition.[159]

The reason is, simply, that the objects of cognition are all constructed, either metaphysically or mathematically, either, we may say, in the science of metaphysics or in that of nature; whereas in metaphysics as philosophy, where we do *not* deal with schematized but with pure concepts of the understanding, we do not encounter constructions, that is, real possibility of objects, but only logical possibility. The concept of a figure enclosed within two straight lines is not contradictory and hence not logically impossible (for the concept of two straight lines coming together contains no negation of a figure), but it is impossible of realization as a construction in space. "The impossibility does not rest on the concept in itself but on its construction in space, i.e. on the conditions of space and its determination."[160] We thus have constructive as against logical possibility; but also constructive as against logical actuality, necessity, and in short, constructive as against logical categories. Construction, says Kant,[161] is in transcendental logic what meaning is in general logic. Construction incorporates existence into meaning. In constructive necessity, we have "that which in its connection with the actual is determined according to universal conditions of experience,"[162] i.e. that existence which is universally and necessarily connected with all other existents. And this is Nature. "By nature (empirically understood) we understand the connection of appearances as to their existence according to necessary rules, i.e. laws."[163]

With this constructive definition we have returned to our point of departure, the determination of Nature as such, as against that of particular natural things. We see that both are constructed. But we also have seen that, in another sense, one

159. Buchdahl, *Metaphysics and the Philosophy of Science*, p. 562.
160. B 268.
161. B 298, 299.
162. B 266.
163. B 263.

of pure metaphysics unmixed with particular applied elements, Nature may be conceived without construction.

There is thus an ambiguity in the Metaphysics of Nature, or at least a subtlety of distinction which is difficult to detect in the Analytic. On the other hand, the course of the argument in the Analytic, which in the deductions "deviates" toward the construction of Nature, resumes—again in a supposedly scientific manner—in the Dialectic in certain thought-experiments which, from the strict point of view of the logical distinction between philosophy and science in the *Logic* and in the Methodology of the *Critique,* are no experiments at all, and are philosophy rather than science.

Thus, for reasons lying in both the Analytic and the Dialectic, the *Critique* must be regarded as both philosophy and science. We shall therefore consider the role of analysis and synthesis in both aspects.

b) Analysis and Synthesis in Kant's Transcendental Philosophy

In the transcendental philosophy, as against the science of metaphysics, analysis and synthesis appear as they do in general logic. This does not mean that they play no role as critical philosophy; they do, but only in the Dialectic. In the Analytic, reason, insofar as it remains unapplied schematically, is in its speculative employment only, and as such "does not contain a single direct-synthetic judgment out of concepts,"[164] for this would be possible only by experience. And the analytic judgments reason deals with in this employment "teach us nothing more about the object than what the concept we have of it already contains."[165] Reason, in this employment, is subjectively a system by means of analytic concepts only, "a system of investigation according to principles of unity"[166] only, while the materials of this activity must be supplied by experience alone. No wonder, then, that Kant gives us very scant information about the method of transcendental philosophy which deals with speculative rea-

164. B 764.
165. *Ibid.*
166. B 766.

son only and is a matter of general logic. All he can say about this method is negative: "Because the mere form of cognition, as much as it may accord with logical laws, is far from sufficient to make out material (objective) truth for cognition, no one can venture merely with logic to judge objects and to assert anything, without having previously secured well-founded information about them outside logic. . . ."[167] The idea of arriving at any material (as against formal) truth through general logic alone must be given up. We have another equally negative but very direct answer to our quest for the method of transcendental philosophy: "Of the peculiar method of a transcendental philosophy, however, nothing can be said here, since we are concerned only with a critique of our circumstances, whether we can build at all and to what height we can carry our edifice with the material we possess (the pure concepts a *priori*)."[168]

The *Critique,* seen as transcendental philosophy, comes into its own in the Transcendental Dialectic, not in the Analytic. In the Dialectic, the very method of the *Critique,* as determination of the formal conditions of a complete system of pure reason, becomes effective in what may be called a formally "scientific" manner—described by Kant as "imitating the natural scientist" —but not a materially constructive scientific manner, as in the Analytic.

Kant set out to determine the possibility of metaphysical cognition, that is, of cognizing the objects of transcendental ideas (God, freedom, immortality). He ended by establishing a metaphysics of nature. The objects of transcendental ideas were found to lie beyond the reach of theoretical knowledge, due to principal limitations in man's theoretical reason. "Though we had a tower in mind that was to reach to the heavens, the supply of materials was sufficient only for a dwelling house roomy enough for our business on the plain of experience and high enough to survey it."[169] The metaphysics of nature which is not related to any special objects of experience, thus indeterminate

167. B 85.
168. B 766.
169. B 735. .

in respect of the nature of this or that thing, is, as we have seen, transcendental metaphysics of nature. It establishes the principles or most general laws that first make the concept of nature possible. A metaphysics of nature, on the other hand, which determines the special nature of a particular kind of things, for instance of matter or of the thinking being (*res extensa, res cogitans*), is a special metaphysical science in which the principles of transcendental metaphysics are applied to a particular kind of objects of our sensibility. The special metaphysics, for instance of corporeal (external) things, presupposes the general transcendental metaphysics; it is "an off-shoot sprouting from its root." This science is contained in the *Metaphysical Foundations of Natural Science.*

If the transcendental metaphysics of nature, in the total framework of the *Critique,* was, if not a by-product at least only a means to the end of Kant's "plan,"[170] then, by the same token, the scientific procedure of the Analytic was the same. It enters at the point at which Kant, rather than arguing that reason could *not* by itself cognize things, demonstrates how it *can* cognize things by a special schematic procedure.

What, then, is the method of the *Critique* leading to this result? It encounters elements a priori and finds itself compelled, by the "nature" of the conditions under investigation, to concede that these a priori elements are only of empirical use, and acquire meaning solely in this use. Subsequently, it shows that certain a priori elements—pure concepts, the categories—are applicable to empirical data by way of transcendental schemata, the schemata being two-sided presentations capable of forming a link between a priori elements and appearances. This provides the outline of a method which accounts also for the schematic construction of mathematics. For mathematics proceeds through a synthetic construction of its objects in the a priori forms of space and time under which things appear to us. But all this is the determination of a method *within* the method proper of the *Critique*—or even the determination of two

170. *Ibid.*

methods, that of the general application of categories, a constructive epistemology or doctrine of metaphysical constructions, and that of mathematical construction. This method is not that of the *Critique* itself, in the sense that the latter describes rather than uses this method. The method it uses is the formally "scientific" method of the Dialectic. We may perhaps say that the materially constructive scientific method of the Analytic is a subject matter of the *Critique,* whereas the formally "scientific" method of the Dialectic, which is transcendental philosophy rather than science of metaphysics, is the *Critique's* own method.

For there is more to transcendental philosophy than its furnishing us with a general metaphysics of nature. The *Critique of Pure Reason* is a "traité de la méthode, not a system of the science itself," namely, of metaphysics.[171] Just because of this "propaedeutic" character (as compared with the doctrinal one which would supply the entire system of metaphysics itself) the *Critique* gives the entire outline (*Umriss*) of metaphysics, in regard to its limits as well as to its inner structure (*Gliederbau*), the inner structure comprising the general metaphysics of nature. But the "outline" goes beyond the latter and is meant, as far as transcendental knowledge is concerned, to be exhaustive. If it is true that in every cognition of nature there is only as much science as there is mathematics, there must still be a philosophical (non-mathematical) method that enables the *Critique of Pure Reason* to *establish* itself as a science. In this role, it cannot gain its results by schematic construction after the example of mathematics, through construction of concepts in an *a priori* intuition, because mathematics itself is here an object, not the subject of cognition. When the *Critique* tells us how metaphysics as a science is possible, it must have a method of rational cognition, merely through concepts, that is all its own.

Everything determined by the Transcendental Doctrine of Method of the *Critique* as a characteristic of *philosophical* as distinguished from mathematical cognition must, of course, ap-

171. B xxii.

ply to the *Critique of Pure Reason* as transcendental *philosophy* itself. All the differences between philosophy and mathematics enumerated there, of akroamata and axiomata, of exposition and definition, of various kinds of proof, are general characteristics of any philosophical cognition and can also be found, often verbatim, in the Doctrine of Method of our text. The Transcendental Doctrine of Method has its own systematic program, it is "a determination of the *formal* conditions of a complete system of pure reason."[172] The Transcendental Doctrine of Elements had taken stock of the materials, the supply at hand for the edifice of metaphysics: pure forms of intuition, categories and principles of the understanding. The Transcendental Doctrine of Method gives certain directions for avoiding the dogmatic method and the imitating of mathematicians (in philosophy), for exercising restraint in the polemical use of pure (transcendent) reason and in its hypotheses. It introduces the vicarious *canon* of pure *practical* reason, resumes the methodological thread with an a priori architectonic of the sciences, and ends with a brief review of the historical elaborations of pure reason ("more ruins than edifice") from a transcendental viewpoint. These are technical-formal conditions of a complete system of pure reason and therefore should be fulfilled in any metaphysical science.

The method of a particular science can normally be determined only after it has discovered the secure road of steadily advancing knowledge. Metaphysics, having led a rather doubtful existence through the centuries and being open to serious questioning of its scientific character, requires a special investigation of its very possibility as a science. We know the outcome: the "great" metaphysics is impossible as a theoretical science, the "little" metaphysics in this field remains.

The revealing Preface to the second edition, with its explanation of the reasons for the revolution of thinking (*der Denkart*) which promises to make metaphysics a science, can be used to justify both notions of science we are discussing, the construc-

172. B 735.

tive material, and the abstractive formal one. Let us here justify
the latter. Kant describes the impossibility of cognition a priori
if this cognition must conform to objects, but the possibility of
such cognition if the objects of experience must conform to the
conditions of our cognizing them, the Copernican turn of seeking the origin of certain objective knowledge in the subject.
"We do not cognize in things anything a priori except what we
put into them ourselves."[173] There follows a more specific explanation of his procedure: "This method imitating the natural
scientist thus consists in this: to seek the elements of pure reason in *what can be confirmed or refuted by an experiment*."[174]
The experiment is carried out, not as in physics with objects,
but with *concepts* and *propositions,* which are so arranged that
their objects may be considered from two distinct viewpoints:
on the one hand as objects of the senses and the understanding
for experience, on the other hand as objects merely thought by
reason alone in striving beyond the limits of experience. If it
turns out that by contemplating things from that twofold viewpoint, "agreement with the principle of pure reason takes place,
but that from a unitary viewpoint an inevitable conflict arises
of reason with itself, then the experiment decides in favor of the
correctness of that distinction."[175] What is the principle of reason that enables us to conduct experiments of this kind? It is
the *unconditioned* or, logically, the maxim to find for the conditioned of the understanding the unconditioned that completes
its unity (by subsuming the condition of a proposition under a
general rule, which in turn is subject to another subsumption in
finding the condition of *its* condition). This logical *maxim* (of all
syllogisms) becomes a *principle* of pure reason by the assumption: "If the conditioned is given, the whole series of the
conditions subordinated to one another, which is thus itself
unconditioned, is also given (i.e. contained in the object and its
connection)."[176] This assumption can be tested: concepts and

173. B xviii.
174. *Ibid.*
175. *Ibid.,* note.
176. B 364.

fundamental propositions a priori are so arranged that they may
be submitted to an experiment as to their agreement with the
principle of pure reason, i.e. with unconditioned unity; and this
agreement becomes possible only by a distinction of their objects as appearances and as things in themselves.

> If we find that the *unconditioned cannot be thought without con-*
> *tradiction,* once we assume that our experiential cognition conforms
> to objects as things in themselves; that the *contradiction, however,*
> *disappears,* once we assume that our presentations of things, as they
> are given to us, conform not to these as things in themselves but
> that these objects, as appearances, rather conform to our manner of
> presentation, . . . then it becomes clear that what initially was as-
> sumed by us only for the sake of an experiment, is justified.[177]

Here the law of contradiction is adduced as a criterion. Is this,
then, analysis? In one sense it is, and it is so in terms of general
logic. In the transcendental enterprises of pure reason which
are all carried on within the domain proper to dialectical
illusion, "concerning synthetic propositions, it can never be
permissible to justify one's assertions by disproving the opposite."[178] For both parties here base their assertions on an impossible, i.e. contradictory concept of the object, and in such cases
"what had been asserted of the object, both positively as well
as negatively, is erroneous."[179] This goes not only for the Kantian
examples, e.g. of *appearances* which are yet to be given *in them-*
selves, but for anything which is self-contradictory; and hence
the dialectic here uses analysis in terms of general logic. The
illicit apagogic "proofs" of the metaphysician are disproved by
the dictum that non-being has no predicates, *non entis nulla*
sunt predicata.

On the other hand, Kant compares the analysis of the metaphysician to that of the chemist. "The *analysis* of the *metaphysi-*
cian separated the pure cognition *a priori* into two very heterogeneous elements, namely that of the things as appearances,
and that of the things in themselves." This analysis, which may

177. B xx.
178. B 820.
179. B 821.

be seen summed up in the chapter "Of the Ground of the Distinction of all Objects in General into Phenomena and Nou-
mena," is not, says Kant, the same kind as that of concepts in
general logic, of which he says in the Introduction to the
Critique that he carries such analysis only so far as is necessary
for his prime task of synthesis. It is rather "analysis similar to
that of the chemist, which they sometimes call the experiment
of *reduction,* but in general the *synthetic procedure.*"[180] It is, in
other words, the scientific method applied to the material of
logic. Here is not meant the object-constructing procedure of
the Preface to the second edition, or of transcendental logic, for
the dialectic uses general logic. On the other hand, the logical
procedure of reason leads to the assumption of reason which
is to be tested, and this test refers to the nature of objects and
hence to their schematic construction. In this sense the procedure of the dialectic may be called indirectly scientific or, as we
call it, "formally 'scientific.' " Its "analysis" does not reduce material entities to formal ones as the chemist does, but traces
formal ones back to material and pseudo-material ones; and its
"synthesis" is not genuine transcendental synthesis but the
demonstration of an illusion. It shows up the illusory, the pseu-
do-synthesis of contradictory marks in one concept. When one
tries to prove either of these concepts by excluding the other
then the dialectic dispels this illicit apagogical procedure. In
this sense Kant's dialectic method is *sui generis* and different
from the scientific method in the strict sense. It is in the latter
where alone apagogical proofs, as in mathematics, "have their
proper place."[181] The dialectic uses general logic to dispel a
logically illicit procedure.

True transcendental synthesis, on the other hand, leads to
direct ostensive proof. This synthesis indicates a relation to material cognition and refers to our interest in expanding our
knowledge; in it a new dimension is added to that of general
logic. Genuine synthesis belongs to transcendental logic. This

180. B xxi, note.
181. B 820.

kind of synthesis gives *proof* in scientific cognition. This proof must be unique, and based on either a priori intuition or the possibility of experience.

> Now every transcendental proposition starts merely from one concept and states the synthetic condition of the possibility of the object according to this concept. The ground of proof therefore can also be only one, because beside the concept there is nothing further by which the object could be determined; the proof thus cannot contain anything but the determination of an object in general according to this concept which itself is only one.[182]

The manner of proving ostensively or directly proceeds from grounds to consequences, i.e. in the progressive method, "by reviewing the whole series of grounds that can lead us to the truth of a cognition by means of complete insight into its possibility."[183] While in mathematics it is a priori intuition that guides synthesis, "in transcendental knowledge, so long as we are concerned only with concepts of the understanding, our guide is the possibility of experience";[184] and the proof proceeds by showing that experience itself, and therefore the object of experience, would be impossible without a connection not empirically contained in the concepts. In this way the a priori connections make for apodeictic certainty because the elements of experience, through transcendental analysis, have been extended[185] in terms of the necessary and universal conditions of experience itself. Transcendental analysis makes for transcendental synthesis.

Although our summary presentation cannot convey the far more subtle and systematic articulation of Kant's determinations as compared with those of his predecessors, at this point there nevertheless appear certain parallels with Descartes' and Leibniz' determinations. We recognize that all three deal with the same set of conditions and show certain similarities in their results, that all three, in one way or another, must pay tribute

182. B 815.
183. B 819.
184. B 810 f.
185. See B 810.

to that oscillation of human cognition around the center of the concept that is analysis and synthesis. Kant, however, is not satisfied without a "strictly proving" synthesis in apodeictic proofs. The "simples" in his critique are time and space (because of their axiomatic nature, although containing a manifold), the categories, and, as regulative principles, the Ideas of reason. In one passage Kant speaks of the categories as original and "primitive" concepts.[186]

The method of the *Critique* as a process of segregating pure (a priori) elements of reason from empirical elements under its principle of unconditioned unity leads, in the Analytic, to a directly scientific procedure. The method of following a *Leitfaden,* a "guiding thread," to assure completeness of the categories is a true derivation from a principle (judgment), its result being the identification of logical function with, or rather *as,* the transcendental function in creating unity of the manifold in intuition. Identification takes place here in the sense of a cognition of identity, of cognizing that two supposedly separate functions are the same. This identifying cognition is similar to the abovementioned identification of a geometric line with a ray of light. It does not superimpose a new entity on another, but discovers something where it had not previously been seen; for the ray of light, after the identification, is not what it had been before, namely an empirical entity: it has become a construction. In the same way, in identifying the logical as the transcendental function we discover something where it had not previously been seen; and it is here, in the deductions of the Analytic, that the materially scientific element enters the *Critique.* In this respect, the method of the segregation of rational from empirical elements deserves the name of an experimental method—after Newton's example—for here also pure presentations are proved by passing the test, not of an agreement of presentations with their actual objects, but of agreement with the possibility of experience, of cognizing objects as appearances in general. This is the experiment of an agreement with a real, not only a

186. B 108.

logical possibility. Real possibility presupposes a principle a priori as its condition. "To cognize something a priori means to cognize it out of its mere possibility."[187] The elements that guarantee the possibility of objective cognition must themselves be true and objective.

But the agreement of the theory confirmed by the experiment goes further than that. It stands the test of leaving reason's idea of the unconditioned intact as something that can be *thought* without contradiction. This idea must be accounted for, not only in its prior undeniable logical maxim but also as underlying the concept of the thing in itself and as a regulative principle. The non-contradictoriness that every theory must possess goes hand in hand with the general requirement of proof, which must here be ostensive, apodeictic proof. After the elements of pure reason have been found in their completeness (analysis), the method of the *Critique* can build up the inner structure, the *Gliederbau* of a finite system of transcendental cognition (synthesis), because for every transcendental proposition only *one* proof is possible.

Human cognition was for Kant not only a "faculty" but possessed, in the subject, a center of truly constitutive acts. "Transcendental philosophy is the doctrine of synthetic cognition a priori through concepts in a subject determining itself absolutely in a system of the possibility of experience. . . ." "The subjective-analytic unity of possible experience is at the same time the objective-synthetic unity of the objects of experience. . . ." "Transcendental philosophy is an analytic doctrine of synthetic self-documentation,"[188] *eine sich selbst in der Analysis synthetisch dokumentierende Vernunftlehre.* Documentation, we should remember, is derived from *documentum,* which means proof.

Thus, the new science of metaphysics is established, which owes so much to general logic in its progress from formal logical to transcendental principles. The *Critique of Pure Reason* in

---

187. *Metaphysical Foundations of Natural Sciences,* Akad. IV, 470.
188. *Opus Postumum,* Akad. XXI, 104, 514, 158.

relation to metaphysics has two hinges, attached, as it were, to the post of reason's concept of the totality of all conditions: first, the doctrine of space and time as forms of our intuiting things as appearances, which points to the supersensuous as the—theoretically—unknowable; second, the doctrine of the reality of the concept of freedom as the concept of a—practically—knowable supersensuous. To the twelve categories of nature correspond twelve categories of freedom, the "given" of these practical categories not being the intuition of space and time but the form of a pure will.

On these two hinges the *Critique* opens, as it were, on the one hand to the world of the senses, on the other to that of the supersensuous. The sensuous appears apodeictically certain by the construction of the schemata. We shall now turn to the role of analysis and synthesis in this aspect of the *Critique*.

c) Analysis and Synthesis in Kant's Science of Metaphysics

Kant, in constructing his science of metaphysics, followed the general Newtonian method of analysis and synthesis. Hence, disregarding the specific requirements of his own specific science, we can find in Kant's procedure the universal method of any science: empirical analysis followed by a priori synthesis. In this sense, as Körner rightly held,[189] the procedure as well as the message of the *Critique of Pure Reason* are still, and will always be, valid for scientific procedure. Let us first summarize the Cartesian-Newtonian procedure of analysis and synthesis.

When an axiom of a science is posited, the phenomenal core of the subject matter is identified with a formula which gives rise to a system. The phenomenal core is the result of analysis and is presented, or rather represented in the Leibnizian sense, in terms of a structure which is identical with a mathematical or logical structure—a formula (e.g. the Galilean formula for velocity). The formula contains in itself a procedure by which the system of which it is part can unfold. And with the latter unfolds systematically the subject matter formalized.

189. Stephan Körner, "Zur kantischen Begründung der Mathematik und der Naturwissenschaften," *Kant-Studien*, LVI (1966), Heft 3–4.

In the Kantian terminology, such an identification of analytic with synthetic structure is a *schema;* and the schema, as a generative process, unfolds the synthesis which corresponds to its analytic content (from the analytic viewpoint, the schema is called an image). Both, sensibility and understanding, are of two kinds, material and formal, a posteriori and a priori, represented, respectively, by analytic or synthetic judgments (with analytic concepts) and by synthetic a priori judgments (with synthetic concepts). The schema, either sensorial or conceptual, is the fusion of these two aspects, that is, of material with formal sensibility (form of intuition expressed in mathematical judgments), or of material with formal understanding (categories and schemata in the strict sense, expressed in principles of pure understanding). The schemata that arise from the fusion of material and formal sensibility produce spaces and times; the schemata that arise from the fusion of material and formal understanding produce the principles of mechanics, i.e. the connection of objects in and as Nature. The forms of sensibility are Space and Time, represented in geometry and arithmetic; the forms of the understanding are the schematized categories, represented in mechanics.

The Kantian science of metaphysics is only one specific science; and its constructive procedure, or schematism, is applicable to any science. *The axiom of any science is a schema.* It fuses the empirical and the formal, it is always an identification of something non-formal with something formal. The non-formal is the material aspect, the phenomenon, by analysis reduced to its most simple structure, the Cartesian simple or the Leibnizian primary concept; the formal aspect is this structure seen as element of a formal system (logic, geometry, etc.). The identification of both, the material and the formal aspects, is a formula which generates a system (optics, mechanics, etc.). In the specific case of a logic accounting for the construction of objects, the material aspect is thought analyzed as judgment in a logic of judgments, a general logic, reduced to, and ending with, a table of judgments; and the formal aspect, the system that constructs Nature, transcendental logic, begins with this

table, but in its function with respect to constructive application, namely a table of categories. The relation between these
two tables may be regarded as the schematism of the *Critique*
of Pure Reason as itself a science, or rather a meta-science—the
science the subject matter of which is the science of metaphysics. From these tables, by addition, further tables are formed
until, in the schematism of the pure concepts of the understanding, Nature itself is constructed and the system which is the
subject matter of the *Critique* is complete.

We thus seem to have two schematisms in the *Critique*, that
of the *Critique* itself as a system and that of the system with
which the *Critique* deals, transcendental logic. The latter constructs Nature. The *Critique* does not construct Nature, it constructs transcendental logic. The schematism *of the Critique* is
the metaphysical deduction, the schematism of transcendental
logic is that of the pure concepts of the understanding. Let us
now in somewhat greater detail examine all this.

**Schematic Parallelism of Transcendental Aesthetic
and Analytic:** The synthetic method, Kant tells us, begins with an
apodeictic certainty. Rational certainty, he says, is either mathematical or philosophical. The former is intuitive, the latter discursive. The mathematical certainty is also called evidence, because an intuitive cognition is clearer than a discursive one.
Rational certainty is distinguished from empirical certainty
through the consciousness of the necessity connected with it.
It is apodeictic while empirical certainty is only assertoric. Kant
calls mathematical certainty intuitive, as did Descartes and Leibniz, but he defines clearly what he means by it. It is a *formal*
intuition, as in his predecessors, but one which involves a spatial
and temporal foundation. Indeed, the intuition, as formal, is
the intuition of Space and Time. (Kant could have pointed to the
Leibnizian notion of representation, which necessarily involves
a spatial element, instead of his somewhat abstract Expositions
in the Aesthetic of the *Critique;* or to the general notion of the
schematism, as he does in other contexts. He could not, of
course, refer to actual experience, as we can today in the case of
persons coming out of electric shock treatment. Such persons,

first of all, sense the immensity of Space and of Time. Next, they have the experience of "I am," the transcendental apperception. These experiences seem to confirm the Kantian epistemology.)

The fact that geometry and arithmetic, as all mathematics, need construction which is necessarily in space, points powerfully to the correctness of the Kantian notion. It also shows up as fallacies the arguments that the development of non-Euclidean geometries refutes the Kantian Aesthetic. Even non-Euclidean geometries must be written in symbols in Euclidean space and hence be subject to the intuition of that space. They are not written within non-Euclidean space; the books of Bolyai and Lobachevski have no saddle form. Their axioms are not "independent of spatial intuition."[190] Any axiom, not only one of geometry, is a spatial construction in form, no matter what its content.[191] It is this formal structure of an axiom, the structure of its symbolic form, which Kant meant by formal intuition, not the content the axiom deals with. This content may be anything, from musical harmonies to non-Euclidean spaces; but an axiom of a science of harmony does not sound, and one of non-Euclidean geometry is not curved. The arguments against Kant in this respect confuse the *method* of a science with its *content* and commit what has been called the *fallacy of method.*[192]

Kant does not tie mathematics to *intuition* but to *pure intuition,* not to sensibility but to the form of sensibility. This form is, precisely, the kind of construction which is the heart of synthesis and of the synthetic concept; it is the intuition of a sign and the symbolic structure inherent in it. When Kant says that "to *construct* a concept means: to exhibit a priori the intuition corresponding to it"[193] he means exactly what he says, namely, to *exhibit a priori,* that is to show up in symbols in (Euclidean)

190. L. Susan Stebbing, *A Modern Introduction to Logic* (London: Methuen, 1948), p. 486.

191. See Ernst Mach, *Space and Geometry* (LaSalle, Ill.: Open Court Publishing Co., 1906), pp. 132 ff.

192. See Robert S. Hartman, *The Structure of Value* (Carbondale: So. Illinois University Press, 1969), pp. 126 ff.

193. B 741.

space and time, a *schema* which brings about both the concept and the corresponding object, e.g. the concept "geometrical circle" with the schema *circle,* or the concept "substance" with the schema *permanence,* etc. The concept here in question is not an abstracted or analytic concept of general logic but a synthetic or constructed one of transcendental logic.

The form of intuition is a dynamic form which Kant discusses not only in the Methodology and in our text, but also in the Transcendental Doctrine of Elements. A synthetic concept arises *together with its object* and such concept-objects (*conjects* one is tempted to say) are called schemata. The schema is the synthetic concept of transcendental logic in its characteristic role of *synthesizing, that is, constructing its own reality.* The synthetic concept is a form generative of its own matter.

> The transcendental use of a concept in any principle is this one: that the concept is related to things as such and *in themselves;* the empirical use, however: that it is merely related to *appearances,* i.e. objects of a possible *experience.* That only the latter use can take place at all becomes clear from the following. For every concept is required, first, the logical form of a concept (of thought) generatim and, secondly, the possibility of giving it an object to which it relates. Without the latter the concept has no sense and is completely empty of content, though it may still contain the logical function to make a concept out of eventual data. Now the object of a concept cannot be given otherwise than in intuition, and if a pure intuition is possible a priori even before the object [is given], it itself can receive its object, hence objective validity, only through empirical intuition, of which it is the mere form. All concepts, therefore, and with them all principles, much as they may be possible a priori, relate nevertheless to empirical intuitions, i.e. to data of a possible experience. . . . One requires therefore that an abstracted concept be *made sensible,* i.e. that the object corresponding to it be shown in intuition, because without this the concept would remain (as one says) without *sense,* i.e. without meaning. Mathematics fulfills this requirement by construction of the figure, which, although brought about a priori, is an appearance present to the senses. The concept of quantity, in the same science, seeks support and sense in number, the latter in turn in the fingers, the beads of the abacus, or in the strokes and points which are placed before the eyes. The concept always remains produced a priori together with synthetic principles or formulas out of such concepts; but their use and relation

to purported objects can in the end be sought nowhere but in experience, whose possibility (as to form) is contained in those mathematical principles or formulas. . . . No one can explain the concept
of quantity in general except perhaps by saying: it is that determination of a thing by which can be thought how many times a unit is
posited in it. But, this how-many-times is founded on successive
repetition, hence on time and the synthesis (of the heterogeneous)
in it. Reality in opposition to negation can be explained only if we
think a time (as the complex concept of all being) which is either
filled with something or empty. If I leave out permanence (which is
a being at all times), nothing remains for the concept of substance
but the logical presentation of subject.[194]

The schematism, thus, is a matter of both intuition and understanding; indeed, it is the heart of the analytic-synthetic method.

Formal intuition, in its exposition (*Auseinanderlegung*) by
mathematics, has the schemata of Space and Time as its content. Geometry and arithmetic are symbolic forms the elements
of which constructively *mean,* i.e. are the schemata of, Space
and Time. These schemata are the "unique objects" of this kind
of intuition. In general, the uniqueness or singularity of the object of a construction has nothing whatsoever to do with the
singular or particular aspect of an abstracted or analytic concept; and when Kant says, in B 742 that "die philosophische Erkenntnis betrachtet also das Besondere nur in Allgemeinen, die
mathematische das Allgemeine im Besonderen, ja gar im ein-
zelnen, gleichwohl doch a priori und vermittelst der Vernunft,"
then the former, the philosophically *Besondere und Allgemeine,*
has nothing to do with the latter, the mathematically *Allgemeine
und Besondere.* It is thus false to say, as is sometimes done, that
the individual in a mathematical intuition has anything to do
with the individual of an abstract concept, or that the mathematical uses a special case of general concepts, or that "in a
mathematical argument general concepts are considered by
means of their individual representatives." For what Kant does
say is that to construct a concept is the same as to exhibit, that
is, show up in space and time, *darstellen,* a priori an intuition
which corresponds to the concept; that this is the construction

194. B 298–300.

of a schema; that this process is one of transcendental logic as opposed to one of general logic (abstraction and specification); and that the same opposition also defines the difference between philosophy and science. Finally, he is clear about his intent of writing a *science* of metaphysics and proceeding in the *Critique* by the synthetic method, i.e. by construction. What is constructed is transcendental logic as a system which constructs Nature as a set of schemata, together with its (their) corresponding set of concepts, the (unschematized) categories. Knowledge from pure reason, Kant reminds us in the *Prolegomena*, is "not . . . analytic but solely synthetic knowledge."[195]

The *schemata of* geometry and arithmetic (circles, numbers, etc. and signs in general[196]) are a priori connected in geometry and in arithmetic, as the forms of intuition, which isomorphically—by construction—mean Space and Time. In the same way the constructs of the schemata of the understanding, the objects of nature, are connected by what Kant calls transcendental affinity,[197] the necessary synthetic unity of appearance leading to the uniformity of nature.[198] Space and Time are the "individuals" of formal intuition, as Nature is the "individual" of formal understanding. Nature is the result of schematization in the same way as are Space and Time, i.e. it receives spatio-temporal existence by scientific construction of a set of schemata, out of unschematized categories of the understanding. In this sense the schematized categories are the *forms* of the unschematized, as formal intuition is of the forms of intuition.

There is thus, in Kant's *Critique*, a complete parallelism between the construction of Space and Time in the Aesthetic and that of Nature in the Analytic. Category and schema are connected by the procedure of construction, as are sensibility and the forms of sensibility. Just as the mathematical schemata brought forth space and time and thus, as is stressed by Gottfried Martin,[199] the intuitive character of mathematics means

195. *Prolegomena,* trans. L. W. Beck, § 5. Cf. B 762 f.
196. *Inquiry,* Akad. II, 278 f., 284, 291 f.
197. A 122.
198. See Paton, *Kant's Metaphysic of Experience,* I, 71, 482.
199. *Kant's Metaphysics and Theory of Science,* p. 23.

that mathematics is limited to objects which can be constructed, so the schemata of nature bring forth nature by construction, and the schematic character of metaphysics consists in metaphysics being limited to objects which can be constructed. What Kant says, or implies, about the schematization of intuition in the Aesthetics is, *mutatis mutandis,* applicable to the Transcendental Deduction, and vice versa.

This parallelism appears clearly not only in the Kantian text but also in sensitive expositions, such as Martin's. Martin stresses, in the third paragraph of his work, the constructive character of geometry in the Aesthetic and shows that the synthetic procedure is the bringing about of the schema by construction. In the twelfth paragraph, where he speaks of the a priority of Newtonian Nature, he calls the connection of category and schema a synthetic procedure; he does not, however, draw the conclusion that the connection between category and schema is, precisely, that of construction. He states that

> for Kant himself there is not first a pure category and then something added to it in the schema, but the temporal determination of the categories is something originally and inseparably given for us, which is merely analyzed. . . . The decisive result for us is that the categories only have meaning if they have a temporal modification and this temporal modification of the categories in the schema at the same time limits the application of the categories to what can be temporally determined.[200]

This means, however, that category and schema are a construction.

Indeed, one may even go a step further. One may say that the table of judgments, on the level of the *Critique* rather than of its subject matter, is part of the construction. For these judgments may well be regarded as the end products of the analysis of thought.[201] As such, however, they would be primary concepts in both the Leibnizian and the Kantian sense and, at the same time, become elements of a synthesis.[202] This synthesis begins in the Metaphysical Deduction, the transition from General to

200. *Ibid.,* p. 85.
201. See B 107.
202. See B 108.

Transcendental Logic. The table of the categories, then, is the first step in the construction of the system which constructs objects, the first step, that is, in the construction of the object. The relation between the two first tables, then, is the fundamental one of the axiomatic identification of analytic with synthetic simple, in the Cartesian sense, which in Kant becomes that of judgment with understanding and, in the schematism, with cognition. The constructive character of the second table is quite clear in Kant.[203] But if we take the analytic-synthetic process of science-creation seriously, then this table of synthetic simples must be preceded by a table of analytic simples, and this by an analysis of the nature of thought; and it must be followed by the synthesis, out of the synthetic simples, of that same nature.

All this we find in Kant. Hence the relation between categories and predicables is not insoluble, as Kant seems to have thought, e.g. in the *Opus Postumum*. Rather, an exact application of the analytic-synthetic procedure gives us the solution, as it does in the parallelism of Transcendental Aesthetic and Analytic. The schematism of the categories is merely the third part of the construction which includes, in addition, the table of judgments and that of the categories, as well as that of the principles. The four tables, thus, of the judgments, categories, schemata, and principles, are all parts of one whole, *a schematic construction* that stands between the analysis of thought and its synthesis in the system which is the *Critique*. It deals with the construction of Nature out of the material of thought. The Aesthetic adds to this the necessary prerequisite, in the parallel construction of Space and Time out of the material of intuition.

In thus inserting the Kantian constructions into the process of analysis and synthesis we solve, in a natural way, a great number of difficulties in the *Critique*. Besides that of the relation of

203. See Gottfried Martin, *Kant's Metaphysics and Theory of Science*, p. 81. On the analytic-synthetic character of the table of categories see Paton, *Kant's Metaphysic of Experience*, I, 307, n. 3; 315, n. 3; 336, n. 1. The "formal-material" Janus-character of the categories has been developed, on a different basis from ours (and from Kant's), by Thomas Swing, *Kant's Transcendental Logic* (New Haven: Yale University Press, 1969).

predicable and category it would explain the question of the completeness of both the tables and the system; for the completeness of a system consists in its presenting its object completely, which is a matter of course when it brings forth its object together with itself, as is the case in any schematic construction. Many details of the system would appear more clearly, such as the relation of formal and transcendental logic (which is in a certain sense still significant today), and the contribution of the Marburg School, especially of Cohen. Finally, it would correspond exactly to Kant's purpose of writing a *science* of metaphysics. The reason that he did not apply his definition of science with all the strictness he could have is probably the same which accounts for the fact that the Doctrine of Method in the *Critique,* though recognized as the equal counterpart to the Doctrine of Elements,[204] is only given one sixth of the space of the latter. Kant probably was much more conscious of breaking with the Cartesian-Leibnizian tradition than he was of continuing it. And the Methodology contains what is in this tradition, clarified and elaborated, whereas the Doctrine of Elements contains what is not. Actually, as we have seen, the Doctrine of Elements cannot be understood except in the framework of the Methodology. The core of the system of pure reason is the notion of schematic construction; and this Kant developed out of the Methodology, and taught in his classes in Logic.

Axiomatic and Akroamatic: The reason that the synthetic concept is different from the analytic concept is, precisely, that the synthetic concept brings forth its object together with itself. The synthetic concept *is* a schema. This has a twofold fundamental significance: one, that this kind of concept brings forth, or is part of, a synthetic procedure and, two, that this procedure is the only one that guarantees the possibility of complete definition. The synthetic procedure is part of the constructive nature of the synthetic concept. This procedure, then, strictly speaking, ought to proceed from synthetic concept to synthetic concept and not contain any analytic concepts.

204. B 29.

Since analytic propositions are possible only with analytic concepts (only such concepts have a "content" which could "contain" a predicate), it follows that within a synthetic system no such propositions could possibly appear.

Yet Kant holds occasionally that within the synthetic procedure there may appear analytic, rather than synthetic a priori, propositions. But the examples he gives do not bear this out. Thus, he mentions the propositions $a = a$, the whole is equal to itself, and $(a + b) > a$, that is, the whole is greater than its part.[205] But none of the concepts here in question are analytic in the sense of the *Logic* and the Methodology; "a", "b", etc. are not abstractions, but variables, and the operations that connect them are not those of predicables but systemic operators. Moreover, even a proposition such as "Socrates is Socrates" is not an analytic but an identical one, a tautology, which Kant in our text strictly distinguishes from an analytic proposition. And even such a tautology is not necessarily correct, i.e. tautological, if, namely, one of the terms is taken extensionally and the other intensionally.[206] Actually, in a synthetic system, such as algebra or logic, "$a = a$" means really " 'a' = 'a'," that is, "the symbol 'a' is to be taken in any argument in the same sense." This is a nominal definition in one of the Leibnizian meanings of this term, and it is the very essence of what Kant calls a synthetic or constructive definition, that is, the kind used in mathematics.[207] The second example, "the whole is equal to itself", when taken synthetically rather than analytically, as it must be in mathematics, is false since in transfinite mathematics any operation with A,[208] except exponentiation by A, is equal to A. Thus, $A + a = A$, $A + A = A$, $A \times a = A$, $A^a = A$. Which aleph, then, is the "whole"? The proposition must be understood as synthetic a

205. B 16f. We take "$a = a$" and "the whole is equal to itself" as two different propositions.
206. For details see Robert S. Hartman, "Singular and Particular," *Critica,* II, 4 (January 1968), pp. 15–50, National University of Mexico.
207. See below, § 103.
208. "A" stands for "aleph."

priori.[209] This also goes for the third example: $(a + b) > a$, which is true if and only if a is finite. Kant thus built better than he knew, and perhaps could know at the time, even though Galileo had already pointed out the particular arithmetic of the infinite. In a synthetic procedure there can appear only synthetic concepts; and whatever appears in a synthetic procedure is a synthetic concept.

The role of the synthetic concept in the definition is the fundamental characteristic which arises from this concept's schematic nature. It makes this concept a fundamental term in Kant's general as well as transcendental logic. Kant does not explicitly discuss the transition from the analytic to the synthetic definition, which precisely is the transition from the last analytic deduction in the sense of Descartes to the absolute simple that is the formula by which the new science starts, the axiom that gives rise to the scientific system. But the doctrine of the schematism supplies this transition. It shows us that both the axiom of a science and the theorems following from it are schemata; and that the *fiat* which brings about the axiom is informed by, and hence applicable to, reality, in the degree in which the analysis that led to it was informed. The "arbitrariness" of this *fiat* is not mere *Willkür* in today's German usage, that is, random choice, but rather *Willkür* in the original German sense, still in use in Kant's day, meaning the will's *Küren*, its deliberately choosing and selecting. Considering that the matrix of this deliberate choice and selection is what is given, and that this deliberate choice and selection is the very process of analysis, *Willkür* in this sense may be taken as a synonym for analysis.

That the axiom of a science is a schema, that is, a synthetic construction, appears clearly in the axiomatic character of geometry and arithmetic in the Transcendental Aesthetic. Axioms, according to Kant, are *intuitive principles*. He distinguishes, in our text, undemonstrable and demonstrable propositions. The latter can, the former cannot be proved. Immediately certain

209. Cf. Gottfried Martin, *Klassische Ontologie der Zahl* (Köln: Kölner Universitätsverlag, 1956), p. 90.

judgments are undemonstrable and called *elementary proposi-tions*. Immediately certain judgments *a priori* are *principles* or *fundamental propositions*. Other judgments can be demon-strated through them but they themselves cannot be subordi-nated under any other judgment. Fundamental propositions or principles are either intuitive or discursive. The former can be represented in intuition and are called *axioms*. The latter can only b́e expressed through concepts and are called *akroams*.[210] Axioms, then, are synthetic a priori principles, that is, principles exhibited in symbols,[211] while akroams are principles not so ex-hibited but expressed in words.[212] Philosophy, which is merely what reason knows by means of concepts, cannot have axioms.

> Mathematics, on the other hand, is capable of axioms, because by means of the construction of concepts in the intuition of the ob-ject it can connect its predicates a priori and immediately, e.g. [in the proposition] that three points always lie in a plane. But a syn-thetic principle out of mere concepts can never be immediately certain, e.g. the proposition: everything that happens has a cause, since I must look around for some third thing, the condition, namely of the time-determination in an experience, and could not cognize such a principle directly out of the concepts alone. Discursive prin-ciples are thus something quite different from intuitive principles, i.e. axioms. The former always require a deduction, with which the latter can entirely dispense. . . . For the same reason axioms are evident.[213]

The basis of, and for, the axiomatic view of mathematics is fourfold. (1) Mathematical judgments cannot be proved analyti-cally, that is, as Leibniz had held, from the principle of contra-diction.[214] (2) The connection between subject and predicate of a mathematical proposition is not analytically necessary, i.e. by the nature of their concepts if they are understood analytically; indeed, thus conceived nothing follows from them.[215] (3) Yet,

---

210. Below, §§ 33–35. From Greek *Akroama*, "recital." See above, n. 140.
211. See B 760, 762f.
212. *Ibid.* Cf. B 744 and *Inquiry*, Akad. II, 277.
213. B 760f.
214. See G. Martin, *Klassische Ontologie der Zahl*, pp. 18 ff.
215. See B 744; *Inquiry*, Akad. II, 277.

once these concepts are seen synthetically, the judgments are both universal and necessary. The reason is, precisely, their schematic character: The *fiat* that gave rise to them grew out of an analysis which began with observation and ended in an a priori elementary proposition. The latter, as the primary element of a subsequent synthetic process, is an intuitive principle, an intuitive fundamental proposition or *formula* which generates the system of which any mathematical proposition is a part. Such a proposition then, as Duhem has shown,[216] carries the entire system within it, including its material connection, and thus its applicability, guaranteed to it by the process of analysis. (4) Even when seen as synthetic concepts, and hence as subject and predicate of a synthetic a priori judgment, the connection between them is not of the necessity of an analytic judgment. For there is always contained either more or less in the axioms of a mathematical system—depending on the viewpoint—than the system can manifest, that is, than can be read out of its principles without trial and error. It is, for example, impossible to determine the sequence of decimals of a transcendental number by any formula; or the sequence of primes; or to prove the consistency of the system, etc.—and it can be proved, in some of these cases, that there cannot be the procedure in question. Even here, in the very heart of mathematics, the conception of a system as an expanded schema may one day help us to understand as yet unexplained features of a priori syntheticity.

The nature of formal thought itself, thus, contains its syntheticity; and this is due to the necessity of this kind of thinking *to make use of the forms of space and time,* that is, to be exhibited by symbols in Euclidean space and constructibility in Euclidean time.[217] On this exhibition, *Darstellung,* rest the natures both of construction and of demonstration, in science and philosophy, respectively. The science of metaphysics is be-

216. Pierre Duhem, *The Aims and Structure of Physical Theory* (Princeton: Princeton University Press, 1954).

217. See G. Martin, *Klassische Ontologie der Zahl*, pp. 96f.; Kant, *Über eine Entdeckung . . . ,* Akad. VIII, 192n.

tween both; it is not mathematical because it is not presented in symbols; it is akroamatic rather than axiomatic. But it becomes axiomatic, that is schematic, after a deduction which shows construction to be possible; for the latter is not self-evident as in axiomatics, e.g. mathematics. Once the deduction has been made, axioms, and indeed mathematics, are seen as possible.

> All our cognition finally relates to possible intuitions, for through these alone an object is given. Now a concept a priori (a non-empirical concept) either already contains a pure intuition in it, and in that case can be constructed, or contains nothing but the synthesis of possible intuitions that are not given a priori, and in that case one can indeed judge through it synthetically and a priori, but only discursively according to concepts and never intuitively through the construction of concepts.[218]

Insofar as the propositions of transcendental philosophy are expressed in words they cannot claim the self-evidence of mathematical demonstration.

> Mathematics arrives at its concepts synthetically and can say with certainty: what it had not wanted to present to itself in the object through the definition, that is indeed not contained in it. For the concept of the matter to be explained arises precisely and only through the explanation itself and has absolutely no other significance but the one the definition gives it.[219]

Philosophy, and in particular metaphysics, is far more uncertain in its explanations, for the concept of the subject to be explained is not made but given. Hence, if one overlooks a characteristic the definition becomes erroneous. Secondly, and connected with this,

> mathematics considers in its conclusions and demonstrations its universal cognitions within its signs *in concreto*, philosophy, however, *beside* its signs ever *in abstracto*. This means a significant difference in the way of both to reach certainty. For since the signs of mathematics are sensorial means of cognition one is able to know with the same confidence one is assured of that which one sees with his eyes, that one has not left any concept out of consideration, that

---

218. B 747 f.
219. *Inquiry*, Akad. II, 291.

every single comparison occurred according to simple rules etc. In this way attention is greatly relieved by the fact that it does not have to attend to things in their abstract conceptualization but to signs in their individual cognition which is sensorial. Against this, the words which are the signs of philosophical cognition serve for nothing but the remembrance of the general concepts signified.[220]

Philosophy, thus, finds its concepts *beside* its signs in abstraction while mathematics finds its concepts *among* or *within* the signs it uses, in concretion. The same train of thought is found some twenty years later in both versions of the *Critique:*

> . . . Any synthetic proposition of pure and transcendental reason is infinitely far from being as evident (though this is obstinately claimed for it) as the proposition that *twice two makes four.* In the Analytic, in the table of the fundamental propositions of the pure understanding, I did mention also certain axioms of intuition: but the fundamental proposition introduced there was not itself an axiom but served only to state the principle of the possibility of axioms as such and was itself merely a fundamental proposition out of concepts. For even the possibility of mathematics must be shown in transcendental philosophy.[221]

Hence, true proofs or demonstrations are possible only in mathematics, not in philosophy, for in the former the nature of space itself carries along the argument. It fuses concept and object and thus gives apodeictic certainty.

> Only an apodeictic proof so far as it is intuitive can be called a demonstration. Experience indeed tells us what there is, but not that it could not in any way be otherwise. Empirical grounds of proof can therefore not provide an apodeictic proof. Intuitive certainty, i.e. evidence, can never spring (in discursive cognition) out of concepts a priori, however apodeictically certain the judgment may otherwise be. Only mathematics, thus, contains demonstrations, because it derives its cognition not from concepts but from their construction, i.e. from intuition that can be given a priori in accordance with the concepts. Even the procedure of algebra with its equations, from which it brings forth, by reduction, the truth together with its proof, is indeed not a geometrical but yet a characteristic construction in which one presents the concepts by signs in

220. *Ibid.* Emphasis added.
221. B 761f.

intution, especially of the relationships of quantities, and, without mentioning its heuristic [side], safeguards all conclusions against mistakes by setting each one before our eyes. Philosophic cognition, on the other hand, must do without this advantage, in that it must consider the general always in abstracto (through concepts), while mathematics can ponder the general in concreto (in the single intuition) and yet through pure presentation a priori, whereby every error becomes visible. I would therefore call the former *akroamatic* (discursive) proofs, because they can be conducted only through words and nothing but words (the object [being pursued] in thought), rather than calling them *demonstrations,* which, as the expression itself indicates, proceed in the intuition of the object.[222]

Obviously, these demonstrations proceed in Euclidean space, even though they may be about non-Euclidean spaces. It follows then that "it is quite inappropriate to the nature of philosophy . . . to adorn itself with the titles and ribbons of mathematics, in whose league it does not belong, though it has all cause to hope for a sisterly union with it."[223]

Perhaps here Kant was too modest; again, perhaps, he built more firmly than he believed. The union may well be more than sisterly. It is now known that spatial intuition inheres necessarily not only in mathematical calculation but also in the logic of discursive argument. Modern physiological research has empirically verified Kant's spatial intuition not only in mathematics but also in grammar logic; so that, after all, akroamata may be as certain as axiomata. "Behavioral processes," writes a Nobel prize–winning neurophysiologist, A. R. Luria,

> that seem to have nothing in common may actually be related through dependence on a particular brain factor. *What can there be in common between the capacities for orientation in space, for doing computations and for dealing with complexities in grammar logic?* Yet all three of these abilities are affected by the same lesion in the lower part of the left parietal lobe. Why so? A close analysis of the three processes suggests an explanation. Computation and the ability to handle language structure depend, like orientation, *on the ability to grasp spatial relations.* In order to subtract 7 from 31, for example, one first performs the operation $30 - 7 = 23$ and

222. B 762 f.
223. B 763.

then adds the 1 to this preliminary result. There is a spatial factor here: one indicates unambiguously that the 1 is to be *added* by placing it to the right of the 23. A patient with a lesion disturbing his capacity for spatial organization is unable to cope with the problem because he is at a loss whether to place the 1 to the left or the right—in other words, whether to add it or subtract it.

The same principle applies to understanding complex grammatical constructions. In order to grasp the difference between "father's brother" and "brother's father" or between "summer comes after spring" and "spring comes after summer," for example, one must make a clear analysis of the quasi-spatial relations between the elements in each expression."[224]

What Luria calls "quasi-spatial" is formally spatial, or the formal intuition of space. Formal thinking is based universally and necessarily on formally spatial relations. This universal necessity of thought links thought with nature, where the same relations appear as principles of organization. What Kant thus shows is the construction of nature out of the material of thought—the merging of the abstract with the concrete in a *formal system applicable to sense reality.* Moreover, however, any system, even one not referring to nature and, indeed, not to anything sensible—such as non-Euclidean space or a symbolic science of value—ties its concepts to symbols in Euclidean space and time, finding them *unter ihnen,* among or within them, and thus presenting them in intuition, making possible their demonstrative, that is apodeictic validity. For, any symbolism adequate to a given field structures this field synthetically a priori, thus releasing attention from what is thought analytically and abstractly in the corresponding concepts and making it "pass beyond this concept to properties which are not [analytically] contained in this concept, but yet belong to it"[225] synthetically, that is, are found in the symbol or sign of it. The latter does not have to have the same form as the thing it refers to— such isomorphism is found in geometry, as between the concept of parallels and the sign for them, or the concept "triangle" and

224. A. R. Luria, "The Functional Organization of the Brain," *Scientific American,* CXXIV, No. 3 (March 1970), p. 78. First two emphases added.
225. B 746.

the form of triangle, but is not found even in algebra.[226] Rather, the object constructed by the synthetic concept may, in its sign, appear in its *symbolic essence;* and the vision of this essence within the symbol is the one which mathematicians, such as Descartes and Lambert, celebrated.[227]

Formal intuition, thus, becomes ever more formalized. The process by which this generalized formal intuition works is both post-Kantian and pre-Kantian, both non-Euclidean and Leibnizian. It has been described, and exhibited, by Ernst Cassirer. The philosophy of symbolic forms is the natural matrix of the universal—rather than metaphysically specific—Kantian procedure. What in both the *Logic* and the *Critique of Pure Reason* was regarded as axiomatic, because *formally intuitive,* now becomes *symbolically intuitive* in such a way that the system developed from the axiom brings about the object in question, in an ever more formalized intuition. What in Kant was formally *intuitive* now becomes formally *intuitable*—what was *anschaulich* now becomes *anschaubar.* The axiom becomes a *norm for* rather than a vehicle of intuition. The system builds up the object as a symbolic construction. Thus, what was sensorial space may now become a pure construction, "the geometrical logos reaches through and beyond the given;"[228] though not beyond time in which even a purely intellectual construction, synthetically a priori, must proceed.[229] Any symbolic system, in other words, may have any kind of content, which is seen and developed in a formal vision but which need not be sensorial at all. Only its construction must be in time to be existing at all.[230] In this sense Kant has shown not only the construction of nature but of any subject matter out of the

---

226. B 762. But see B 745. Also see *Inquiry,* Akad. II, 292.

227. See above, nn.118, 140.

228. Ernst Cassirer, *The Philosophy of Symbolic Forms* (New Haven: Yale University Press, 1957), III, 429.

229. See G. Martin, *Klassische Ontologie der Zahl,* p. 97.

230. Cf. Hermann Weyl, *Philosophy of Mathematics and Natural Science* (Princeton: Princeton University Press, 1949), pp. 65 f.; and his *The Open World* (New Haven, Yale University Press, 1932), pp. 83 f.

material of thought—the merging of the abstract and the concrete in any formal system that is applicable to a subject matter.[231] The latter, even if non-sensorial, is yet concrete in being the subject matter in question. Conversely, any subject matter presentable by a symbolism in this sense is, on account of this fact, constructible. Cantorian transfinite arithmetic and non-Euclidean spaces, thus, are constructible in this sense.[232] All our science, in other words, is finite sensorial and in Euclidean time and space; but it may be *about* the infinite, the nonsensorial and non-Euclidean spaces.

In this generalized view, the Kantian science of analysis and synthesis reaches forward into modern systems of thought; but it also merges backward with those of its predecessors, Descartes and Leibniz; and it illuminates the method of Newton and Galileo.

231. Cf. Stephan Körner, "Zur kantischen Begründung der Mathematik und der Naturwissenschaften," *Kant-Studien,* LVI (1966), Heft 3–4, p. 473.

232. The Cantorian construction of the Infinite proceeds in the finite. Cantor's books *are* not transfinite, they *deal with* it. To deny the constructibility of the transfinite because it is not constructible in the finite (G. Martin, *Klassische Ontologie der Zahl,* p. 98) is committing the same fallacy observed above (n.192) with respect to non-Euclidean spaces, the fallacy of method. Hilbert's foundations of mathematics, inspired by Kant, elaborate the difference between constructions of perceptual objects and theories about them.

Immanuel Kants

Logik

ein

Handbuch zu Vorlesungen.

Königsberg,
bey Friedrich Nicolovius,
1800.

Immanuel Kant's
LOGIC
A Manual for Lectures

Sr. Excellenz

dem

Herrn

Herrn Eberhard Julius E. von Massow,

Königl. Preuß. Geheimen Staats- und Justizminister, Chef
des geistlichen Departements in evangelisch-lutherischen Kir-
chen- und Schul-, auch allen Stifts- und Klöster-, inglei-
chen katholischen Geistlichkeits-Sachen, Erstem Präsident des
evangelisch-lutherischen Ober-Consistorii, Ober-
Curator der Universitäten rc. rc.

ehrfurchtsvoll gewidmet

vom

Herausgeber

Gottlob Benjamin Jäsche,

Doctor und Privatdocent auf der Universität in Königsberg,
Mitgliede der gelehrten Gesellschaft zu Frankfurt
an der Oder.

Preface

It is already a year and a half since Kant instructed me to edit his *Logic* for the press as presented by him in public lectures to his listeners, and to submit it to the public in the form of a *compendious manual*. To that end I received from him the very manuscript he had used in his lectures, with an expression of the special honorable confidence in me that I, familiar with the principles of his system generally, would readily enter into the course of his ideas; and that I would not distort or falsify his thoughts but exhibit them with the requisite clarity and definiteness and at the same time in the appropriate order. In undertaking the honorable assignment and trying, as best I could, to carry it out in accordance with the wish and expectation of the *celebrated wise man,* my much revered teacher and friend, everything concerning the presentation—the style and execution, the exhibition and arrangement of the thoughts—must thus be charged in part to *my* account. It therefore also falls naturally to me to render account thereof to the reader of this new Kantian work. On this point a few explanations are in order.

Since 1765, without interruption, Professor Kant had based his lectures on logic on Meier's textbook as a guide (Georg Friedrich Meier's *Auszug aus der Vernunftlehre,* Halle, at Gebauer, 1752), for reasons which he had explained in a program announcing his lectures in 1765. The copy of said compendium of which he availed himself in his lectures, like all other textbooks used by him for the same purpose is interleaved with sheets of paper; his general notes and explanations as well as the more special ones that stand in close relation to the text of individual paragraphs may be found partly on these sheets, partly on the margins of the book itself. And these handwritten records of scattered notes and explanations now make up the *store of materials* which Kant assembled for his lectures and from time to time expanded by new ideas, revising and improving it again and again in respect of various particular matters. It thus contains at least the essentials of everything the famous commentator of Meier's textbook used to communicate to his listeners in his freely delivered lectures on logic, and considered worth writing down.

As concerns the presentation and arrangement of matters in this work, I believed that I would carry out the ideas and principles of the great man most accurately, if, in respect to the economy and division of the whole generally, I kept to his express explanation. Accordingly there must be included, in the actual treatise of logic and especially of the *doctrine of elements,* nothing but the theory of the three essential main functions of thinking—*concepts, judgments,* and *conclusions.*[1] Anything dealing with cognition in general and its logical perfections, which in Meier's textbook precedes the doctrine of concepts and occupies almost one half of the whole, must therefore be assigned to the Introduction. As Kant remarks right at the beginning of the eighth section in which Meier presents the doctrine of concepts: "So far cognition in general has been dealt with, as the *propaedeutic* of logic; now follows logic itself."

As a result of this express indication I have taken into the Introduction everything up to the said section. The Introduction, for that reason, has gained much greater length than it usually occupies in manuals of logic. Another consequence of this has been that the Doctrine of Method, the second main part of the treatise, had to turn out the shorter, the greater the amount of material that had already been treated in the Introduction, as, e.g., the doctrine of proof, and the like—which incidentally by our modern logicians is now rightly considered as belonging to the field of the doctrine of method. It would have been a repetition as unnecessary as improper to mention these matters

---

1. *Schlüssen,* comprising both conclusions of the understanding and conclusions of reason or syllogisms. We translate *Schluss* by "conclusion," where the genus is meant (in preference to "inference").

once more in their right spot, only to make the incomplete complete and to put everything in its proper place. The latter, however, has nevertheless been done by me in respect to the doctrine of *definition* and the *logical division of concepts,* which in Meier's compendium is treated as early as the eighth section, namely, the doctrine of elements regarding concepts, an order which Kant also left unchanged in his presentation.

It probably goes without saying that the great reformer of philosophy and—regarding the economy and external form of logic—also of this special part of theoretical philosophy would have worked out a logic after *his* architectonic design, whose essential outline is recorded in the *Critique of Pure Reason,* if it had so pleased him. His task of a scientific foundation of the entire system of philosophy proper—the philosophy of what is *realiter* true and certain—that incomparably more important and more difficult task, which only he alone could carry out in *his* originality, did not permit him to think of working out a logic by his own hand. He could, however, very well leave this work to others who with insight and unbiased judgment could use his architectonic ideas for a truly well adapted and well ordered treatment of that science. This was to be expected of several thorough and unbiased thinkers among our German philosophers, and this expectation has indeed not disappointed Kant and the friends of his philosophy. In economy and disposition of the whole, several new textbooks on logic must be regarded as a fruit of those Kantian ideas on logic. For the conviction must enter everyone through even the most superficial comparison of the old with the new textbooks of logic treated after Kantian principles—if only he has correct and clear concepts of the peculiar character and lawful limits of logic—that this science has really gained thereby, though it is true that it has become neither richer, nor more solid in content or better grounded in itself. But it has become more purified, partly of all foreign matter, partly of many useless subtleties and mere dialectical trifles; it has become more *systematic* and yet, with all scientific rigorousness of method, at the same time simpler. For, much as some old manuals of this science have won distinction by scientific strictness of method, clarity, definiteness and precision in explanations, and conclusiveness and evidence of proofs, there is hardly one among them in which the boundaries of various domains belonging to general logic in its wider extension, of the merely *propaedeutic*, the *dogmatic* and *technical*, the *pure* and *empirical*, do not run into and across one another in such a manner as to make it impossible to distinguish one from the other.

Herr Jacob, in the Preface to the first edition of his logic, remarks: "Wolff has excellently grasped the idea of a general logic, and if this great man had embarked on an entirely separate presentation of pure logic, he would have furnished us, due to his systematic mind, with a masterpiece that would have made all future work of this kind superfluous." But he just did not carry out this idea and none of his successors has carried it out, great and well-founded as, by the way, the merit is that the Wolffian school has acquired concerning the properly *logical*, the *formal* perfection in philosophical cognition.

But apart from what still could and had to be done to perfect logic in respect of external form by the necessary separation of pure and merely formal propositions from real or metaphysical propositions, when the adjudication and determination of the inner content of this science, as a science, is at issue, Kant's judgment on this point is not in doubt. Several times he has expressed himself definitively and explicitly: logic is to be regarded as a separate, self-contained science grounded in itself, and from its origin and first development, beginning with Aristotle up to our times, it has not been able to gain anything in scientific grounding. According to this assertion, Kant thought neither of grounding the logical principles of identity and contradiction in a higher principle, nor of deducing the logical forms of judgments. He has recognized and treated the principle of contradiction as a self-evident premise not in need of any derivation from a higher principle. Only the use, the validity of this principle, was restricted by him, in expelling it from the domain of metaphysics where dogmatism had tried to establish it, and limiting it to the merely logical use of reason, as valid for this use alone.

Whether now the logical premise of identity and contradiction is, in itself and absolutely, neither capable nor in need of further deduction, that is another question, which leads to the much more significant question: Is there an *absolutely first* principle of all cognition and science at all; is such a principle possible and can it be found?

The *Science of Knowledge*[2] believes that it has discovered such a principle in the *pure absolute I,* thus having established all philosophical knowledge not only as to mere form but also as to content. And on the supposition of the possibility and apodeictic validity of this absolutely sole and unconditioned principle it therefore proceeds quite consistently, when it does not admit the logical principles of identity and contradiction, the propositions $A = A$ and $-A = -A$ as unconditionally valid but declares them as mere subaltern propositions, which through it and its highest proposition, *I am,* can and must first be demonstrated and determined (cf. *Foundation of the Science of Knowledge,* pp. 13 ff.). In an equally consistent manner also Schelling, in his system of transcendental idealism, declares himself against the presupposition of logical principles as *unconditioned,* that is, as not derived from a higher one, in that logic generally can originate only by abstraction from determinate propositions and—so far as it originates in a scientific manner—only by abstraction from the *supreme* principles of knowledge, and consequently presupposes these highest principles of knowledge and, thus, the *Science of Knowledge* itself. Since, however, on the other hand, these highest principles of knowledge, considered as *principia,* presuppose the logical form with as much necessity, the very circle arises which science cannot solve but nevertheless can explain, namely by acknowl-

2. This title of J. G. Fichte's work is variously translated, e.g. "Science of Knowledge", or "Doctrine de la Science". Fichte's work had been defended by the young Schelling (cf. further below, this paragraph); and Jäsche, without mentioning Fichte's name, uses the word *Wissenschaftslehre* here almost generally for a philosophy that presupposes a both formal and material first principle. Further below in this paragraph, Jäsche refers to the *Grundlage der Wissenschaftslehre,* probably the *Grundlage der gesammten Wissenschaftslehre* (Leipzig, 1794), *Foundation of the Entire Science of Knowledge.*

edging a principle of philosophy which is first both as to form and content (formal and material), in which both form and content condition and ground each other reciprocally. In this principle, then, would lie the point in which the subjective and the objective, identical[3] and synthetic knowledge, would be one and the same.

On the supposition of the dignity which undoubtedly must be due such a principle, logic, as every science, would have to be subordinated to the *Science of Knowledge* and its principles.

Be this as it may, so much is certain: At the core of its region, as concerns essentials, logic remains at all events unchanged; and the transcendental question, whether the logical propositions are capable and in need of derivation from a higher absolute principle, can have no more influence on it and the validity and evidence of its laws, than the transcendental task, *How are synthetic judgments a priori possible in mathematics?* can have on pure mathematics in respect of its scientific content.

Just as the mathematician as mathematician, so the logician as logician, within the scope of his science, can safely and assuredly continue his course of explaining and proving without bothering about the transcendental question of the transcendental philosopher and the teacher of *Science of Knowledge,* a question which lies outside his own sphere: *How is pure mathematics or pure logic as a science possible?*

Under this general acknowledgment of the rightness of general logic, the dispute between skeptics and dogmatics about the last grounds of philosophical knowledge has therefore never been carried out in the domain of logic but always in the domain of metaphysics; the rules of logic have been acknowledged as valid by every reasonable skeptic just as well as by the dogmatist. And how could it be otherwise? The highest task of philosophy proper concerns not at all subjective but objective knowledge—not identical but synthetic knowledge. Logic *as such,* therefore, is here not affected at all; and it could occur

3. See below §§ 36, 37.

neither to the *Critique* nor to the *Science of Knowledge*—nor will it ever occur to a philosophy capable of distinguishing the transcendental standpoint from the merely logical—to seek the last grounds of real philosophic knowledge within the domain of mere logic and to pick from a proposition of logic, considered merely as such, a *real object.*

Anyone who has firmly grasped and never lost sight of the world of difference that lies between (general) logic proper as a mere formal science—the science of mere thinking as thinking—and transcendental philosophy, the sole material or real pure science of reason—the science of knowledge proper[4]—can readily judge what is to be thought of the recent attempt undertaken by Mr. Bardili (in his *Ground-Plan of First Logic*[5]) to determine a *prius* for logic, in the expectation of finding on this road: "a *real object,* either posited by *it* (mere logic) or else none that can be posited at all; the key to nature's essence, either given by *it* or otherwise no logic and no philosophy being possible at all." One fails to see, in truth, in what possible manner Mr. Bardili can find a real object in the *prius* of logic he sets forth, namely the principle of the absolute possibility of thinking, according to which we can repeat *one,* as *one and the same* in a *many* (not a manifold), an infinite number of times. This alleged newly discovered *prius* of logic is obviously nothing more nor less than the old long-since recognized principle of identity situated within the domain of logic and placed at the top of this science: *What I think, I think,* and just this and nothing else I can then think, *repeated to infinity.* Who would, in the well understood logical proposition of identity, think of a manifold and not of a *mere many* that indeed arises and can arise in no other way but by mere repetition of one and the same thought—the mere repeated positing of an $A = A = A,$ and so forth to infinity. We should therefore hardly find on *that* road chosen by Mr. Bardili, and by the heuristic method of which he has availed himself, that which is of the greatest inter-

4. *des eigentlichen Wissens* or, in another possible translation, "of actual knowledge."

5. *Grundriss der ersten Logik* (Stuttgart, 1800).

est to philosophizing reason: the *starting point* and the *terminal* from which it must proceed and to which it must return in its investigation.

The most significant and chief objections raised by Mr. Bardili against Kant and his method of philosophizing would therefore concern not so much Kant the *logician* as Kant the *transcendental philosopher* and *metaphysician*. We can therefore leave them here for consideration in their proper place.

Finally I wish to add that as soon as my leisure permits, I shall edit, in the same manner, Kant's metaphysics, the manuscript of which is already in my hands.

Königsberg, the 20th of September 1800.

Gottlob Benjamin Jäsche
Doctor and Faculty Lecturer at the University
of Königsberg, Member of the Learned Society
at Frankfort on the Oder.

Introduction

I. The Concept of Logic

Everything in nature, in the inanimate as well as the animate world, happens *according to rules,* although we do not always know these rules. Water falls according to the laws of gravity, and the locomotion of animals also takes place according to rules. The fish in the water, the bird in the air move according to rules. All nature actually is nothing but a nexus of appearances according to rules; and there is nothing at all *without rules.* When we believe that we have come across an absence of rules, we can only say that the rules are unknown to us.

The exercise of our own powers also takes place according to certain rules which we first follow without being conscious of them, until we gradually come to cognize them through experiments and long use of our powers, and finally make them so familiar to us that it costs us great effort to think them in abstraction. Thus, for example, general grammar is the form of a language as such. One also speaks, however, without knowing grammar, and he who speaks without knowing it actually does have a grammar and speaks according to rules, even though he is not conscious of them.

Like all our powers, *the understanding* in particular is bound in its acts to rules we can investigate. Indeed, the understanding is to be regarded as the source and faculty of thinking rules generatim. For, just as sensibility is the faculty of intuitions, so the understanding is the faculty of thinking, that is, of bringing the presentations of the senses under rules. It therefore is avid to seek rules, and satisfied when it has found them. The question then is, since the understanding is the source of rules, *according to what rules does it proceed itself?*[6]

For there cannot be any doubt: We cannot think or use our understanding otherwise than according to certain rules. Now these rules we can think by themselves, e.g., we can think them *without their application* or *in abstracto.* Which then are these rules?

All rules according to which the understanding proceeds are either *necessary* or *contingent.* The former are those without which no use of the understanding would be possible at all; the latter are those without which a certain use of the understanding would not take place. The contingent rules which depend on a certain object of cognition are as variegated as these objects themselves. Thus, for example, there is a use of the understanding in mathematics, metaphysics, morality, etc. The rules of such special determinate use of the understanding in the said sciences are contingent, because it is contingent whether I think this or that object to which these rules relate.

If, now, we set aside all cognition that we must borrow from *objects* and reflect solely upon the use of the understanding in itself, we discover those of its rules which are necessary throughout, in every respect and regardless of any special objects, because without them we would not think at all. Insight into these rules can therefore be gained a priori and *independently of any experience,* because they contain, *without discrimination between objects,* merely the conditions of the use of the understanding itself, be it *pure* or *empirical.* And it also follows from this that the universal and necessary rules of

---

6. Emphasis of the translators. "General laws of nature have their ground in our understanding, which prescribes them to nature (though only according to the general concept of it as nature)," *Critique of Judgment,* Introduction, IV. Special empirical laws or rules "with which experience supplies us" (B 677) contain something that is left undetermined by those most general laws of nature. In the sense of "prescribing laws to nature" and as the "faculty of thinking rules generatim," the understanding can be said to be the source of rules. (On the use of "generatim" throughout the translation, see "Note on the Translation," above, p. xii.)

thought in general can concern solely its *form,* and not in any way its *matter.* Accordingly, the science containing these universal and necessary rules is a science of the mere form of our intellectual cognition or of thinking. And we can therefore form for ourselves the idea of the possibility of such a science, just as that of a *general grammar* which contains nothing beyond the mere form of a language in general, without words, which belong to the matter of language.

Now this science of the necessary laws of the understanding and reason in general, or—which is the same—of the mere form of thinking, we call *logic.*

As a science concerning all thinking in general, regardless of objects as the matter of thinking, logic is to be considered as

    1) the *basis* of all other sciences and the *propaedeutic* of all use of the understanding. For this very reason, however, because it abstracts entirely from all objects, it can be

    2) no *organon* of the sciences.

By *organon* namely we understand an instruction for bringing about a certain cognition.[7] This implies, however, that I already know the object of the cognition that is to be produced according to certain rules. An organon of the sciences is therefore not mere logic, because it presupposes the exact knowledge of the sciences, of their objects and sources. Thus mathematics, for example, is an excellent organon as a science containing the ground of the expansion of our cognition in regard to a certain use of reason. But since logic, as a universal propaedeutic of all use of the understanding and of reason in general, need not go into the sciences and anticipate their subject matter, it is only a *universal art of reason (Canonica Epicuri),* to make cognition in general conform with the form of the understanding; and only to that extent may it be called an organon, which, however, serves not the *expansion* but merely the *judging* and *correction* of our cognition.

    3) As a science of the necessary laws of thinking without which no use of the understanding and of reason takes

---

7. See B 24 ff., 76 ff., 85, 823.

place at all, which consequently are the conditions under which alone the understanding can and shall agree with itself—the necessary laws and conditions of its right use—logic, however, is a *canon*.[8] And as a canon of the understanding and of reason it need not borrow any principles, either from any science or from any experience; it must contain nothing but laws a priori that are necessary and concern the understanding in general.

Some logicians presuppose *psychological* principles in logic. But to bring such principles into logic is as absurd as taking morality from life. If we took the principles from psychology, i.e. from observations about our understanding, we would merely see *how* thinking occurs and *how* it *is* under manifold hindrances and conditions; this would therefore lead to the cognition of merely *contingent* laws. In logic, however, the question is not one of *contingent* but of *necessary* rules, not how we think, but how we ought to think. The rules of logic, therefore, must be taken not from the *contingent* but from the *necessary* use of the understanding, which one finds, without any psychology, in oneself. In logic we do not want to know how the understanding is and thinks, and how it hitherto has proceeded in thinking, but how it ought to proceed in thinking. Logic shall teach us the right use of the understanding, i.e. the one that agrees with itself.

From the foregoing explanation of logic the other essential properties of this science can also be gathered, namely that it is

4) a science of reason not as to mere form but *as to matter,* since its rules are not taken from experience and since at the same time it has reason as its subject matter.[9] Logic is therefore a self-cognition of the understanding and of reason, not, however, as to their faculty in respect of objects, but solely as to form. In logic I shall not ask: *What* does the understanding cognize and *how much* can it cognize or *how far* does its cognition go? for that would be self-cognition in respect of its

8. See B 77, 88, 170 f., 823 ff.

9. *Objekt.* Reason as its own subject matter must be distinguished from the material use of reason which belongs to metaphysics. Kant's text here is univocally correct, as Heinze holds, as against Kinkel's emendation, *Philosophische Bibliothek,* Vol. XLII (Leipzig: Verlag von Felix Meiner, 1920), p. 15.

material use, and belongs to metaphysics. In logic the question is only: *How will the understanding cognize itself?* Being a rational science, both as to matter and form, logic finally is

    5) a *doctrine* or *demonstrated theory*. For since it is not occupied with the common and as such merely empirical use of the understanding and of reason, but solely with the universal and necessary laws of thinking in general, it rests on principles a priori from which all its rules can be derived and proved as rules to which all cognition of reason should conform.

Since logic, as a science a priori or as a doctrine, must be taken to be a canon of the use of the understanding and of reason, it differs essentially from *aesthetics,* which as a mere *critique* of taste has no *canon* (law) but only a *norm* (model or standard of judging) which consists in general agreement. Aesthetics namely contains the rules of the agreement of cognition with the laws of sensibility; logic, on the contrary, contains the rules of the agreement of cognition with the laws of the understanding and of reason. The former has only empirical principles and therefore can never be a science or doctrine, if by doctrine one understands a dogmatic instruction out of principles *a priori,* in which one has insight into everything through the understanding without further lessons from experience, and which gives us rules whose observance provides the desired perfection.

Some have tried, especially orators and poets, to discourse upon taste, but they have never been able to pass a decisive judgment on it. The philosopher Baumgarten[10] in Frankfort has made the plan for a science of aesthetics. More correctly, Home[11] has called aesthetics a *Criticism,* since it does not give, as logic does, rules *a priori* that sufficiently determine the judg-

---

10. Alexander Gottlieb Baumgarten (1714–1762), *Aesthetica,* 2 vols. (1750, 1758).

11. Henry Home (1696–1782), *Elements of Criticism* (1762). These statements about the empirical character of judgments of taste are not contradicted but supplemented by the theory of an a priori heautonomy in Kant's *Critique of Judgment,* Introduction, V, that is, the self-prescription of reflective judgment concerning its interpretation of nature.

ment but takes up its rules a *posteriori* and generalizes, through comparisons, the empirical laws by which we cognize the less perfect and the perfect (the beautiful).

Logic therefore is more than mere criticism; it is a canon that afterwards serves criticism, i.e. serves as the principle of judging all use of the understanding as such, although only as to its rightness in respect of mere form, it being no more an organon than general grammar.

Viewed from another angle, as a propaedeutic of all use of the understanding as such, general logic at the same time differs also from *transcendental logic,* in which the object itself is presented as an object of the mere understanding, whereas general logic concerns all objects generatim.

If, then, we summarize all essential characteristics belonging to a full determination of the concept of logic, we shall have to set up the following concept of it:

Logic is a science of reason not only as to mere form but also as to matter; a science a priori of the necessary laws of thinking, not, however, in respect of particular objects but all objects generatim; it is a science, therefore, of the right use of the understanding and of reason as such, not subjectively, i.e. not according to empirical (psychological) principles of how the understanding thinks, but objectively, i.e. according to a priori principles of how it ought to think.

II. Main Divisions of Logic / Different Ways of Its Presentation / Usefulness of This Science / Outline of Its History

One divides logic into
    1) *analytic* and *dialectic.*

The *analytic* brings to light, by sundering them, all acts of reason that we exercise in thinking. It therefore is an analytic of the form of the understanding and of reason and is rightly called the logic of truth, because it contains the necessary rules of all (formal) truth, without which our cognition, regardless of objects, is also untrue in itself. It is therefore nothing but a canon of adjudication (of the formal rightness of our cognition).

If one wanted to use this merely theoretical and universal doctrine as a practical art, i.e. as an organon, it would become a *dialectic*, a *logic of semblance* (*ars sophistica, disputatoria*)[12] which springs from a mere abuse of the analytic, inasmuch as the semblance of a true cognition, whose characteristics must be taken from agreement with objects and therefore from *content*, is contrived after *the mere logical form*.

In former times, dialectic was studied with great diligence; This art put forward false premises under the semblance of truth and sought, in accordance with them and by the same semblance, to pretend things. Among the Greeks, dialecticians were advocates and orators who could lead the people wherever they wanted, because people allow themselves to be deceived by semblance. The dialectic of that time was thus the art of semblance. In logic it was put forward for some time under the name of the *art of disputation*, and during that period all logic and philosophy was a cultivation of certain loquacious individuals to contrive any kind of semblance. Nothing, however, can be more unworthy of a philosopher than cultivating such an art. It must therefore be dropped altogether, and instead, a critique of this semblance must be introduced into logic.

We would then have two parts of logic: the *analytic*, containing the formal criteria of truth, and the *dialectic*, containing the characteristics and rules by which we can tell that something does not agree with the formal criteria of truth, although it seems to. Dialectic in this sense would then have its good use as a cathartic of the understanding.

Logic is commonly divided also into

   2) *natural* or *popular* and *formal*[13] or *scientific* logic (*logica naturalis; logica scholastica s. artificialis*).

---

12. Cf. B 86.

13. *Künstlich*, from *Kunst*, "art," and *können*, "to be able, to know how," in the sense of the Greek τέχνη, "art," distinguishing man's from nature's production. In this sense "technical" would have been a good translation.

But this division is inadmissible. For natural logic or the logic of common reason (*sensus communis*) is actually no logic but an anthropological science that has empirical principles only, in that it deals with the rules of the natural use of the understanding and of reason, which can be cognized only *in concreto*, thus without their consciousness *in abstracto*. Therefore, the formal or scientific logic alone deserves this name [of logic], as a science of the necessary and universal rules of thinking which can and must be cognized a *priori* independently of the natural use of the understanding and of reason *in concreto*, although they can be found at first only by observing that natural use.

3) Still another division of logic is that into *theoretical* and *practical* logic. This division, however, is also incorrect.

General logic, as a mere canon abstracting from all objects, can have no practical part. This would be a *contradictio in adjecto*, because a practical logic presupposes knowledge of a certain kind of objects to which one applies it. We therefore may call every science a *practical logic,* for in every one we must have a form of thinking. General logic, considered as practical, can therefore be nothing more than a *technique of learning*[14] *generatim—an organon of scholastic method.*

As a consequence of this division, logic would have a *dogmatic* and a *technical part*. The first could be called the *doctrine of elements,* the second, *doctrine of method.*[15] The practical or technical part of logic would be a logical art in respect of orderly arrangement, and logical terminology and distinction to facilitate thereby the acts of the understanding.

Since Jäsche, however, in the following explanation (3) uses the word *technisch* himself in this meaning, "the technical part of logic would be a logical art . . . ," we have retained "technical" for *technisch* in that context and translated *künstlich* here by "formal." It would be rather misleading to translate by the English "artificial" a meaning almost lost in that English word, notwithstanding the Latin *artificialis* given in the parenthesis, which should also be read merely as characterizing art production.

14. *der Gelehrsamkeit,* i.e. of the body of profound knowledge acquired by study, which then makes for learned men.

15. This is also the division of the *Critique of Pure Reason.*

In both parts, however, the technical as well as the dogmatic, not the slightest consideration would have to be given to objects, nor to the subject of thinking. In the latter relation logic might be divided into

4) *pure and applied logic.*

In pure logic we segregate the understanding from the other powers of the mind and contemplate what it does by itself. Applied logic contemplates the understanding so far as it is intermingled with other powers of the mind that influence its acts and slant it in some direction, so that it does not proceed according to the laws which its own insight knows are the right ones. Applied logic actually should not be called logic. It is a psychology in which we contemplate how things usually work in our thinking, not how they are to work. Admittedly, it does say in the end what one has to do in order to make a right use of one's understanding under the manifold subjective hindrances and restrictions; we can also learn from applied logic what furthers the right use of the understanding, the aids to it or the cures of mistakes and errors. But a propaedeutic it is not. For psychology, from which everything in applied logic must be derived, is part of the philosophical sciences[16] to which logic shall be the propaedeutic.

One says that the technique [method] or manner of building a science should be presented in applied logic. But this is futile, and even harmful. One then begins to build before one has the material, and one gives the form, but content is lacking.[17] The technique must be presented together with [the subject matter of] every science.

Finally, as to

16. There is a place for psychology in a chart of the system or architectonic of pure reason. Kant did not think, however, that either rational or empirical psychology was a science in the light of transcendental philosophy (cf. *Critique of Pure Reason,* B 874 ff.; *Metaphysical Foundations of Natural Science,* Preface; *Critique of Judgment,* § 89). True empirical psychology becomes anthropology.

17. Cf. Friedrich Gauss: "Demonstration is based on notions, not on notations."

5) the division of logic into a logic of the *common* understanding and of *speculative* understanding, we note that it can not be divided in that way at all.

It can not be a science of the speculative understanding. For as a logic of speculative cognition or of the speculative use of reason it would be an organon of other sciences and not merely a propaedeutic concerned with all possible use of the understanding and of reason.

No more can logic be *a product of the common understanding.* Common understanding is the faculty of insight into the rules of cognition *in concreto.* Logic, however, is to be a science of the rules of thinking *in abstracto.*

One can, however, assume general human understanding to be the subject of logic, and in this case logic would abstract from the special rules of speculative reason and differ from logic of *speculative understanding.*

As concerns the *presentation* of logic, it can be either [academic or] *scholastic,* or *popular.*

The presentation is *scholastic* so far as it is commensurate with the desire for knowledge, the capacities, and the culture of those who wish to treat the cognition of logical rules as a science. *Popular,* however, it is, if it condescends to the capacities and needs of those who do not want to study logic as a science but want to use it only to enlighten their understanding. In scholastic presentation the rules must be exhibited *in their universality* or *in abstracto;* in the popular one, *in particular,* or *in concreto.* The scholastic presentation is the foundation of the popular one, for he alone can present something in a popular manner who can also present it more thoroughly.

We are distinguishing here, by the way, *presentation* from *method.* By *method* is to be understood the manner in which we can completely cognize a certain object to the cognition of which the method is to be applied. Method grows out of the nature of the science itself and, as a necessary order of thinking determined by that nature, can not be changed. *Presentation* means only the mode of communicating one's thoughts to others in order to make a doctrine understood.

From what we have said so far about the essence and the

purpose of logic, the value of this science and the usefulness of its study may now be gauged by a correct and definite standard.

Logic then is indeed not a universal art of inventing and not an organon of truth, not an algebra that might help us to the discovery of hidden truth. It is, however, useful and indispensable as a *critique of cognition,* or for judging common as well as speculative reason, not in order to teach it, but to make it *correct* and agreeing with itself. For the logical principle of truth is agreement of the understanding with its own general laws.

As concerns the history of logic, we are citing only the following:

Present-day logic has developed out of Aristotle's *Analytic.* This philosopher may be regarded as the father of logic. He presented it as an organon and divided it into *Analytic* and *Dialectic.* His manner of teaching is very academic and directed toward the development of the most general concepts underlying logic, from which, however, no profit is derived, because almost everything amounts to mere subtleties, except that the names of various acts of the understanding have been extracted from it.

Logic, by the way, has not gained much in *content* since Aristotle's times and indeed it cannot, due to its nature. But it may well gain in *exactness, definiteness* and *distinctness.* There are but few sciences that can come into a permanent state beyond which they undergo no further change. To these belong logic, and also metaphysics. Aristotle had omitted no moment[18] of the understanding; we are herein only more exact, methodical, and orderly.

Of Lambert's *Organon,*[19] one believed that it would augment

---

18. *Critique of Pure Reason,* B 210: "the degree of reality as a cause is called a moment," or momentum. By analogy, Kant speaks of "moments of thinking," B 101. A point may be made for saying that Aristotle in his own way, has left out no moment of thinking, and that in this sense all logic is a footnote on Aristotle even though many of these footnotes have today, in complexity, profundity, and range, surpassed the whole of the original treatise.

19. Johann Heinrich Lambert (1728–1777), Kant's friend. *New Organon or Thoughts on the Exploration and Designation of the True and Its Distinction from Error and Illusion (Neues Organon, oder Gedanken über die Erforschung*

logic very much. It contains, however, nothing but subtler divisions which, as all correct subtleties do, sharpen the understanding but are of no essential use.

Among the more recent philosophers there are two who have set general logic going, Leibniz and Wolff.

Malebranche and Locke have not actually written a logic, as they deal also with the content of cognition and the origin of concepts.

Wolff's general logic is the best we have. Some have connected it with Aristotle's, as, for instance, Reusch.[20]

Baumgarten,[21] a man who has much merit, condensed the Wolffian logic, and Meier in turn commented on Baumgarten.

To the more recent logicians also belongs Crusius[22] who did not consider, however, what logic is all about. For his logic contains metaphysical principles and thus transgresses, in so far, the limits of this science; moreover, it sets up a criterion of truth that cannot be a criterion, and thus gives rein to all kinds of fancies.

In present times there has been no famous logician, and we do not indeed need any new inventions for logic, because it contains merely the form of thinking.

und *Bezeichnung des Wahren, und dessen Unterscheidung von Irrtum und Schein)*, 2 vols. (1764).

20. Johann Peter Reusch (1691–1754).

21. Cf. above, n. 10.

22. Christian August Crusius (1712–1775).

III. Concept of Philosophy in General / Philosophy According to the School Concept and According to the World Concept / Essential Requirements and Goals of Philosophizing / The Most General and Highest Tasks of This Science

It is sometimes difficult to explain what is understood by a science. A science gains in precision by establishing its definite concept; and quite a few mistakes are thus avoided, which for various reasons slip in when one is not yet able to distinguish the science from those related to it.

Before we try to give a definition of philosophy, we must first investigate the character of the different cognitions themselves; and since philosophic cognitions belong to the cognitions of reason, we must explain what is to be understood by the latter.

Cognitions of reason are opposed to *historical* cognitions. The former are cognitions out of *principles* (*ex principiis*), the latter out of *data* (*ex datis*). A cognition, however, may have arisen out of reason and notwithstanding be historical; when a mere copyist,[23] for example, learns the products of the reason of others, his cognition of such rational products is merely historical.

Cognitions may be distinguished

1) according to their *objective* origin, i.e. according to the sources from which alone a cognition is possible. In this respect all cognitions are either *rational* or *empirical;*

2) according to their *subjective* origin, i.e. according to the manner in which a cognition can be acquired by man. When seen from this latter viewpoint, cognitions are either *rational* or *historical*, whichever way they in themselves may

23. *Literator.*

have arisen. Something that *subjectively* is mere historical cognition, may therefore *objectively* be a cognition of reason.

It is harmful to know some rational cognitions merely historically; this does not matter with others. For example, the navigator knows the rules of navigation historically from his tables, and that is enough for him. But if a lawyer knows jurisprudence merely historically, he is completely ruined for being truly a judge, let alone a legislator.

From the aforementioned distinction between *objectively* and *subjectively* rational cognitions it becomes clear that, in a certain way, one can learn philosophy without being able to philosophize. He who truly wants to become a philosopher must practice the free use of his reason and not merely an imitative and, so to speak, mechanical use.

We have explained cognitions of reason as cognitions out of principles; and from this follows that they must be *a priori*. There are, however, two kinds of cognition which both are *a priori* and yet have many pronounced differences, namely, mathematics and philosophy.[24]

One customarily maintains that mathematics and philosophy are distinguished from one another *by their subject,* in that the former deals with *quantity,* the latter with *quality*. This, however,[25] is wrong. The difference between these sciences cannot rest on the subject, for philosophy is directed toward everything, therefore also toward *quanta,* and mathematics in part also [toward everything], as far as everything has a quantity. Only *the different manner of rational cognition or of the use of reason* in mathematics and philosophy is decisive for the specific difference between these two sciences. Philosophy, namely, is the *cognition of reason out of mere concepts;* mathematics, on the contrary, is the *cognition of reason out of the construction of concepts.*

We *construct* concepts when we exhibit them in intuition *a*

24. See B 740–747. Mathematics there serves as the prototype of an intuitive science, as against discursive philosophy.

25. Reading, with the list of printer's errors, *Allein* instead of the original *Alles*.

priori without experience or when we exhibit in intuition the object that corresponds to our concept.[26] The mathematician can never avail himself of his reason according to mere concepts, the philosopher can never avail himself of it through construction of concepts. In mathematics one uses reason *in concreto,* but the [corresponding] intuition is not empirical; rather one here constructs something for himself, *a priori,* as object of intuition.

And herein, as we see, mathematics has an advantage over philosophy, in that the cognitions of the former are *intuitive,* those of the latter, on the contrary, only *discursive.* The reason, however, why in mathematics we ponder more the quantities lies in this, that quantities can be constructed *a priori* in intuition, whereas qualities cannot be exhibited in intuition.[27]

Philosophy, thus, is the system of philosophic cognitions or of cognitions of reason out of concepts. This is the *scholastic* [or *school*] concept of this science. According to its *world concept*[28] it is the science of the ultimate ends of human reason. This high concept gives philosophy its *dignity,* i.e. an absolute value. And actually it is philosophy alone that has an inner value and first gives value to all other cognitions.

In the end the question is always, What is philosophizing good for and what is its ultimate end? and this even when philosophy is considered as a science according to the *scholastic concept.*

In this scholastic meaning of the word, philosophy relates

26. These sentences are transliterated in B 741.

27. But see Anticipations of Perception, B 207–218.

28. In the *Critique of Pure Reason,* B 867, Kant says: "World concept [*Weltbegriff*] is called here the concept that concerns what necessarily interests everyone." Probably influenced by the Latin equivalent given by Kant in B 866, *conceptus cosmicus,* all translators of the *Critique of Pure Reason* and Abbott have rendered *Weltbegriff* by "cosmical concept." Since these translators also call the *transcendental* (not practical) *Weltbegriffe,* or cosmological concepts, "cosmical concepts" (B 434), the confusion is complete. We have preferred "world concept" for *Weltbegriff,* analogous to "world language," "world state," etc., as it is less physically and more practically oriented than "cosmical concept." Cf. also just below, n.31, "cosmopolitan meaning."

only to *skill;* in reference to the world concept, on the contrary, it relates to *usefulness.* In the former respect it is a *doctrine of skill;* in the latter a *doctrine of wisdom,* the *lawgiver* of reason, and to that extent the philosopher is not a *theoretician of reason,*[29] but *lawgiver.*

The mere theoretician or, as *Socrates* calls him, the *philodoxus,* strives only after speculative knowledge, without caring how much his knowledge contributes to the ultimate end of human reason; he gives rules for the use of reason to all kinds of ends. The practical philosopher, the teacher of wisdom through doctrine and example, is the philosopher in the true sense.[30] For philosophy is the idea of a perfect wisdom that shows us the ultimate ends of human reason.

Two things belong to philosophy according to the scholastic concept:

First, a sufficient store of cognitions of reason; *second,* systematic coherence of these cognitions, or their conjunction in the idea of a whole.

Philosophy not only provides such strictly systematic coherence, but is the only science that has systematic coherence in the proper sense and gives systematic unity to all other sciences.

As concerns philosophy according to the world concept, however (*in sensu cosmico*), one may call it a *science of the highest maxim of the use of our reason,* if by maxim one understands the inner principle of choice among different ends.

For, in the latter meaning, philosophy is the science of relating all cognition and every use of reason to the ultimate end of human reason, to which, as the supreme end, all others are subordinated and in which they must be joined into unity.

The field of philosophy in this cosmopolitan[31] meaning may be summed up in the following questions:

29. *Vernunftkünstler,* literally "artist of reason."
30. This, Kant thought, was a well-nigh extinct species: "Nobody cares about wisdom, because it makes science, which is a tool of vanity, rather small" (Akad. XVI, 1652).
31. *weltbürgerlich,* "of world citizens."

1) *What can I know?*—
2) *What ought I to do?*
3) What may I hope?
4) What is man?[32]

The first question is answered by *metaphysics,* the second by *morality,* the third by *religion,* and the fourth by *anthropology.* At bottom all this could be reckoned to be anthropology, because the first three questions are related to the last.

The philosopher, therefore, must be able to determine

1) the sources of human knowledge,

2) the extent of the possible and advantageous use of all knowledge, and finally

3) the limits of reason.

The last is the most urgent but also the most difficult task, of which the *philodoxus,* however, takes no notice.

Two things, primarily, make the philosopher. (1) Cultivation of talents and skill to use them for various ends. (2) Readiness in the use of all means to any ends one may choose.[33] Both must be united, for without knowledge one never becomes a philosopher, but knowledge alone will never make the philosopher, unless there is added a purposeful joining of all cognitions and skills into unity, and an insight into their agreement with the highest ends of human reason.

No one at all can call himself a philosopher who cannot philosophize. Philosophizing, however, can be learned only through practice and the use of one's own reason.

How, indeed, should it be possible to learn philosophy? Every philosophical thinker builds his own work, so to speak, on the ruins of another; never, however, has a work come about that would have lasted in all its parts. Merely for that reason one cannot learn philosophy, because *it is not yet given.* Supposing, however, there *actually* were a philosophy: then no one who

32. The typography of the four questions—italics for (1) and (2) and the dash between them—follows the original. Note that the anthropological question (4) is not included in B 833.

33. *zu beliebigen Zwecken,* within the permissible, of course (cf. next sentence).

learned it could yet say of himself that he is a philosopher, for his knowledge of it would still be only *subjective-historical.*

In mathematics things are different. This science can in a certain way be learned, for here the proofs are so evident that everyone can become convinced of them; and because of its evidence it also can, as it were, be preserved as a *certain* and *permanent* doctrine.

He who wants to learn to philosophize must, on the contrary, regard all systems of philosophy only as the *history of the use of reason* and as objects for exercising his philosophical talent.

The true philosopher, as self-thinker, thus must make free, not slavishly imitating use of his reason. But not a *dialectical* use, i.e. one that aims only at giving cognitions a *semblance* of *truth* and *wisdom.* This is the business of the mere sophist, totally incompatible though with the dignity of the philosopher as one who knows and teaches wisdom.

For science has a true inner value only as an *organ of wisdom.* As such, however, it is indispensable, so that one may well maintain that wisdom without science is the shadowy outline of a perfection that we shall never reach.

He who hates science and so much the more loves wisdom is called a *misologist.* Misology usually springs from an emptiness of scientific attainments and a certain kind of vanity coupled with it. Sometimes, however, those also fall into the mistake of misology who at first pursued the sciences with much diligence and fortunate results but in the end found no satisfaction in all their knowledge.

Philosophy is the only science that can provide this inner satisfaction, for it closes, as it were, the scientific circle, and only through it do the sciences receive order and coherence.

For the sake of practice in self-thinking or philosophizing, we shall, therefore, have to look more to the *method* of our use of reason than to the propositions themselves that we have attained through it.

IV. Short Outline of a History of Philosophy

There is some difficulty in determining the borderline at which the *common* use of the understanding ends and the *speculative* begins, or where the common cognition of reason becomes philosophy.

There is, however, a fairly certain criterion here, namely the following:

Cognition of the general *in abstracto* is speculative cognition; cognition of the general *in concreto* is common cognition. Philosophy is speculative cognition and it therefore begins where the common use of reason sets out to make attempts at cognition of the general *in abstracto*.

Based on this determination of the difference between the common and the speculative use of reason, we can judge with which people the beginning of philosophizing must be dated. Among all peoples the Greeks first began to philosophize. For they first attempted to cultivate the cognition of reason *in abstracto* without the guiding thread of pictures, while other peoples sought instead to make concepts intelligible to themselves *in concreto by pictures* only. Even nowadays there are peoples like the Chinese and some Indians who indeed treat of things taken from mere reason, such as God, the immortality of the soul, and the like, but nevertheless do not seek to investigate the nature of these objects *in abstracto* according to concepts and rules. They make no separation between the use of reason *in concreto* and that *in abstracto*. Among the Persians and the Arabs one finds some speculative use of reason, but they borrowed its rules from Aristotle, thus from the Greeks. In the *Zend Avesta* of Zoroaster one does not detect the slightest trace of philosophy. This holds good also of the eulogized Egyptian wisdom, which in comparison with Greek philosophy was mere child's play.

As in philosophy, so in respect of mathematics, the Greeks have been the first to cultivate this part of reason's cognition in accordance with a speculative scientific method, by demonstrating every theorem out of elements.

However, *when* and *where* among the Greeks the philosophical spirit first sprang up—this cannot be determined.

The first who introduced the speculative use of reason, and to whom one has traced back the first steps of the human understanding toward a scientific culture, is Thales, the author of the Ionic sect.[34] He carried the surname "physicist," though he was also a mathematician, just as, in general, mathematics has always preceded philosophy.

The first philosophers, by the way, clothed everything in pictures. For poetry, which is nothing but thoughts in the clothing of pictures, is older than *prose*. Therefore, even for things that are solely objects of pure reason, one had to avail oneself at first of a picture language and poetic style. Pherecydes is said to have been the first prose writer.

The Ionian philosophers were followed by the Eleatics. The principle of Eleatic philosophy and its founder Xenophanes was: *In the senses is deception and illusion, in the understanding alone lies the source of truth.*

Among the philosophers of this school Zeno distinguished himself as a man of great intellect and acumen and as a subtle dialectician.

Dialectic at first meant the art of the pure use of the understanding in respect of abstract concepts segregated from all sensibility. Hence the many eulogies of this art among the ancients. Subsequently, when the philosophers who altogether rejected the testimony of the senses had, of necessity, to resort to many subtleties, dialectic degenerated into the art of asserting and disputing any proposition. And thus it became a mere exercise for the sophists, who wanted to argue about everything and tried to give the varnish of truth to illusion and turn black into white. For that reason the name *sophist,* under which otherwise one thought of a man capable of speaking reasonably and

34. See B xi.

with insight about all matters, became hated and contemptible, and in its stead the name *philosopher* was introduced.

Around the time of the Ionian school there arose in Greece a man of rare genius, who not only established a school but at the same time designed and carried out a project the like of which had never been before. This was Pythagoras, born on the isle of Samos. He founded a society of philosophers who were united in a league by the law of secrecy. His students were divided by him into two classes, the Acusmatics (ἀκουσματικοί), who had only to listen, and the Akroamatics (ἀκρουμμτικοί), who were also allowed to ask questions.[35]

Among his doctrines some were *exoteric,* which he presented to the entire people; others were secret and *esoteric,* meant for the members of his league alone, several of whom he received into his most intimate friendship and separated entirely from the rest. *Physics* and *theology,* the doctrine of the visible and the invisible, became the vehicle of his secret teachings. He also had various symbols, which presumably were nothing but certain signs serving the Pythagoreans to communicate with each other.

The object of his league seems to have been none other than *to purify religion from the delusions of the people, to moderate tyranny, and to introduce greater legality in the states.* This league, however, which the tyrants began to fear, was destroyed shortly before the death of Pythagoras, and the philosophical society was dissolved, partly by execution, partly by flight and exile of most of its members. The few who remained were novices. And since they did not know much of the peculiar doctrines of Pythagoras, nothing certain and definite can be said about these. Subsequently, many teachings were ascribed to Pythagoras, who indeed was a great mathematician, but they are certainly ficticious.

---

35. Kant himself opposes akroams (recitals) to axioms, the former being discursive, the latter intuitive principles. See below, § 35 and B 761–763. For details see the Translators' Introduction, pp. cv–cxv above.

The most important epoch of Greek philosophy finally began with Socrates. It was he who gave an entirely new *practical*
direction to the philosophic spirit and to all speculation. He
stands almost alone among men as the one whose conduct
came closest to *the idea of a wise man.*

The most famous among his disciples is Plato, who dealt particularly with the practical teachings of Socrates, and among the
disciples of Plato, Aristotle, who raised speculative philosophy
to a higher level.

Plato and Aristotle were succeeded by the Epicureans and
the Stoics, who were the most irreconcilable enemies of each
other. The *former* placed the highest good in a cheerful heart,
which they called pleasure;[36] the *latter* found it in *nobility* and
strength of soul, which enables one to do without the pleasur-
able things of life.

The Stoics, by the way, were *dialectical* in speculative philosophy, dogmatic in moral philosophy, and showed an unusual
dignity in their practical principles, by which they sowed the
seeds of the most sublime ethos that ever existed. The founder
of the Stoic school was Zeno of Citium. The most famous men
of this school of Greek philosophers are Cleanthes and Chrysippus.

The Epicurean school never gained the same reputation as the
Stoic. Whatever may be said of the Epicureans, however, this
much is certain: they showed the greatest moderation in pleasure and were the *best philosophers of nature* among Greek
thinkers.

We may still mention here that the most exclusive Greek
schools had special names. Thus, the school of Plato was called
Academy, that of Aristotle *Lyceum,* the school of the Stoics
Porticus (στοά), a covered walk from which the name Stoic is derived, the school of Epicurus *Horti,* because he taught in *gar-
dens.*

Plato's Academy was succeeded by three other academies

---

36. *Wollust,* which in earlier German did not have the censorious meaning
it has today.

that were founded by his disciples, the first by Speusippus, the second by Arcesilaus, the third by Carneades.

These academies tended toward scepticism. Speusippus and Arcesilaus both attuned their way of thinking to scepticism, and Carneades went even further in this respect. For that reason the sceptics, those subtle, dialectical philosophers, are also called *Academicians*. The academicians thus followed the first great doubter, Pyrrho and his successors. The occasion for this had been given them by their teacher Plato himself when he presented many of his teachings as dialogues, so that reasons *pro* and *contra* were adduced without his deciding on them, even though otherwise he was quite *dogmatic*.

If we let the epoch of scepticism begin with Pyrrho, one gets an entire school of sceptics who differed essentially from the dogmatics in their turn of mind and method of philosophizing, by making this the first maxim of the philosophizing use of reason: *to reserve one's judgment even in face of the greatest semblance of truth,* and by setting up this principle: *philosophy consists in the equilibrium of judging and teaches us to uncover illusion.* Of these sceptics, however, nothing is left except the two works of Sextus Empiricus in which he has put together all doubts.

When subsequently philosophy passed from the Greeks to the Romans, it did not develop further, for the Romans always remained disciples.

Cicero was in speculative philosophy a disciple of Plato, in morality a Stoic. To the Stoic sect belonged Epictetus, Antoninus the philosopher, and Seneca, the most famous.

There were no philosophers of nature among the Romans, except Plinius the Elder,[37] who has left us a natural history.

At last, culture disappeared among the Romans, and *barbarism* spread, until the Arabs, in the sixth and seventh centuries, began to apply themselves to the sciences and to revive

37. In the original, *dem Jüngern,* "the Younger." Both Plinii were called *Secundus,* the surname also used by Kant according to a transcript of his lecture (Akad. IX, 506), which Jäsche apparently misinterpreted as the younger (the Elder wrote the *Natural History*).

Aristotle. Now a resurgence of the sciences and particularly of Aristotle's reputation took place in the occident. In the eleventh and twelfth centuries the *scholastics* entered the scene, expounding Aristotle and carrying his subtleties *ad infinitum*. They were occupied with nothing but abstractions. This scholastic method of pseudo-philosophizing was displaced at the time of the Reformation, and now *eclectics* appeared in philosophy, i.e. such self-thinkers as confessed no school but sought and accepted the truth where they found it.

Philosophy owes its improvement in recent times partly to the intensified study of nature, partly to the connection of mathematics with natural science.[38] The orderly thinking that arose through the study of these sciences spread over the special branches and parts of philosophy proper. The first and greatest student of nature in modern times was Bacon of Verulam. In his inquiries he entered upon the road of experience and called attention to the importance and indispensability of *observation* and *experiment* for the discovery of truth. It is, by the way, difficult to say where the improvement of speculative philosophy actually originated. No small merit is due to Descartes, who contributed much that gave *distinctness to thinking* by his criterion of truth, which he placed in *clarity and evidence of cognition*.

Among the greatest and most meritorious reformers of philosophy in our times are to be reckoned Leibniz and Locke. The latter tried to analyze the human understanding and to show what powers of the soul and which of their operations belong to this or that cognition. But he did not complete the work of his enquiry; his procedure, moreover, is dogmatic, although he initiated the beginning of a better and more thorough study of the nature of the soul.

The special dogmatic method of philosophizing characteristic of Leibniz and Wolff was faulty. There is so much in it that is deceptive that it may well be necessary to suspend the entire procedure and to set in motion something else—*the method of*

38. At this point Kant's own work begins.

critical philosophizing, which consists in investigating the procedure of reason itself, in analyzing and examining the entire human faculty of cognition itself: how far its *limits* extend.

In our age the *philosophy of nature* flourishes, and among natural scientists there are great names, such as Newton. More recent philosophers of distinguished and lasting name cannot be cited at present, because here everything is, as it were, in flux. What one builds, another tears down.

In moral philosophy we have not advanced beyond the ancients. As concerns metaphysics, it seems as if we had become perplexed in the investigation of metaphysical truths. A kind of *indifferentism*[39] is shown toward this science, as one seems to take honor in speaking contemptuously of metaphysical investigations as though they were mere ruminating. And yet, metaphysics is actually the true philosophy!

Our age is the age of *criticism,* and it remains to be seen what will come of the critical attempts of our time in respect to philosophy and to metaphysics in particular.

V. Cognition in General / Intuitive and Discursive Cognition; Intuition and Concept and Their Difference in Particular / Logical and Aesthetic Perfection of Cognition

All our cognition has a *twofold* relation, *first* to the *object,* *second* to the *subject.* In the former respect it is related to *presentation,* in the latter to *consciousness,* the general condition of all cognition in general. (Actually, consciousness is a presentation that another presentation is in me.)

In every cognition there is to be distinguished *matter,* i.e. the object, and *form,* i.e. the manner *how* we cognize the object. For example, when a savage sees a house in the distance,

39. *Indifferentism,* as in A 10.

the use of which he does not know, he has the same object before him as another who knows it as a dwelling furnished for men. But as to form, this cognition of one and the same object is different in both. In the one it is *mere intuition,* in the other *intuition* and *concept* at the same time.

The difference in the form of cognition rests on a condition that accompanies all cognizing—*consciousness.* When I am conscious of a presentation, it is *clear;* when I am not conscious of it, it is *obscure.*

Since consciousness is the essential condition of all logical form of cognition, logic can and must be occupied only with clear, not with obscure presentations. In logic we do not see how presentations arise but solely how they agree with the logical form. Generally, logic cannot treat of mere presentations and their possibility. This it leaves to metaphysics. It is merely occupied with the rules of thinking—in concepts, judgments, and conclusions—through which all thinking takes place. Something precedes, indeed, before a presentation becomes a concept. This we shall also indicate in its proper place. We shall not investigate, however, how presentations arise. Logic does treat of cognition also, because in cognition thinking already takes place. But presentation is not yet cognition, rather cognition always presupposes presentation. And this latter cannot be explained at all. For, *what presentation is* would have to be explained again through another presentation.

All clear presentation to which alone the logical rules can be applied can be distinguished in regard to *distinctness* and *indistinctness.* When we are conscious of the whole presentation but not of the manifold contained in it, then the presentation is indistinct. First, by way of explanation, an example of intuition.

We see a cottage in the distance. When we are conscious that the intuited object is a house, we must necessarily have a presentation of the various parts of this house—windows, doors, and so forth. For, if we did not see the parts, we would not see the house itself either. But we are not conscious of this presentation of the manifold of its parts, and our presentation of the said object is therefore an indistinct presentation.

If further we want an example of indistinctness in concepts, the concept of beauty may serve us. Everybody has a clear concept of beauty. Several characteristics, however, occur in this concept, among others, that the beautiful must be something that (1) strikes the senses and (2) generally pleases. If now we are unable to expound the manifold of these and other characteristics of the beautiful, our concept of it is still indistinct.

The indistinct presentation is called by Wolff's disciples a *confused* presentation. This expression, however, is unsuitable, because the opposite of confusion is not distinctness, but order. Distinctness is indeed an effect of order, and indistinctness an effect of confusion, and every confused presentation is therefore also indistinct. But the converse of the sentence is not true: Not every indistinct presentation is a confused one. For in cognitions in which there is no manifold, there is no order, but also no confusion.

This is the case with all *simple* presentations that never become distinct, not because there is confusion in them, but because we do not meet with a manifold in them. One must call them, therefore, indistinct, but not confused.

And even in the most complex presentations in which a manifold of characteristics may be distinguished, indistinctness is often not the result of confusion but of *weakness of consciousness*. Something, namely, may be distinct as to *form*, i.e., I may be conscious of the manifold in the presentation, but the distinctness may decrease as to *matter*, if the degree of consciousness becomes less although all order is there. This is the case with abstract presentations.

Distinctness itself may be twofold:

1. *Sensible distinctness.* This consists in consciousness of the manifold in intuition. I see the Milky Way as a white band; the rays from the individual stars in it must necessarily have entered my eye. But the presentation thereof was only clear; it becomes distinct through the telescope, because now I see the individual stars comprised in that milky band.

2. *Intellectual distinctness, distinctness in concepts,* or *distinctness of the understanding.* This rests on analysis of the concept in respect of the manifold that lies in it as its content. Thus, for example, the concept of *virtue* contains as characteristics (1) the concept of freedom, (2) the concept of adherence to rules (duty), and (3) the concept of subduing the force of inclinations, inasmuch as they run counter to those rules. When thus resolving the concept of virtue into its individual components, we make it distinct by this very analysis. By this process of making distinct, however, we add nothing to a concept, we only explain it. Through distinctness, therefore, concepts are not improved as to *matter,* but only as to *form.*[40]

When we reflect on our cognitions in respect of the two essentially different basic faculties of sensibility and understanding from which they spring, we meet with the difference between intuitions and concepts. All our cognitions, viewed in this respect, are either *intuitions* or *concepts.* The former have their source in *sensibility*—the faculty of intuitions; the latter in the *understanding*—the faculty of concepts. This is the *logical*[41] distinction between the understanding and sensibility, according to which the latter furnishes nothing but intuitions, the former nothing but concepts. Both basic faculties may be viewed, of course, in another aspect and defined in a different manner, namely, sensibility as a faculty of *receptivity,* the understanding as a faculty of *spontaneity.* This manner of explanation, however, is not logical, but *metaphysical.*[42] Commonly, one also calls sensibility the *lower,* the understanding, however, the *higher* faculty; on the ground that sensibility gives the mere material to thinking, the understanding, on the other hand, disposes of this material and brings it under rules and concepts.

On the difference here stated between *intuitive* and *discursive* cognitions, or between intuitions and concepts, is based the difference between the *aesthetic* and the *logical perfection* of cognition.

A cognition can be perfect either according to laws of sensi-

40. The notion of analysis is here connected with the notion of distinctness of conceptual content, that is, quality of cognition.

41. Underlying is the distinction between singular presentations and general presentations. See below, § 1.

42. See B 33, 61, 74–75.

bility or according to laws of the understanding; in the former case it is *aesthetically* perfect, in the latter *logically* perfect. Both aesthetic and logical perfection are thus of different kinds, the former having reference to sensibility, the latter to the understanding. The logical perfection of cognition rests on its agreement with the object,[43] therefore on *universally valid* laws, and can thus be judged by norms a priori. Aesthetic perfection consists in the agreement of cognition with the subject and is based on the special sensibility of man. In aesthetic perfection, therefore, no objectively and universally valid laws can be applied, in accordance with which this kind of perfection could be judged a priori in a manner universally valid for all thinking beings as such. So far as there are, however, also general laws of sensibility that are valid, though not objectively for all thinking beings, yet subjectively for all mankind, an aesthetic perfection may be conceived which contains the ground of a subjective-general pleasure. This perfection is *beauty:* that which pleases the senses in *intuition* and for that very reason can be the object of a general pleasure, because the laws of intuition are general laws of sensibility.

Through this agreement with the general laws of sensibility, the *actually, independently beautiful* whose essence consists in the *mere form* is distinguished, as to kind, from the *agreeable,* which pleases solely in sensation by stimulus or emotion and for that reason can be the ground of private pleasure only.[44]

It is this essential aesthetic perfection which among all perfections is compatible with logical perfection and may best be combined with it.

Viewed under this aspect, aesthetic perfection in respect of essential beauty may be advantageous to logical perfection. In another respect, however, it is also detrimental to it, so far as we look in aesthetic perfection only to what is *extra-essential* in the beautiful—the *stimulating* or the *moving* that pleases the senses in mere sensation and is related not to mere form but to the matter of sensibility. For stimulus and emotion, more than

43. See above, p. 16, n. 9.
44. For details see Analytic of the Beautiful, *Critique of Judgment,* §§ 1–9.

anything else, can ruin logical perfection in our cognition and judgment.

Conceivably, between the aesthetical and the logical perfection of our cognition there will always remain a kind of conflict that cannot be entirely overcome. The understanding wants to be instructed, sensibility wants to be animated; the first desires insight, the second ease of apprehension.[45] If cognitions are to instruct, they must in so far be thorough; if at the same time they are to entertain, they must also be beautiful. If a speech is beautiful but shallow, it pleases only our sensibility, but not the understanding; if, conversely, it is thorough but dry, it can please only the understanding, and not the sensibility.

Since, however, the need of human nature and the purpose of popularizing cognition require that we try to unite both perfections with each other, we must also see to it that we provide an aesthetic perfection for those cognitions which are at all capable of it and that we popularize a scholastic, logically perfect cognition through the aesthetic form. In this endeavor of combining in our cognitions aesthetic perfection with logical perfection, we must, however, not overlook the following rules, namely, (1) that logical perfection is the basis of all other perfections and therefore must not be entirely placed second or sacrificed to any other; (2) that one pay attention chiefly to *formal* aesthetic perfection—agreement of a cognition with the laws of intuition—because it is just herein that the essentially beautiful consists which can best be united with logical perfection; (3) that one be very sparing with *stimulation* and *emotion* by which a cognition acts on sensation and sustains interest, otherwise attention may easily be drawn from the object to the subject, whence obviously a very detrimental influence on the logical perfection of cognition must arise.

In order to make the essential differences between logical and aesthetic perfection of cognition even clearer, not merely in general but in certain special aspects, we shall compare them

45. *Fasslichkeit.*

both in regard to the four principal moments of quantity, quality, relation, and modality, on which the judging of perfection of cognition turns.

A cognition is perfect as to (1) quantity, if it is *universal;* (2) quality, if it is *distinct;* (3) relation, if it is *true;* and finally (4) modality, if it is *certain.*

Viewed from these angles, a cognition will be logically perfect when it has: as to quantity, objective universality (universality of the concept or rule); as to quality, objective distinctness (distinctness in the concept); as to relation, objective truth; and as to modality, objective certainty.

Now to these logical perfections, in reference to those four principal moments the following aesthetic perfections correspond, namely:

1) *aesthetic generality.* This consists in the applicability of a cognition to a multitude of objects that serve as examples, to which that cognition may be applied and whereby it becomes at the same time useful for the purpose of popularity;

2) *aesthetic distinctness.* This is the distinctness in intuition in which through examples an abstract concept is exhibited and explained *in concreto;*[46]

3) *aesthetic truth.* A merely subjective truth, which consists only in the agreement of cognition with the subject and the laws of semblance in the senses and consequently is nothing but a general seeming;[47]

4) *aesthetic certainty.* This rests on what is necessary according to the testimony of the senses, i.e. what is confirmed by sensation and experience.

In the aforementioned perfections there are always two ele-

---

46. The formal aspect of this is the basis of construction and schematism in the *Critique of Pure Reason,* see B 172, 176 ff.; 741, 761.

47. When, for example, Kant says of the starry sky that it has the semblance of a dome, then the semblance means "the subjective in the presentation of a thing, which can be the cause of falsely taking it for objective in a judgment" (Akad. XX, 269). Cf.: "Aesthetically true: what actually is described as it appears, or as what all people say" (Akad. XVI, 2205).

ments which in their harmonious union make up perfection in itself, namely, *manifoldness* and *unity*. With the understanding the unity lies in the concept; with the senses, in intuition.

Mere manifoldness without unity cannot satisfy us. And therefore among all perfections truth is the chief perfection, because it is the ground of unity by reference of our cognition to the object.[48] Even in aesthetic perfection, truth remains always the *conditio sine qua non,* the supreme negative condition, without which something cannot generally please the taste. Nobody therefore should hope to advance in the belles lettres[49] unless he has founded his cognition on logical perfection. The character and art of genius truly manifest themselves in the greatest possible coordination of logical perfection with aesthetic perfection as such, in regard to such cognitions as are to instruct and at the same time entertain.

VI. Specific Logical Perfections of Cognition
A) Logical Perfection of Cognition as to Quantity / Magnitude / Extensive and Intensive Magnitude / Range and Thoroughness or Importance and Fruitfulness of Cognition
Determination of the Horizon of Our Cognitions

The magnitude of cognition may be understood in a twofold way, either as *extensive* or as *intensive*[50] magnitude. The former

---

48. This is the basis of Transcendental Logic as well as of its discussion of analytic and synthetic unity.

49. *schönen Wissenschaften,* a popular 18th-century expression fashioned, after the French, for literature and art.

50. *intensive.* It should be borne in mind that these and the following determinations of "quantity" in this chapter refer, first of all, to cognition generally, rather than only to concepts. Cf. Akad. XVI, 1999: "extensive: cog-

refers to the *extension* of cognition and therefore consists in its volume and manifoldness; the latter refers to its *content*, which concerns the *manifold validity* or logical importance and fruitfulness of a cognition, as far as it is considered as a ground of many and great consequences (*non multa sed multum*).

In expanding our cognitions or in perfecting them as to their extensive magnitude, it is well to estimate how far a cognition conforms with our ends and capacities. This reflection concerns the determination of the *horizon* of our cognitions, by which is to be understood the *commensurateness of the magnitude of all cognitions with the capacities and ends of the subject.*

The horizon may be determined:

1) *logically,* according to the faculty and the powers of cognition in reference to the *interest of the understanding.* Here we have to judge: How far can we get in our cognitions, how far do we have to go, and to what extent do certain cognitions serve, in logical respect, as means to this or that kind of main cognitions as our ends.

2) *aesthetically,* according to taste in reference to the *interest of feeling.* He who determines his horizon aesthetically seeks to arrange science according to the taste of the public, i.e. to make it *popular,* or in general, to acquire only such cognitions as can be communicated to all and in which also the class of the unlearned takes pleasure and interest.

3) *practically,* according to usefulness in reference to the *interest* of the *will.* The practical horizon, so far as it is determined according to the influence of a cognition on our morality, is *pragmatic,* and of the greatest importance.

The horizon thus concerns judgment on, and determination of, what man *can* know, what he *needs* to know, and what he *should* know.

As concerns especially the theoretically or logically deter-

---

nition spread either internally in one man or externally among many men, intensive: the degree, i.e. the magnitude as ground of many and great consequences."

mined horizon—and of this alone can we speak here—we may consider it either from the *objective* or *subjective* point of view.

In respect of objects, the horizon is either *historical* or *rational*. The former is much wider than the latter, indeed it is immeasurably large, for our historical cognition has no boundaries. The rational horizon, on the contrary, can be fixed; we can determine, for example, to what kind of objects mathematical cognition cannot be extended. So also in respect to the philosophical cognition of reason: [we can determine] how far reason may advance a priori without any experience.

In reference to the *subject,* the horizon is either the *universal* and *absolute* horizon, or a *particular* and *conditioned* (private) horizon.

By the absolute and universal horizon is to be understood the congruence of the limits of human cognitions with the limits of the complete human perfection as such, and here the question is: What can man, as man, know at all?

The determination of the private horizon depends on various empirical conditions and special considerations, e.g. age, sex, position, way of life, and the like. Every special class of men, therefore, has its special horizon in reference to its special powers of cognition, ends and standpoints; every mind has its own horizon as dictated by the individuality of its powers and standpoint. Lastly, we can think a horizon of *sound reason* and a horizon of *science,* which latter still requires *principles* in order to determine according to them *what we can know, and what we can not know.*[51]

What we are *unable* to know is *above*[52] our horizon; what we *need* not or are not required to know is *outside* our horizon.

---

51. The notion of horizon has been taken up in our time by Husserl's phenomenology.

52. Cf. Akad. XVI, 1962: "Incorrectness of the expression above [*über*] the horizon." Kant continues, however, to use this expression in other *Reflections,* as a concession to German usage, *das geht über meinen Horizont,* literally, "something goes above my horizon," i.e. that is *beyond* me. Cf. also *quae supra nos, nihil ad nos.* Cf. Akad. XVI, 1977.

The latter, however, can hold good only *relatively* in reference to this or that particular private end, to the attainment of which certain cognitions not only contribute nothing but can even be a hindrance. For no cognition is altogether and in every respect useless and unavailing, although we may not always have insight into its use. It is therefore a reproach as unwise as unjust, voiced by shallow minds against great men who work with laborious diligence at the sciences, when they ask: *What is that good for?* If one wants to apply oneself to science, this question must never be raised. Supposing a science could make disclosures only about some possible object; it would be, for that reason, already useful enough. Every logically perfect cognition has always some possible use which, although as yet unknown to *us,* may perhaps be found by posterity. If in the cultivation of sciences one had always looked for material gain or their usefulness, we should have no arithmetic or geometry. Moreover, our understanding is so organized that it finds satisfaction in mere insight, even more than in the utility arising from it. Plato had already observed this. Man herein feels his own excellence, he sees what it means to have understanding. Men who lack this sense must envy animals. The intrinsic value that cognitions possess through logical perfection is not to be compared with their extrinsic value in application.

Both that which lies *outside* our horizon, so far as we *need* not know it as dispensable to us according to our intentions, and which lies *under* our horizon, so far as we *shall* not know it as harmful to us, must be understood in a *relative* and by no means an *absolute* sense.[53]

In respect to expansion and demarcation of our cognition the following rules are to be recommended. One should, regarding one's horizon,

1) determine it early, but nevertheless only when one is able to determine it for oneself, which usually is not before the age of twenty;

---

53. Akad. XVI, 1964: "Nothing is under the horizon (of learned cognition) but that which, one knows, learned cognition cannot and need not advance further than common cognition."

2) not change it easily and frequently (not jump from one thing to another);

3) not measure the horizon of others by one's own and not consider useless what is of no use to *us*. It would be impertinent to intend to determine the horizon of others, because one does not sufficiently know their capacities, on the one hand, and their purposes, on the other;

4) neither expand nor restrict it too much. For he who wants to know too much knows in the end nothing, and he who conversely believes that some things do not concern him, often victimizes himself, when, for example, the philosopher believes that history is dispensable to him.

One should also

5) determine in advance the absolute horizon of the entire human race (as to past and future), and in particular also

6) determine the place occupied by our science in the horizon of all cognition. This purpose is served by a *Universal Encyclopedia* as a universal chart (*mappe-monde*) of the sciences; [one should also]

7) examine carefully, in determining one's own special horizon, for which part of cognition one has the best capacities and with which he feels the greatest satisfaction; what is more or less necessary in respect of certain duties; what cannot coexist with necessary duties; and finally,

8) always try rather to expand than to narrow one's horizon.

What d'Alembert fears from the expansion of cognition is not at all to be feared. For it is not the weight of our cognitions which oppresses us, but the lack of space for them that cramps us. Critique of reason, of history and historical writing, a universal spirit which goes into human cognition comprehensively and not merely in detail, will reduce the extent without diminishing content. Merely the dross falls away from the metal, or the coarser vehicle, the husk, that had been needed so long. With the expansion of natural history, mathematics, etc., new methods will be found that shorten the old and make the multitude of books dispensable. On the invention of such new methods and principles will depend our ability to find, through them, everything we wish without burdening our memory. Therefore he deserves well of history, like a genius,[54] who captures it under ideas that can last forever.

Opposed to the perfection of cognition in respect of its extension is *ignorance, a negative* imperfection or imperfection of *want,*[55] which remains inseparable from our cognition because of the limits of our understanding.

We may consider ignorance from an *objective* and from a *subjective* point of view.

1) Taken objectively, ignorance is either *material* or *formal.* The former consists in a lack of historical, the latter in a lack of rational cognitions. One ought not to be totally ignorant of any subject matter; but one may well limit historical knowledge in order to devote oneself so much the more to rational knowledge, or vice versa.

2) In its *subjective* meaning, ignorance is either erudite, *scientific* ignorance, or *common* ignorance. He who has distinct insight into the limits of cognition, thus into the field of ignorance, where this begins—the philosopher, who has the insight and proves how little one can know, for want of the requisite data, for example in respect of the structure of gold—is ignorant in an expert way[56] or in a learned manner. On the other hand, he who is ignorant without insight into the grounds of the limits of ignorance and without paying heed to them, is ignorant in a common, unscientific manner. Such a man does not even know that he knows nothing. For one can never present to oneself one's ignorance other than by science,[57] just as

54. Since to Kant *Genie* means the faculty of *aesthetic* Ideas, we take this sentence to imply an analogy between the inventor of philosophic Ideas and the creator of aesthetic Ideas, the genius (on Kant's concept of genius cf. *Critique of Judgment,* §§ 46–57).

55. As distinguished from the positive imperfection of cognition, namely error, which is falsity regarded as truth. See below, Sec. VII.

56. *kunstmässig.*

57. *Wissenschaft,* "science," which may be used here in its original unsystematic meaning of a "particular knowledge," still current in the 18th century.

the blind cannot present to himself darkness until he has gained sight.

Being cognizant of one's ignorance therefore presupposes science and at the same time makes one modest, whereas imagined knowledge puffs one up. So Socrates' want of knowledge was a commendable ignorance, actually a knowledge of not knowing, according to his own confession. Those, therefore, who possess much knowledge and in spite of it are amazed at what they do not know, do not come under the reproach of ignorance.

Irreproachable (*inculpabilis*) in general is ignorance of things whose cognition reaches *above* our horizon; and it can be allowable (though only in a relative sense) in respect of the speculative [theoretical] use of our faculty of cognition, so far as here the objects do not lie *above* but yet *outside* our horizon. *Ignominious,* however, is ignorance in things which are necessary and also easy for us to know.

There is a difference between *not knowing* something, and *ignoring* it, i.e. *not taking notice of something*. It is good to ignore much that is not good for us to know. Distinguished from both is *abstraction*. One abstracts from a cognition when one ignores its application, whereby one obtains it *in abstracto* and can consider it better in its generality as a principle. Such an abstraction from what does not belong to our purpose in the cognition of a matter, is useful and commendable.

Historically ignorant are commonly the teachers of reason [of merely rational knowledge].

Historical knowledge without determinate limits is *polyhistory;* this makes one puffed up. *Polymathy* is directed to the cognition of reason. Both historical and rational knowledge, when extended without definite limits, may be called *pansophy.* To historical knowledge belongs the science of the tools of learning—*philosophy,* which comprises a critical knowledge of books and languages (*literature* and *linguistics*).

Mere polyhistory is a *cyclopean* erudition that lacks one eye, the eye of philosophy; and a cyclops of mathematics, history, natural history, philology, and languages is a learned man who is great in all these fields but takes philosophy to be dispensable.

Part of philology is made up by the *humaniora,* understood as cognizance of the ancients, which furthers the *unification of science with taste,* polishes roughness, and furthers the communicability and urbanity in which *humaneness* consists.

The *humaniora* therefore concern the instruction in what serves the cultivation of taste after the models of the ancients. To this belongs, for example, rhetoric, poetry, being well read in the classical authors, and the like. All this humanist knowledge may be counted with the *practical* part of philology, which aims at the cultivation of taste. If, however, we maintain a separation of the mere philologist from the humanist, he would be distinguished from the latter in that he seeks the tools of *learning* with the ancients; the humanist, however, seeks the tools for the *cultivation of taste.*

The man of *belles lettres* or *bel esprit* is a humanist according to contemporary models in living languages. He is not an erudite man—for only *dead languages* are now erudite languages —but a mere *dillettante* of knowledge in fashionable taste without needing the ancients. One could call him the *ape* of the humanist. The polyhistor as a philologist must be a *linguist* and *literary* man, and as a humanist he must be a *classical* scholar and interpreter of the ancient authors. As philologist he is *cultivated,* as humanist, *civilized.*

In respect of the sciences there are two degenerations of the prevailing taste: *pedantry* and *galanterie.*[58] The one pursues the sciences merely for the *school* and thereby limits them in regard to their *use;* the *other* pursues them merely for *social relations* or the *world* and thereby restricts them in respect to *content.*

The pedant is either, as the man of learning, set off against the man of the world and in so far is the arrogant erudite without knowledge of the world, i.e. without knowing how to communicate his science to others; or he is to be considered as the man of skill, but only in *formalities,* not as to essence and ends. In the latter meaning he picks at formalities and is narrow-

58. *Galanterie,* an 18th-century catchword borrowed from the French, synonymous with the characteristics of "gallantry" other than those denoting bravery.

minded in respect of the core of things, looking only to the dress and the shell. He is the unsuccessful imitator or *caricature* of a *methodical* man. One may therefore also call pedantry a ruminating fastidiousness and useless exactitude (micrology) in matters of form. And such scholastic formality outside the school is to be met with not only in learned men and in the learned community but also in other estates and affairs. The *ceremonial at courts,* in *social relations*—what is it but a chase of formalities and finicalities. In the military it is not quite so, although it seems that way. But in conversation, dress, religion, there is often much pedantry.

A purposeful exactness in matters of form is *thoroughness* (scholastic perfection). Pedantry is thus an *affectation* of thoroughness, just as galanterie is mere pandering to the plaudits of taste, nothing but an affectation of popularity. For galanterie strives only to win favours from the reader and therefore not to perturb him by even one difficult word.

To avoid pedantry there is required wide knowledge not only in the sciences themselves but also in respect of their use. Only the truly learned man can therefore free himself from pedantry, which is always the property of a narrow mind.

In striving to give our cognition the perfection of scholastic thoroughness and at the same time that of popularity without falling into the mistakes of an affected thoroughness or affected popularity, we must above all look to the scholastic perfection of our cognition—the scholarly form of thoroughness—and only then care about how to make the methodically learned cognition of the school truly popular, i.e. easily and generally communicable to others, yet not supplanting thoroughness with popularity. For scholastic perfection, without which all science would be mere toying and trifling, must not be sacrificed for the sake of popular perfection, to please people.

To learn true popularity, however, one must read the ancients, e.g. Cicero's philosophical writings, the poets Horace, Virgil, etc., among the moderns, Hume, Shaftesbury, and others, men who were all coming and going in the refined world, without which one cannot be popular. For true popularity requires much practical knowledge of the world and of men, knowledge of the concepts, the taste, and the inclinations of men, to which constant regard must be given in presentation and even in the choice of fitting expressions commensurate with popularity. Such a condescension to the mental capacity of the public and to accustomed expressions, such true popularity of cognition is indeed a great and rare perfection that betokens much insight into the sciences, when scholastic perfection does not come second but the clothing of the thoughts is so arranged that the skeleton— the scholarly and technical part of that perfection— remains invisible (just as one draws lines with a pencil to write on them, which then are rubbed out). Beside many other merits it also has this, that it may give proof of a complete insight into a matter. For the mere scholastic test of a cognition leaves the doubt whether the test is not one-sided and whether the cognition really has a value conceded to it by all men. Schools have their prejudices just as common understanding has them. One side here corrects the other. It is important therefore to test a cognition with men whose understanding does not depend on any school.

This perfection of cognition by which it qualifies for easy and general communication could also be called the *external extension* or the extensive magnitude of a cognition, so far as it is spread *externally* among men.

Since there are so many and manifold cognitions, one will be well advised to make for oneself a plan according to which one orders the sciences in a manner best suiting one's purposes and best contributing to their advancement. All cognitions stand in a certain natural connection with one another. If in the striving after expansion of cognitions one does not heed their connection, all pansophy will become nothing but mere *rhapsody*.[59] If, however, one makes a particular science one's principal end and considers all other cognitions only as a means of attaining it, then one brings a certain systematic character into one's knowledge. In order to proceed in expanding one's cognitions

59. Cf. B 106, 860.

according to such an orderly and purposeful plan, one must try to understand the connection of cognitions with one another. Herein we get advice from the *architectonic* of sciences, a *system according to ideas*[60] in which *the sciences are considered in respect of their relationship and systematic connection in a whole of cognition that is of interest to mankind.*

Now, as concerns the *intensive* magnitude of cognition, i.e. its contents or its import and logical importance—which, as noted above, are essentially different from its mere range—we will add the following few remarks.

1) A cognition directed toward *the large*, i.e. *the whole* in the use of the understanding, is to be distinguished from *subtlety in small things* (micrology).

2) Every cognition is to be called *logically important* which furthers logical perfection *as to form*, e.g. every mathematical proposition, every law of nature into which we have distinct insight, every correct philosophical explanation. *Practical* importance cannot be *foreseen* but must be *waited for.*[61]

3) Importance must not be confounded with *difficulty*. A cognition may be difficult without being important, and *vice versa*. Difficulty therefore decides neither *for* nor *against* the value and the importance of a cognition. This rests on the magnitude and multiplicity of consequences. The more and the greater logical consequences a cognition has, and the more use can be made of it, the more important it is. A cognition without important consequences is called a rumination, such as was, for example, scholastic philosophy.

60. See B 860.
61. Cf. the modern notion of serendipity.

VII. B) Logical Perfection of Cognition as to Relation[62] / <u>Truth</u> / Material and Formal or Logical Truth / Criteria of Logical Truth / Falsity and Error / Semblance as the Source of Error / Means of Avoiding Errors

A main perfection of cognition, indeed the essential and inseparable condition of all perfection, is *truth*. Truth, one says, consists in the agreement of cognition with the object.[63] According to this mere verbal explanation, my cognition, then, in order to pass as true, shall agree with the object. Now I can, however, compare the object with my cognition only by *cognizing it*. My cognition thus shall confirm itself, which is yet far from sufficient for truth. For since the object is outside me and the cognition in me, I can judge only whether my cognition of the object agrees with my cognition of the object. Such a circle in explanation was called by the ancients *diallelus*. And really it was this mistake for which the logicians were always reproached by the skeptics, who noted that with this explanation it was the same as if someone testified in court and appealed to a witness whom no one knows, but who wants to gain credibility by maintaining that the one who called him as a witness is an honest man. The charge was well founded indeed; but the solution of the task in question is completely impossible for anyone.

The question, namely, is whether and how far there is an unfailing, universal criterion of truth usable in application. For that is the meaning of the question: *What is truth?*

62. As against the *Critique of Pure Reason, relation* is here treated before *quality*, which follows as Sec. VIII, corresponding to the order of Meier's *Vernunftlehre.* Cf. Akad. XVI, 2154: "Truth may be drawn to relation."

63. Here the object meant is the external object of a specific cognition. This kind of object cannot be reached by cognition in formal logic. Note that truth is a perfection of cognition, although it is the essential one. See above, p. 16, n. 9.

In order to be able to decide this important question, we must carefully distinguish what belongs in our cognition to its *matter* and refers to the object, from what concerns the *mere form* as the condition without which a cognition would not be a cognition at all.[64] With regard to this distinction, between the *objective, material* and the *subjective, formal* relation in any cognition, the above question divides itself into these two particular questions:

1) Is there a universal, material, and

2) is there a universal, formal criterion of truth?

A universal, material criterion of truth is not possible—indeed, it is even self-contradictory. For as *universal* and valid for all objects as such, it would have to abstract from all differences of objects, and yet at the same time, as a material criterion, have to pertain to these differences in order to be able to determine whether a cognition agrees with the very object to which it is referred, and not merely with some object in general, whereby actually nothing would be said at all. But material truth must consist in the agreement of a cognition with that definite object to which it refers. For a cognition that is true in respect of one object may be false in reference to another. It is therefore absurd to demand a universal, material criterion of truth, which should at once abstract and again not abstract from all differences of objects.

But if the question concerns *universal, formal* criteria of truth, then the decision is easy: indeed there can be such criteria. For *formal* truth consists solely in the agreement of cognition with itself when abstraction is made completely from all objects and any differences among them. And the universal, formal criteria of truth accordingly are nothing but universal, logical characteristics of the agreement of cognition with itself, or—which is the same[65]—with the universal laws of the understanding and of reason.

64. This is the question of the *Critique of Pure Reason*.

65. Here a universalized set of rules of inner consistency is equated with the "universal laws of the understanding," thus formalizing the answer without recourse to faculties. This is the very core of the solution of the problem of the *Critique of Pure Reason*, namely the identification of judgment with

These formal, universal criteria are not sufficient for objective truth, to be sure, but yet they are to be considered as its *conditio sine qua non*.

For before the question whether the cognition agrees with the object, must come the question whether it agrees with itself (as to form). And this is the business of logic.

The formal criteria of logic are:

> **1)** *the principle of contradiction,*
> **2)** *the principle of sufficient reason.*

By the former is determined the *logical possibility,* by the latter, the *logical actuality* of a cognition.

To the logical truth of a cognition, namely, belongs:

First: That it be logically possible, that is, *not contradict* itself. This characteristic of the *internal* logical truth, however, is only *negative;* for a cognition that contradicts itself is indeed false, but if it does not contradict itself, it is not always true.

Second: That it be logically grounded, that is, have (a) reasons, and (b) no false consequences.

This second criterion of the *external* logical truth or of the *rationality* of cognition, which concerns the logical connection of a cognition with reasons and consequences, is *positive*. And here the following rules hold good.

> **1)** From the *truth of the consequence* may be concluded the *truth* of the cognition as a *ground,* but only negatively: If one false consequence follows from a cognition, then the cognition itself is false. For if the ground were true, the consequence would also have to be true, because the consequence is determined by the ground.

But one cannot conclude conversely: If no false consequence follows from a cognition, it is true; for from a false ground true consequences may be drawn.

> **2)** *If all consequences of a cognition are true, the cognition is also true.* For if anything false were in the cognition, there would be a false consequence.

---

the nature of the understanding. See B 133–134. The identification is here meant formally logically. The clarification of understanding and reason in this connection led to transcendental logic.

From the consequence a ground may indeed be concluded, but without our being able to determine this ground. Only from the sum total of all consequences can a *definite ground* be concluded, that this be the true one.

The first mode of conclusion, according to which the consequence can only be a *negative* and *indirectly* sufficient criterion of the truth of a cognition, is called in logic the *apagogic* mode (*modus tollens*).

This procedure, of which frequent use is made in geometry, has the advantage that I need derive only one false consequence from a cognition to prove its falsity. In order to show, for example, that the earth is not flat, I only need to conclude apagogically and indirectly, without advancing positive and direct reasons, thus: If the earth were flat, the Polar Star would have to be always equally high; now this is not the case, therefore the earth is not flat.

With the other, the *positive* and *direct* mode of conclusion (*modus ponens*), the difficulty enters that the totality of consequences cannot be cognized apodeictically,[66] and that therefore the said mode of conclusion leads one only to a probable and *hypothetically* true cognition (*hypotheses*), on the supposition that where many consequences are true, the rest may also be true.

We shall thus be able to state here three principles as universal, merely formal or logical criteria of truth; these are

    1) the *principle of contradiction and identity* (*principium contradictionis* and *identitatis*), by which the inner possibility of a cognition is determined for *problematic* judgments;

    2) the *principle of sufficient reason* (*principium rationis sufficientis*), on which rests the (logical) *actuality* of a cognition—that it is grounded, as material for *assertoric* judgments;

    3) the *principle of excluded middle* (*principium exclusi medii inter duo contradictoria*), on which the (logical) necessity of a cognition is based—that it is necessary to judge

---

66. This logical fact becomes essential in the Antinomies of the *Critique of Pure Reason*. See below, § 26, and B 387, 388, 434, 821.

thus and not otherwise, i.e. that the opposite is false—for *apo-deictic* judgments.

The opposite of truth is falsity, which, in so far as it is taken for truth, is called *error*. An erroneous judgment—for our error as well as truth is only in judgment—is one which mistakes the semblance of truth for truth itself.

How [logical] *truth is possible*—this is an easy task for our insight, since here the understanding acts according to its own essential laws.

How error in the formal meaning of the word, however, is possible, that is, how a form of thinking contrary to the understanding is possible, that is difficult to comprehend; as indeed how any force should deviate from its own essential laws cannot be comprehended at all. We cannot therefore seek the ground of error in the understanding itself and in its essential laws—not any more than in the *limits* of the understanding, in which lies the cause of *ignorance,* to be sure, but by no means that of error. Now, if we had no other power of cognition beside the understanding, we would never err. However, beside the understanding there is another indispensable source of cognition within us. This is *sensibility,* which gives us the material of thought and thereby acts according to laws that are different from those of the understanding. Out of sensibility, viewed in and by itself, error cannot arise either, because the senses do not judge at all.

The originating ground of all error must therefore be sought solely in the *unnoticed influence of sensibility upon the understanding,* or, more exactly, upon judgment. This influence, namely, causes us to take merely *subjective* grounds in judging for *objective* grounds and consequently to mistake the *mere semblance of truth for truth itself.* For therein consists the very essence of semblance, which on that account is to be considered a ground of holding a false cognition to be true.

What makes error possible is therefore the semblance by which the merely *subjective* is mistaken in judging for the *objective.*[67]

___

67. This is the basis of the Transcendental Dialectic. See B 350, 351.

In a certain sense one may perhaps also declare the understanding the originator of errors, so far namely as from lack of the required attention to the influence of sensibility, it allows itself to be misled into taking subjective determining grounds of judgment for objective, or into accepting as valid by its own laws what is true only according to laws of sensibility.

Only the fault of ignorance, therefore, is due to the limits of the understanding; the fault of error we have to ascribe to ourselves. Nature has indeed denied us much knowledge, leaving us in inevitable ignorance about many things; but she does not cause error. We are misled into this by our own propensity to judge and to decide even where, because of our limitations, we are incapable of judging and deciding.

Every error, however, into which the human understanding may fall is only *partial,* and in every erring judgment there must always lie something true. For a total error would be a complete conflict with the laws of the understanding and of reason. As such, how could it come in any way from the understanding and, so far as it is yet a judgment, be held to be a product of the understanding?

In regard to what is true and erroneous in our cognition, we distinguish an *exact* from a *rough* cognition.

A cognition is *exact* when it is adequate to its object, or when in regard to its object not the slightest error takes place; it is *rough* when there may be errors in it without impeding its purpose.[68]

This distinction concerns the *wider* and *narrower determinacy* of our cognition (*cognitio late vel stricte determinata*). Initially it is sometimes necessary to determine a cognition in a wider extension (*late determinare*), especially in historical matters. In cognitions of reason, however, everything must be exactly (*stricte*) determined. When the *determination* has *latitude,* one says a cognition is determined *praeter propter.* Whether it shall be determined roughly or exactly always depends on the

68. The objects in question correspond to synthetic or constructed, and analytic or abstracted concepts, respectively. See below, Sec. VIII, § 4, §§ 100 ff. Also B 741–760. Exactness, in this sense, is possible only in mathematics.

purpose of a cognition. The latitudinous determination always leaves a margin for error, which yet can have its definite limits. Error takes place particularly where a latitudinous determination is taken for a strict one, e.g. in matters of morality, where everything must be determined strictly. Those who do not do this are called by the English *Latitudinarians*.[69]

From exactness as an objective perfection of cognition—since here the cognition is fully congruent with the object—one may further distinguish *subtlety* as a *subjective* perfection of cognition.

A cognition of a thing is subtle when one discloses in it what usually escapes the attention of others. It therefore requires a higher degree of attention and a greater expenditure of intellectual power.

Many persons find fault with all subtlety, because they cannot attain it. But in itself it always does honor to the understanding and is even meritorious and necessary, as long as it is applied to an object worthy of observation. If, however, one could have attained the same purpose with less attention and effort of the understanding and yet applies more to it, then one makes a useless expenditure and falls into subtleties which are difficult but serve nothing (*nugae difficiles*).

As the *rough* is opposed to the exact, so the *crude* is opposed to the subtle.

From the nature of error, whose concept, as we noted, contains besides falsity the semblance of truth as an essential characteristic, the following important rule results for our cognition:

In order to avoid error—and absolutely *unavoidable* is no error although it may be *relatively* so in cases where, even at the risk of erring, it is unavoidable for us to judge—in order, then, to avoid error, one must try to discover and explain its source, semblance. This has been done by very few philosophers. They have sought to refute the errors themselves without indicating the semblance from which they have sprung. This disclosure and solution of semblance, however, is a far greater service to

69. Cf. Akad. VI, 22.

truth than the direct refutation of the errors themselves, by which one cannot block their source and prevent the same semblance, because one does not know it, from leading again to errors in other cases. For even though we may have been convinced that we have erred, yet when the semblance itself that underlies our error is not removed, there still remain scruples, however little we can put forward to justify them.

By explaining semblance one moreover accords a kind of equity to the erring person. For no one will admit that he has erred without some semblance of truth which might have deceived perhaps even a more perspicacious person; for here the subjective reasons count.

An error in which the semblance is obvious even to the common understanding (*sensus communis*) is called *preposterous* or *absurd*. The reproach of absurdity is always a personal blame that one must avoid, especially in refuting errors.

For, to the one who maintains an absurdity, the semblance underlying this obvious falsity is not obvious. It first has to be *made* obvious to him. If he still persists in it, he is preposterous; but then nothing more can be done for him. He has thereby made himself both incapable and unworthy of all further correction and refutation. For one can actually not *prove* to anyone that he is absurd; here all arguing would be in vain. When proving an absurdity, one no longer talks to an erring but to a rational person. But then disclosure of the absurdity (*deductio ad absurdum*) is not necessary.

One may call a preposterous error one which is not excused by anything, not even by *semblance;* just as a *gross* error is an error that shows ignorance in common cognition or an offense against common attention.

Error in *principles* is greater than in their *application*.

An *external* mark or an *external* touchstone of truth is the comparison of our own judgment with those of others, because what is subjective will not dwell in all others alike; thus semblance may be cleared up by comparison. The *irreconcilability* of the judgments of others with our own is therefore an external mark of error and to be considered as a hint that we should examine our procedure in judgments, without however immediately discarding it. For one may well be right *in re* and only wrong *in the manner*, i.e. in presentation.

Common understanding (*sensus communis*) in itself is also a touchstone to discover the mistakes of the *technical* use of the understanding. This is what it means to *orient* oneself *in thinking*[70] or in the speculative use of reason by common understanding, when *common* understanding is used as a test of judging the correctness of the speculative one.

General rules and conditions of avoiding error are: (1) to think [by] oneself, (2) to think oneself in the place of another, and (3) to think consistently with oneself. The maxim of thinking for oneself may be called the *enlightened* maxim; the maxim of putting oneself into others' viewpoints, the *broadened* maxim; the maxim of always thinking in harmony with oneself, the *consistent* or *conclusive manner of thought.*

VIII. C) Logical Perfection of Cognition as to Quality / Clarity / Concept of a Characteristic as Such / Different Kinds of Characteristics / Determination of the Logical Essence of a Thing / Distinctness, a Higher Degree of Clarity / Aesthetic and Logical Distinctness / Difference Between Analytic and Synthetic Distinctness

Human cognition on the side of the understanding is *discursive*, that is, it takes place through presentations that make what is common to several things the ground of cognition, thus through

---

70. The notion of orientation was extended by Kant from orientation in space in geography to orientation in thinking in logic, both formal and transcendental, in *Was heisst: sich im Denken orientieren?* ("What does it mean: To Orient Oneself in Thinking?" 1786). He there anticipates today's universal use of the notion of *field* in all kinds of sciences. Also see B 324.

characteristics as such. We thus cognize things only *through characteristics;* and this means precisely *cognizing, cog-noscere,* which comes from *noscere,* being cognizant.[71]

A characteristic is that in a thing which makes up part of its cognition, or—which is the same—a *partial presentation so far as it is considered as cognitive ground of the whole presentation.* All our *concepts* therefore are characteristics and all *thinking* is nothing but a presenting through *characteristics.*[72]

Every characteristic may be viewed from two sides:

First, as a presentation in itself;

Second, as belonging *qua* partial concept to the whole presentation of a thing and thereby as a ground of cognition of this thing itself.

All characteristics considered as grounds of cognition are of *twofold* use, either *internal* or *external.*

The *internal* use consists in *derivation*[73] in order to cognize the thing itself through characteristics as grounds of its cognition. The *external* use consists in *comparison,* so far as we can compare, through characteristics, one thing with another according to the rules of *identity* and *diversity.*

There is a variety of specific differences between characteristics, on which the following classification is based.

1) *Analytic* and *synthetic* characteristics.

The former are partial concepts of my *actual* concept (which I already think in it); the latter, on the contrary, are partial concepts of the *merely possible* whole concept (which thus through a synthesis of several parts is to *complete* itself). The former are all *concepts* of *reason;* the latter may be *concepts* of *experience.*[74]

71. *Erkennen, welches von Kennen herkommt.* A plausible translation would seem to be "recognizing, which comes from cognizing." But "recognizing" instead of "cognizing" would not be consistent with "cognition"—our term for *Erkenntnis*—in the immediately preceding sentence. See also p. 71, the degrees of cognition.

72. See B 93–94.

73. A concept derived from another concept augments our cognition of the object. Kant thus means by derivation the derivation of the cognition of a thing from that of some of its characteristics.

74. They may also be concepts of reason regarded as synthetic a priori.

2) *Coordinate* or *subordinate* characteristics. This division concerns their connection one *after* another, or one *under* another.

Characteristics are *coordinate* so far as each of them is presented as an *immediate* characteristic of the matter; and they are *subordinate* so far as a characteristic is presented only by means of another characteristic of the thing. The connection of coordinate characteristics in the whole of a concept is called an *aggregate;* the connection of subordinate characteristics is called a *series.* The former, the aggregation of coordinate characteristics, makes up the totality of a concept, which, however, in respect of synthetic empirical concepts can never be completed, but is like a straight line *without limits.*

The series of subordinate characteristics touches, *a parte ante,* or on the side of grounds, upon irresolvable concepts which, because of their simplicity, cannot be further analyzed; *a parte post,* or in regard to consequences, however, it is *infinite, because we do have a highest genus, but no lowest species.*

With the synthesis of every new concept in the aggregation of coordinate characteristics the *extensive* or *complex* distinctness is increased; with the further analysis of concepts in the series of subordinate characteristics the *intensive* or *deep* distinctness is increased. This latter kind of distinctness, as it necessarily serves the *thoroughness* and *conclusiveness* of cognition, is therefore mainly the business of philosophy and is carried farthest especially in metaphysical investigations.

3) *Affirmative* and *negative* characteristics. By the former we cognize what a thing is; by the latter, what it is not.

Negative characteristics serve to keep us from errors. Therefore they are unnecessary where it is impossible to err, and are necessary and of importance only in those cases where they keep us from an important error into which we might easily fall. Thus, for example, in respect of the concept of a being *such as God,* the negative characteristics are very necessary and important.

Through affirmative characteristics we want to *understand* something; by means of negative characteristics—into which all characteristics may be changed—we want not to *misunderstand* or to *err*, even if we should not get any knowledge of the thing.

4) *Important* and *fecund* or *empty* and *unimportant* characteristics.

A characteristic is important and fecund if it is a cognitive ground of great and numerous consequences, *partly* in respect of its internal use—its use in derivation—so far as it is sufficient to cognize a great deal of the matter itself through it, and *partly* in respect of its external use—its use in comparison—so far as it serves to cognize both the *similarity* of a thing with many others and its *difference* from many others.

Here, by the way, we must distinguish *logical* importance and fecundity from the *practical*—from *usefulness* and *serviceableness*.

5) *Sufficient* and *necessary* or *insufficient* and *contingent characteristics.*

A characteristic is *sufficient* so far as it suffices to distinguish the thing from all others; otherwise it is insufficient, as, for example, the characteristic of barking in a dog.[75] The sufficiency of characteristics, however, as well as their importance, is to be taken only in a relative sense, in relation to the ends intended by a cognition.

Necessary characteristics, finally, are those which must always be found in the matter conceived. Such characteristics are also called *essential* and are opposed to *nonessential* and contingent characteristics, which can be separated from the concept of the thing.

Among the necessary characteristics, however, there is yet another difference.

Some belong to the thing *as grounds* of other characteristics of the same matter; others only as *consequences* of other characteristics.

The former are *primitive* and *constitutive* characteristics (*constitutiva, essentialia in sensu strictissimo*); the others are called *attributes* (*consectaria, rationata*) and belong also to the

---

75. According to Akad. XVI, 2308, Kant knew of a barking bird.

essence of the thing, but only in so far as they are to be derived first from its essential elements, as, for example, the three angles in the concept of a triangle from the three sides.

The nonessential characteristics are also of a *twofold kind:* they concern either *internal* determinations of a thing (*modi*), or its *external relations* (*relationes*). Thus, for example, the characteristic of *learning* is an *internal* determination of man; to be *master* or *servant* only an *external* relation.

The complex concept of all essential components of a thing or the sufficiency of its characteristics as to coordination and subordination is the *essence* (*complexus notarum primitivarum, interne conceptui dato sufficientium; s. complexus notarum, conceptum aliquem primitive constituentium*).

Here in this explanation, however, we must in no way think of the *real* or *natural essence* of the things, into which we can never gain insight. For since logic abstracts from all content of cognition, consequently also from the matter itself, only the *logical* essence of things can be under discussion in this science. And into this we can easily have insight. For to the logical essence belongs nothing but the cognition of all predicates in respect of which an object is determined *by its concept;* the real essence of the thing (*esse rei*), on the other hand, requires the cognition of those predicates on which depends, as determining grounds, everything that belongs to its existence.[76] If, for example, we want to determine the logical essence of a body, we do not have to search out the data for this in nature; we only need to direct our reflection to those characteristics which as essential elements (*constitutiva, rationes*) originally constitute its basic concept. For the logical essence itself is indeed nothing else but the *first fundamental concept of all necessary characteristics of a thing* (*esse conceptus*).

The first level, then, of a perfection of our cognition as to

---

76. The gap between logical and real essence of a thing is bridged in transcendental logic by the schematism which formalizes existence itself in its spatial and temporal aspects. The forms of space and time become necessary elements of thought.

quality is its clarity. A second level, or a higher degree of clarity, is *distinctness*. This consists in the *clarity* of *characteristics*.

Here we must *first* of all distinguish logical distinctness from aesthetic distinctness. Logical distinctness rests on the objective, aesthetic on the subjective clarity of characteristics. The former is clarity *through concepts,* the latter through *intuition*. The latter kind of distinctness therefore consists in a mere *vividness* and *intelligibility,* that is, in a mere clarity through examples *in concreto* (for much can be intelligible that is not distinct, and conversely, much can be distinct that is yet difficult to understand, because it goes back to distant characteristics whose connection with intuition is possible only through a long series).

Objective distinctness often causes subjective obscurity and *vice versa*. Not seldom, objective distinctness is therefore possible only at the expense of aesthetic distinctness and, conversely, aesthetic distinctness—through examples and similes that do not exactly fit but are taken only after some analogy—often harms logical distinctness. Moreover, examples as such are no characteristics and do not belong as parts to a concept, but as intuitions to the use of a concept. Distinctness through examples —mere intelligibility—is therefore of a kind quite different from distinctness through concepts as characteristics. In the combination of the two, aesthetic or popular and scholastic or logical distinctness, consists *lucidity*. For by a *lucid mind* one understands the talent for an illuminating presentation of abstract and thorough cognitions commensurate with the capacities of *common understanding*.

Now, *secondly,* as concerns logical distinctness especially, it is to be called a *complete* distinctness so far as all characteristics which, taken together, make up the whole concept, have come to clarity. A *completely* or *thoroughly* distinct concept again may be so either in respect of the totality of its *coordinate,* or in regard to the totality of its *subordinate* characteristics. In the total clarity of coordinate characteristics consists the *extensively* complete distinctness of a concept, also called *explicitness;* total clarity of subordinate characteristics makes up *intensively* complete distinctness, or *profundity*.

The first kind of logical distinctness may also be called *external completeness* (*completudo externa*), as the other may be called *internal completeness* (*completudo interna*) of the clarity of characteristics. The latter can be attained only in pure concepts of reason and in freely invented[77] concepts, but not in empirical concepts.

The extensive magnitude of distinctness, so far as it is not abundant, is called *precision* (measuredness). Explicitness (*completudo*) and measuredness (*praecisio*) together make up *adequacy* (*cognitionem quae rem adequat*); and in the *intensively adequate* cognition, in *profundity*, joined with the *extensively adequate* cognition, in *explicitness* and *precision*, consists (as to quality) the *consummate perfection of a cognition* (*consummata cognitionis perfectio*).

Since it is the business of logic, as we have noted, *to make clear concepts distinct*, the question now is: *In what manner does it make them distinct?*

Logicians of the Wolffian school believe that to make cognitions distinct is entirely a matter of analysis.[78] But not all distinctness rests on the analysis of a given concept. This is the case only in respect of those characteristics that we have already thought in the concept; not at all, however, in regard to *those* characteristics that are added to the concept as parts of the entire possible concept.

That kind of distinctness which arises not through analysis but through synthesis of characteristics is *synthetic distinctness*. And there is thus an essential difference between the two procedures:[79] *to make a distinct concept*, and *to make a concept distinct*.

---

77. *willkürlichen*. Kant restricts *willkürlich*, i.e. "created at will or freely invented" concepts, to constructed or synthetic, namely mathematical concepts. The free invention of such concepts must follow the a priori laws of reason, not the arbitrariness of sensibility. Only in the former manner can the object arise together with its concept and the latter thus be completely clear. See below, § 102, and B 757.

78. *Zergliederung*.

79. *Sätzen*.

For when I make a distinct concept, I begin with the parts and proceed from these to the whole. There are no characteristics present here; I obtain them first by synthesis. From this synthetic procedure then results synthetic distinctness, which actually expands my concept as to content by what is added as a characteristic *over and above* the concept in intuition (pure or empirical). This synthetic procedure in making distinct concepts is employed by the mathematician and also by the philosopher of nature. For all distinctness of mathematical as well as of experiential cognition rests on expansion through synthesis of characteristics.

But when I make a concept distinct, then my cognition does not in the least increase in its content by this mere analysis. The content remains the same; only the form is changed, in that I learn to distinguish better or with greater clarity of consciousness what already was lying in the given concept. Just as by the mere illumination of a map nothing is added to it, so by the mere elucidation of a given concept by means of analysis of its characteristics no augmentation is made to this concept itself in the least.

To synthesis belongs the making distinct of *objects,* to analysis belongs the making distinct of *concepts*. Here the *whole* precedes the *parts,* there the *parts* precede the *whole*. The philosopher only makes given concepts distinct. Sometimes one proceeds synthetically, even when the concept one wants to make distinct in this manner is already *given*. This often takes place with experiential judgments, when one is not satisfied with the characteristics already thought in a given concept.

The analytic method to produce distinctness, with which alone logic can concern itself, is the first and principal requirement in making our cognition distinct.[80] For the more distinct our cognition of a matter is, the stronger and more effective it can be. Only one must not go so far in analysis that in the end the object itself disappears thereby.

80. The corresponding method concerning constructed concepts is the synthetic method. It belongs to transcendental logic. See below, §§ 94 ff., and B 756, 759.

If we were conscious of all that we know, we would have to be amazed at the great number of our cognitions.

In respect of the objective content of our cognition generatim, the following *degrees* may be thought, by which it may be graded in this regard:

The *first* degree of cognition is to present something to oneself.[81]

The *second:* To present something to oneself with consciousness, or to *perceive* (*percipere*).

The *third:* To be cognizant (*noscere*), or to present something to oneself in conscious comparison with other things both as to *identity* and *disparity*.

The *fourth:* To be cognizant *with consciousness*,[82] that is, to cognize (*cognoscere*). Animals also are cognizant of objects, but they do not *cognize* them.

The *fifth:* To understand (*intellegere*), that is to cognize or conceive through the understanding by means of concepts. This is very different from comprehension. We can conceive many things, although we cannot comprehend them, e.g. a *perpetuum mobile,* whose impossibility is shown in mechanics.

The *sixth:* To cognize something through reason, or to have *insight* into it (*perspicere*). This point we reach in few things, and our cognitions become fewer and fewer the more we wish to perfect them as to content.

Finally, the *seventh* degree: To *comprehend* something (*comprehendere*), that is, to cognize it through reason or *a priori* in *that* degree which is sufficient for our purpose. For all our comprehension is merely *relative,* that is, sufficient for a certain purpose; *absolutely* we do not comprehend anything. We comprehend nothing better than what the mathematician demonstrates, e.g. that all lines in the circle are proportional. And yet he does

---

81. *Sich etwas vorstellen. We have translated literally.* Any implication of a *conscious* act is to be excluded. The German equivalents of these seven degrees of cognition are: (1) *vorstellen,* (2) *wahrnehmen,* (3) *kennen,* (4) *erkennen,* (5) *verstehen,* (6) *einsehen,* (7) *begreifen.*

82. This is a new level of consciousness over and above that of degree three.

not comprehend how it happens that so simple a figure has
these properties. The field of what we understand or of the
understanding is therefore, as such, far greater than the field
of comprehension or of reason.

IX. D) Logical Perfection of Cognition as to Modality / Certainty / Concept of Holding Something to Be True / Modes of Holding-to-Be-True: Opinion, Belief, Knowledge / Conviction and Persuasion / Reservation and Deferment of Judgment / Preliminary Judgment / Prejudice, Its Sources and Main Varieties

Truth is the *objective property* of cognition; the judgment
through which something is *presented* as true, the relation to
an understanding and thus to a special subject, is *subjectively*
the *holding-to-be-true*.

The holding-to-be-true is of two kinds: *certain* or *uncertain*.
A holding-to-be-true which is certain, or *certainty*, is connected
with the consciousness of necessity; the uncertain kind, however, or *uncertainty*, is connected with the consciousness of
contingency or the possibility of the opposite. The latter, again,
is either both *subjectively* and *objectively* insufficient, or *objectively insufficient*, but *subjectively sufficient*. The *former* is
called *opinion*, the *latter* must be called *belief*.

There are, then, three *kinds* or *modes* of holding-to-be-true:
opinion, belief, and *knowledge*. Opinion is *problematic*, believing *assertoric*, and knowing *apodeictic* judging. For what is
merely my opinion, that I hold in the consciousness of my judgment to be problematic; what I believe, I hold to be *assertoric*,

but not as objectively but only as subjectively necessary[83] (valid only for me); finally, what I *know,* I hold to be *apodeictically certain,* i.e. to be universally and objectively certain (valid for all), supposing even that the object to which this certain holding-to-be-true relates were a mere empirical truth.[84] For this distinction of holding-to-be-true according to the three *modes* mentioned concerns only the *faculty of judgment* in regard to the subjective criteria of subsuming a judgment under objective rules.

Thus, for example, our holding immortality to be true would be merely problematic, in case we act only *as if we were immortal;* it would be assertoric, so far as *we believe that we are immortal;* and lastly, *apodeictic, so far as we all know* that there is another life after this.

Hence, there is an essential difference between opinion, belief, and knowing, which we want to expound here in greater exactness and detail.

1) *Opinion.* Opining or holding-to-be-true out of a cognitive ground that is neither subjectively nor objectively sufficient may be regarded as a *preliminary* judging (*sub condi-*

---

83. Cf. Akad. XVI, 2449: "In opinion, one is still free (problematic), in belief assertoric (one declares oneself). . . . In belief I am, as to the subject, already bound."

84. This sentence has prompted the following comment by Klaus Reich, in *Die Vollständigkeit der Kantischen Urteilstafel,* 2d ed. (Berlin: Richard Schoetz, 1948): "If the proposition can nevertheless be an empirical truth, it will be *impossible* to take the necessity whose consciousness is said to be connected with certainty, to be an objective one, but it must be taken again to be a *subjective* necessity of holding-to-be-true" (p. 22). But Reich disregards the twofold relationship expressed by *Kant* as follows (below, p. 78): "Our cognitions, therefore, may concern objects of experience, and the certainty thereof can yet be empirical and rational at the same time, namely so far as we cognize an empirically certain proposition out of principles a priori." Or: "The holding-to-be-true can be apodeictic, without the cognition being objectively apodeictic. The former is only the consciousness that it is impossible that one could have erred in the application of indubitably certain rules, e.g. in experience. It is certain that it [the holding-to-be-true] is experience" (Akad. XVI, 2479).

tione suspensiva ad interim) with which we cannot readily dispense. Before one accepts and asserts, one must first have an opinion, being careful not to take an opinion for more than a mere opinion. In all our cognizing we usually begin with opinions. Sometimes we have an obscure presentiment of the truth; a matter seems to contain characteristics of truth; we already have a *vague awareness* of its truth, before we cognize it with determinate certainty.

Where, however, does mere opinion actually take place? Not in any science that contains cognitions *a priori*, therefore not in mathematics, nor in metaphysics, nor in morality, but solely in *empirical* cognitions—in physics, psychology, and the like. For it is in itself absurd, *to opine a priori*. Nor could anything be more ridiculous indeed than to have, for example, opinions in mathematics. Here, as in metaphysics and morality, the rule holds: *Either to know or not to know. Matters of opinion* therefore can only be the objects of an experiential cognition which *in itself* is possible indeed, but only *for us* impossible due to the empirical limitations and conditions of our faculty of experience and due to the degree we possess of this faculty depending on these conditions. Thus, for example, the *ether* of modern physicists is a mere matter of opinion. For my insight tells me of this as well as of every opinion as such, whatever it may be, that the opposite might possibly yet be proved. My holding-to-be-true then is here both objectively and subjectively insufficient, although, considered in itself, it may become complete.

2) *Belief.* Believing or holding-to-be-true out of a ground that is objectively insufficient but subjectively sufficient relates to objects of which one can not only know nothing but also have no opinion—nay, cannot even allege the probability, but can only be certain that it is not contradictory to think such objects the way one thinks them.[85] The rest is a *free* holding-to-be-true which is needed only in a practical a priori respect—a holding-to-be-true, therefore, of what I adopt on *moral* grounds,

85. The objects here in question either are not present or are transcendent.

and indeed so that I am certain that the *opposite* can never be proved.*

Matters of belief are thus

I) no objects of *empirical cognition*. So-called historical belief can therefore not really be called belief and as such

---

* [Kant's own note follows.] Belief is no special source of cognition. It is a kind of holding-to-be-true with consciousness of its incompleteness; and when it is considered as restricted to special objects (proper to belief only), it is distinguished from opinion not by the degree but by the relation it has as cognition to action. Thus, for example, the merchant, in order to make a deal, not only needs to have the opinion that something is to be gained thereby, but also needs to believe it, i.e. that his opinion is sufficient for an undertaking freighted with uncertainty. Now we do have theoretical cognitions (of the sensuous) in which we can achieve certainty, and this must be possible in respect of everything that we can call human cognition. Just such certain cognitions and, what is more, cognitions wholly a priori, we have in practical laws; but these are based on a supersensuous principle (of freedom), that is, *in ourselves,* as a principle of practical reason. This practical reason is a causality in respect of a likewise supersensuous object, *the highest good,* which in the world of the senses is not possible for us to reach. Nature, however, as an object of our theoretical reason, must agree with it; for in the sensible world the *consequence* or *effect* of this idea shall be met with. We thus ought to act so as to make this end actual.

In the world of the senses we also find traces of an *art-wisdom;* and now we believe that the cause of the world operates also with *moral* wisdom toward the highest good. This is a holding-to-be-true that is sufficient for action, i.e. a *belief.* But we do not need this for acting according to moral laws, for these are given by practical reason alone; we do need adoption of a highest wisdom for the sake of the object of our moral will toward which, beside the mere legality of our actions, we cannot but direct our ends. Although *objectively* this would not be a necessary relation of our choice, the highest good is yet the *subjectively* necessary object of a good (including a human) will, and belief in its attainability is necessarily presupposed.

Between the acquisition of a cognition through experience (a posteriori) and through reason (a priori) there is no middle term. But between the cognition of an object and the mere presupposition of its possibility there is something intermediate, namely a ground, empirical or from reason, for adopting this possibility in relation to a necessary set off against knowledge, for it may itself be knowledge. The holding-to-be-true on the basis of a testimony differs neither in degree nor in kind from the holding-to-be-true through one's own experience.

II) no objects of *rational* cognition (of cognition a priori), neither of reason's theoretical cognition, as in mathematics or metaphysics, nor of its practical cognition in morality.

One may indeed believe mathematical truths of reason on testimony, partly because error here is not readily possible, partly because it can be readily discovered; but one cannot in this manner know them. Philosophical truths of reason, however, cannot even be believed, they must solely be known, for philosophy suffers no persuasion. And as concerns particularly

---

expansion of the field of possible objects over and above those whose cognition is possible for us. This necessity takes place only in respect of that [relation] in which the object is cognized as practical and through reason as practically necessary; for the assumption of something for the purpose of merely expanding theoretical cognition is always *contingent*. This practically necessary presupposition of an object is that of the possibility of the highest good as an object of choice, thus also of the condition of this possibility (God, freedom, and immortality). This is a subjective necessity, namely to adopt the reality of the object for the sake of the necessary determination of the will. This is the *casus extraordinarius*, without which practical reason cannot maintain itself in respect of its necessary end, and here *favor necessitatis* countenances it in its own judgment. It cannot acquire an object through logic but only resist what hinders it in the use of this idea which practically belongs to it.

This belief is the necessity of adopting the objective reality of a concept (of the highest good), i.e. the possibility of its object as an a priori necessary object of [the faculty of] choice. If we merely look to action, we do not need this belief. If, however, we want to expand ourselves through action to the possession of the end thereby possible, we must adopt this end as being possible throughout. I therefore can only say: *I* find myself compelled, through my end according to laws of freedom, to adopt a highest good in the world as possible, but I *cannot compel anyone else by reasons* [to share this belief] (belief is *free*).

The belief of reason consequently can never be directed to theoretical cognition, for there the objectively inadequate holding-to-be-the objects of reason's practical cognition in morality—rights and duties—there can be in respect of these just as little a mere believing. One must be *completely certain* whether something is right or wrong, according to or contrary to duty, licit or illicit. In things moral *nothing* can be ventured on an uncertainty, nothing *at the risk of an offense against the law*. Thus, for example, it is not enough for the judge *merely to believe* that the man accused of a crime has actually committed it. He must (juridically) know it, or he acts unconscionably.

III) those objects alone in which the holding-to-be-true is necessarily free, that is, not determined by objective grounds of truth, independent of the nature and interests of the subject.

Belief, therefore, because of its merely subjective grounds, does not yield a conviction that can be communicated and commands general acclaim, like the conviction that comes from knowledge. *I myself* can be certain only of the validity and immutability of my practical belief; and my belief in the truth of a proposition or the actuality of a thing is what in relation to me takes the place of a cognition, without being one itself.

He is morally *unbelieving* who does not accept what indeed is *impossible* to know but is *morally necessary* to presuppose. A want of moral interest always underlies this kind of unbelief.

---

true is mere *opinion*. It is merely a presupposition of reason in a *subjective*, though absolutely necessary practical respect. The bent[86] toward moral laws leads up to an object of choice determined by pure reason. The adoption of the feasibility of this object and also of the actuality of the cause for it is a *moral* belief or a free holding-to-be-true that is necessary in the moral view directed to the completion of one's ends.

Fides is actually fidelity in *pacto*, or subjective trust in one another, that one will keep his promise to the other—*good faith*. This means faithfulness when the *pactum* has been made, and faith when it is to be concluded.

By analogy, practical reason is, as it were, the *promisor*; man, the *promisee*; the expected good from the deed, the *promissum*.

86. *Gesinnung*.

The stronger a man's moral bent, the more firm and vivid will be his belief in everything he feels himself compelled to accept and to presuppose out of moral interest as practically necessary.

    3) *Knowledge.* The holding-to-be-true out of a cognitive ground that is both objectively and subjectively sufficient, or certainty, is either *empirical* or *rational,* according as it is based on *experience*—one's own as well as that of others—or on *reason.* This distinction thus refers to the two sources from which spring all our cognition: *experience* and *reason.*

Rational certainty, again, is either mathematical or philosophical certainty. The former is *intuitive,* the latter *discursive.*

Mathematical certainty is also called evidence, because an intuitive cognition is clearer than a discursive one. Although both the mathematical and the philosophical cognition of reason are in themselves equally certain, yet the kind of certainty in the two is different.

Empirical certainty is original (*originarie empirica*) as far as I am certain of something *from my own experience,* and *derivative* as far as I become certain of something through others' experience. The latter is also commonly called *historical* certainty.

Rational certainty differs from empirical by the consciousness of *necessity* connected with it; it is thus an *apodeictic* certainty, whereas empirical certainty is only assertoric.[87] One is rationally certain of that into which one would have gained insight a priori even without any experience. Our cognitions, therefore, may concern objects of experience, and the certainty thereof can yet be empirical and rational at the same time, namely so far as we cognize an empirically certain proposition out of principles a priori.

87. Here Reich comments (*Die Vollständigkeit,* p. 22): "If previously we had to equate certainty and apodeictic certainty, we must now distinguish them. Contradictions enough!" However, it was not Kant-Jäsche who ruled that "certainty" equals "apodeictic certainty." Such an equation is arbitrarily inferred by Reich from the determinations of the first three paragraphs of this section, none of which justifies Reich's claim that "one will have to conclude . . . that certainty and apodeictic certainty shall pass for synonymous expressions."

We cannot have rational certainty of everything, but where we can have it, we must prefer it to the empirical.

All certainty is either *mediated* or *not mediated,* that is, it either requires proof or is neither susceptible nor in need of any proof. There may be ever so much in our cognition that is mediately certain only, that is, only through proof, yet there must also be something *indemonstrable* or *immediately certain,* and all our cognition must start from *immediately certain* propositions.

The proofs on which all mediated or mediate certainty of a cognition rests are either *direct proofs* or *indirect,* that is, *apagogic* proofs. When I prove a truth out of its grounds, I furnish a direct proof for it; and when I conclude from the falsity of the opposite to the truth of a proposition, I furnish an apagogic proof. If the latter, however, shall have validity, the propositions must be *contradictorily* or *diametrically* opposed. For two propositions that are merely contrarily opposed (*contrarie opposita*) can both be false. A proof forming the ground of mathematical certainty is called *demonstration,* and one that is the ground of philosophical certainty is called an *akroamatic* proof. The essential components of every proof generatim are its *matter* and its *form,* or the *ground of the proof* and the *consequence.*

From *scire,* knowing, is derived science, by which is to be understood the complex of a cognition as a *system.* Science is contrasted with *common* cognition, that is, the complex of a cognition as a *mere aggregate.* The system rests on the idea of a whole that precedes the parts, whereas in common knowledge or in the mere aggregate of cognitions the parts precede the whole. There are *historical* sciences and sciences *of reason.*

In a science we often *know* only the *cognitions* but not the *things presented* by them; consequently there can be a science of that whereof our cognition is not knowledge.[88]

From the preceding remarks about the nature and the kinds

88. E.g. the transcendental dialectic.

of holding-to-be-true we can now draw the general result that all our conviction is either *logical* or *practical*.[89]

If, namely, we know that we are free from all subjective grounds and that the holding-to-be-true is yet sufficient, then we are *convinced,* that is, *logically* convinced or convinced out of *objective* grounds (the object is certain).

The complete holding-to-be-true out of subjective grounds which, in *practical relation,* are equivalent to objective grounds, is, however, also conviction, only not logical but *practical* conviction (*I am certain*). And this practical conviction or this *moral rational belief* is often firmer than any knowing. In knowing one still listens to counter-reasons, but not in belief, because this turns not on objective grounds but on the moral interest of the subject.*

To conviction is opposed *persuasion,* a holding-to-be-true out of insufficient grounds of which one does not know if they are merely subjective or also objective.

Persuasion often precedes conviction. We are conscious of many cognitions only in a manner that does not enable us to judge whether the grounds of our holding-to-be-true are objective or subjective. In order to be able to advance from mere persuasion to conviction, we therefore must first *reflect,* that is, see, to what power of cognition a cognition belongs,[90] and then

---

* [Kant's own note.] This practical conviction is thus the *moral rational belief* which alone, in the strictest sense, must be called a belief and set as such against knowing and all theoretical or logical conviction in general, because it can never rise to knowing. The so-called historical belief, on the other hand, as noted before, must not be distinguished from knowing, since as a kind of theoretical or logical holding-to-be-true it may itself be a knowing. We accept an empirical truth on the testimony of others with the same certainty as if we had attained it through facts of our own experience. In the first kind of empirical knowledge there is something deceptive, but also in the second.

Historical or mediate empirical knowledge rests on the reliability of testimonies. Among the requirements of an unexceptionable witness are *authenticity* (competence) and *integrity*.

89. The original makes no paragraph break here.
90. See B 316 ff.

investigate, that is, examine whether the grounds in respect of the object are sufficient or insufficient. Many do not get beyond persuasion. Some reach reflection, few investigation. He who knows what belongs to certainty will not readily confuse persuasion with conviction and thus will not allow himself to be readily persuaded either. There is a determining ground of acclaim which is composed of objective and subjective grounds, and most men do not separate this mixed effect.

Although every persuasion is false as to form (*formaliter*), so far, namely, as in it an uncertain cognition seems to be certain, it may yet be true as to matter (*materialiter*). And thus it also differs from opinion, which is an uncertain cognition so far as *it is taken to be uncertain.*

The sufficiency of holding-to-be-true (in belief) can be tested by *wager* or by *oath.* For the first is needed *comparative,* for the second, *absolute* sufficiency of *objective* grounds; instead of which, when they are not present, a subjectively sufficient holding-to-be-true is accepted.[91]

One often uses the expressions: *to concur with someone's judgment; to reserve, suspend, or give up one's judgment.* These and similar phrases seem to suggest that there is something arbitrary in our judgments, in that we are holding something to be true because we want to hold it to be true. Here then the question arises *whether volition has any influence on our judgment.*

The will has no immediate influence on our holding-to-be-true; if it had, that would be very absurd. When it is said, *We easily believe what we wish for,* this refers only to our *good-natured wishes,* e.g. those which a father has of his children. If

---

91. *gilt,* "is valid," referring to that on which men actually have agreed. In his article *On the Failure of All Philosophical Attempts in Theodicy* (Concluding Remark, note, Akad. VIII, 268), Kant says: "The means of extorting veracity in external statements, *the oath* (*tortura spiritualis*), is considered, before a human court of justice, not only as permitted but even as indispensable: a sad proof of the low respect of men for the truth even in the temple of justice, where its mere idea by itself should already instill the greatest respect."

the will had an immediate influence on our conviction of what we wish, we would constantly make chimeras for ourselves of a happy state and then also hold them to be true. The will, however, cannot contend *against* convincing proofs of truths that run counter to its wishes and inclinations.

However, as far as the will impels the understanding to explore a truth or restrains it therein, one must concede to the will an influence on the *use of the understanding* and thus, indirectly, on conviction itself, since this depends so much on the use of the understanding.

As concerns, however, *suspension* or *reservation* of our judgment, it consists in the resolve not to let a merely *provisional* judgment become a *determinate* one. A provisional judgment is one by which I suppose that there are more grounds *for* the truth of something than against it, that these grounds, however, do not suffice for a *determinate* or *definitive* judgment by which I decide straightway for the truth. Provisional judging is therefore a consciously problematic judging.

Reservation of judgment can take place with a twofold intent: *Either* to seek the grounds for a determinate judgment, *or never* to judge. In the first case the reservation of judgment is called critical (*suspensio judicii indagatoria*), in the latter, skeptical (*suspensio judicii sceptica*). For the skeptic renounces all judging, whereas the true philosopher, when he has not yet sufficient reasons for holding something to be true, merely suspends his judgment.

To suspend one's judgment according to *maxims* requires a practiced power of judgment that is found only in advanced age. Generally, withholding our acclaim is very difficult, partly because our understanding is so avid to enlarge and to enrich itself with cognitions by judging, partly because our propensity is always directed more to some things than to others. But he who often has had to take back his acclaim and thereby has become prudent and cautious, will give it less quickly, for fear of having to retract his judgment later on. This *disavowal* is always humiliating and a cause for distrusting all other attainments.

We note here further that to leave one's judgment *in dubio* is something different from leaving it *in suspenso*. In the latter case I am always interested in the matter; in the former, however, to decide whether the thing is true or not does not always conform with my purpose or interests.

Provisional judgments are very necessary, indeed indispensable to the use of the understanding in all meditation and investigation. For they serve to guide the understanding in its searches and to that end place at its disposal various means.

When meditating on a thing, we must always judge provisionally and, as it were, already scent the cognition that will become ours by meditation. And if one is intent on findings and discoveries, one must always make a plan; otherwise our thoughts roam haphazardly.

Provisional judgments may therefore be regarded as *maxims* for the investigation of a matter. One could call them also *anticipations,* because one anticipates the judgment on a matter before one has the determinate judgment. Such [anticipatory] judgments thus have their good use, and it would be possible even to give rules on how to judge an object provisionally.

From provisional judgments are to be distinguished *prejudices.*

Prejudices are provisional judgments *so far as they are adopted as principles.* Every prejudice is to be regarded as a principle of erroneous judgments. The false cognition springing from the prejudice must therefore be distinguished from its source, the prejudice itself. Thus, for example, the significance of dreams is in itself not a prejudice, but an error that springs from accepting the general rule: What sometimes happens, always happens, or is always to be held to be true. And this principle, to which belongs the significance of dreams, is a prejudice.

Occasionally prejudices are true provisional judgments; it is wrong only that we should let them pass as principles or *determining* judgments. The cause of this delusion is to be sought in our taking subjective grounds falsely for objective *out of want of reflection,* which must precede all judging. For even while we can accept some cognitions, e.g., immediately certain propositions, without *investigating* them, that is, without examining the conditions of their truth, yet we cannot and must not judge anything without *reflecting,* that is, without comparing a cognition with the cognizing power from which it is supposed to spring (sensibility or the understanding). If now we adopt judgments without reflection, which is needed even where no investigation takes place, then prejudices or principles of judging out of subjective causes arise which are falsely taken for objective grounds.

The main sources of prejudices are *imitation, habit,* and *inclination.*

Imitation has a general influence on our judgment, for it is a strong ground for taking as true what others have alleged as true. Hence the prejudice: What everyone does is right. As concerns prejudices that have sprung from habit, they can be eradicated only by time, in that the understanding, checked and delayed in its judgments, step by step, by counter-reasons, is thereby gradually brought to an opposite manner of thinking. If, however, a prejudice of habit has at the same time arisen from imitation, then the man who is possessed of it can hardly be cured of it. A prejudice from imitation may also be called a *propensity for the passive use of reason,* or for the *mechanism of reason instead of its spontaneity under laws.*

Reason indeed is an active principle that shall borrow nothing from the mere authority of others, not even, when its *pure* use is at issue, from experience. But the laziness of so many men makes them tread in the footsteps of others rather than exert the powers of their own understanding. Such men can never become anything but copies of others, and if all were of this kind, the world would forever remain on the same spot. It is therefore highly necessary and important not to tie the young, as is usually done, to mere imitation.

There are quite a few things that contribute to habituating us to the maxim of imitation and thereby make reason a fertile soil of prejudice. To these aids of imitation belong:

    1) *Formulas.* These are rules whose expression serves

as a pattern for imitation. They are, by the way, extremely useful in simplifying involved propositions, and the brightest brains seek to invent them.

2) *Sayings,* whose expression has a great conciseness of striking sense, so that it seems one could not capture the sense in fewer words. Sayings of this kind (*dicta*) must always be borrowed from others whom one entrusts with a certain infallibility, and serve, because of this authority, as rule and law. The pronouncements of the Bible are called sayings κατ'ἐξοχήν.

3) *Sentences,* that recommend themselves and preserve their reputation as products of mature judgment often for centuries by the impact of the thoughts embodied in them.

4) *Canones.* These are general teachings underlying the sciences and pointing to something sublime and well thought through. One may express them also in a sententious way in order that they may please the more.

5) *Proverbs (proverbia).* These are popular rules of the common understanding, or expressions that signify popular judgments. As such merely parochial sentences serve only the common mob as *sentences* and *canones,* they are not to be met with among people of refined education.

From the three general sources of prejudices previously mentioned, and especially from imitation, spring various special prejudices, among which we will here touch on the following as the most common.

1) *Prejudices of prestige.* With these are to be reckoned:

a) The prejudice of prestige of the *person.* When in matters resting on experience and testimonies we build our cognition on the prestige of other persons, we do not thereby become guilty of any prejudice; for in matters of this kind, since we cannot ourselves experience and encompass everything with our own understanding, the prestige of the person must be the basis of our judgment. If, however, we make the prestige of others the ground of our holding-to-be-true in respect to cognitions of reason, then we accept these cognitions upon mere prejudice. For rational truths hold good anonymously; here the question is not, *who* has said it, but *what* has he said? It does not count whether a cognition is of noble descent; but the propensity toward the prestige of great men is nevertheless very common, partly because of the limitations of our own insight, partly out of the desire to imitate what is described to us as *great*. To this adds further that the prestige of the person serves to flatter our vanity in an indirect way. Just as the subjects of a powerful despot are proud that they are all treated *alike* by him, in that the lowest may deem himself equal to the most noble person insofar as they are both nothing before the unlimited power of their ruler, so the admirers of a great man also judge themselves equal, insofar as the distinctions among themselves are to be held insignificant before the merits of the great man. For more than one reason, therefore, the much praised great men lend no small countenance to the propensity toward the prejudice of personal prestige.

b) The prejudice of the prestige of the *multitude*. The mob is most inclined to this prejudice. For as it cannot judge the capacities and knowledge of the person, it rather clings to the judgment of the multitude, on the supposition that what everyone says must probably be true. However, with the mob this prejudice refers only to historical things; in matters of religion, in which it is interested itself, it relies on the judgment of the learned.

Generally it is peculiar that the ignorant has a prejudice for learning, and the learned again a prejudice for the common understanding.

When the learned man, after having pretty well completed the circle of the sciences, does not gain due satisfaction from all his labors, he at last distrusts learning particularly in respect of those speculations in which concepts cannot be made sensible and whose foundations are insecure, as, for example, in metaphysics. Since, however, he nevertheless believes that the key to certainty on some special objects should be discoverable somewhere, after he has so long sought it in vain on the road of scientific search, he seeks it in the common understanding.

However, this hope is very deceptive; for if the cultivated

faculty of reason is of no avail with respect to the cognition of certain things, the uncultivated will undoubtedly serve as little. In metaphysics the appeal to pronouncements of the common understanding is always quite inadmissible, because here no case can be exhibited *in concreto*. In morality, however, the situation is different. Not only can all rules in morality be given *in concreto*, but practical reason reveals itself more clearly and correctly through the organ of the common understanding than through that of the use of the speculative understanding. The common understanding, therefore, often judges more correctly about matters of morality and duty than the speculative.

c) The prejudice of the prestige of *the age*. Here the prejudice relating to *antiquity* is one of the most significant. We have reason indeed to judge favorably of antiquity; but it is only a reason for a moderate esteem, the limits of which we all too often transgress by making the ancients the treasurers of cognitions and sciences, elevating the *relative* value of their writings to an absolute value and entrusting ourselves blindly to their guidance. To value the ancients so excessively means leading the understanding back into its childhood and neglecting the use of one's own talent. We would also err very much if we believed that everyone in antiquity wrote as classically as those whose writings have come down to us. As time, namely, sifts everything, and only that survives which has an inner value, we may assume, not without reason, that we possess only the best writings of the ancients.

There are several *causes* that produce and maintain the prejudice relating to antiquity.

When an expectation according to a general rule is surpassed by something, one initially *wonders* at this, and this wonder then often passes into admiration. That is the case with the ancients, when one finds something in them that could not be expected in regard to the circumstance of the time under which they lived. Another cause lies in the circumstances that knowledge of the ancients and antiquity is proof of learning and being well read, which always earn respect, however common and insignificant in themselves the things one has unearthed from the study of the ancients. A third cause is the gratitude we owe to the ancients for having opened the way to many cognitions. It seems fair to show them a special esteem on this account, the measure of which, however, we often overstep. A fourth cause, finally, is to be sought in a certain *envy* of contemporaries. He who cannot compete with the moderns extols, at their expense, the ancients, in order that the moderns may not be able to rise above him.

The opposite of this is the prejudice relating to *novelty*. At times the prestige of antiquity and the prejudice in its favor decreased, especially at the beginning of this century, when the famous Fontenelle sided with the moderns. In cognitions that are capable of expansion it is very natural to place more trust in the moderns than in the ancients. But this judgment is justified only as a provisional judgment. If we make it determinate, it becomes a prejudice.

2) Prejudices of *self-love* or logical *egoism,* according to which one holds that the agreement of one's own judgment with the judgments of others is an unnecessary criterion of truth. They are opposed to the prejudices of prestige, for they express a certain preference for what is the product of one's own understanding, e.g. one's own system of thought.

Is it good and advisable to allow prejudices to persist or perhaps even to favor them? It is astonishing that such questions, particularly the one about favoring prejudices, can still be posed in our time. To favor someone's prejudices is as much as to deceive someone with well-meaning intent. Not to touch prejudices might still pass, for who can make it his business to uncover and dispel everyone's prejudices? But should it not be advisable to work with all our might at eradicating them? That is indeed another question. Old and deep-rooted prejudices are of course hard to fight, because they are self-justifying and, as it were, their own judges. One also tries to excuse the allowed persistence of prejudices on the ground that disadvantages would arise from their eradication. But let us readily admit these disadvantages—the ensuing results will be the more beneficial.

X. Probability / Explanation of the Probable / Difference of Probability from Verisimilitude/ Mathematical and Philosophical Probability / Doubt, Subjective and Objective / Skeptical, Dogmatic, and Critical Manner of Thinking or Method of Philosophizing / Hypotheses

To the doctrine of the certainty of our cognition belongs also the doctrine of the cognition of the probable, which is to be regarded as an approximation to certainty.

By probability is to be understood a holding-to-be-true out of insufficient reasons, which, however, bear a greater proportion to the sufficient ones than the reasons of the opposite. By this explanation we distinguish probability (*probabilitas*) from verisimilitude (*verisimilitudo*), a holding-to-be-true out of insufficient reasons so far as these are greater than the reasons of the opposite.

The reason of a holding-to-be-true can be *objectively* or *subjectively* greater than that of the opposite. Which of the two it is can be found out only by comparing the reasons of holding-to-be-true with the sufficient reasons; for then the reasons of holding-to-be-true are greater than the reasons of the opposite *can be*. In probability the reason of holding-to-be-true is therefore *objectively* valid; in verisimilitude, however, only *subjectively* valid. Verisimilitude is mere magnitude of persuasion; probability is an approximation to certainty. In probability there must always be a standard by which I can estimate it. This standard is *certainty*. For as I shall compare the sufficient with the insufficient reasons, I must know how much is required for certainty. Such a standard, however, does not exist in mere verisimilitude, since here I compare the insufficient reasons not with the sufficient, but only with those of the opposite.

The moments of probability may be either *homogeneous,* or *heterogeneous.* If they are homogeneous, as in mathematical cognition, they must be *numbered;* if they are heterogeneous, as in philosophical cognition, they must be *pondered,* i.e. estimated by their effect, namely by the overcoming of hindrances in the mind. The latter do not give a proportion to certainty, but only of one verisimilitude to another. Hence it follows that only the mathematician can determine the proportion of insufficient to sufficient reasons; the philosopher must be satisfied with verisimilitude as a merely subjective and practically sufficient holding-to-be-true. For in philosophical cognition, because of the heterogeneity of the grounds, probability cannot be estimated; here the weights are, so to speak, not all stamped. Even of *mathematical* probability therefore one can properly say only that *it is more than one half of certainty.*

Much has been said of a logic of probability (*logica probabilium*). But such a logic is not possible; for if the proportion of insufficient reasons to the sufficient reason cannot be mathematically weighed, no rules will help. Nor can one give any general rules of probability at all, except that error will not strike *on one and the same* side, but there must be a ground of agreement in the object; likewise *if two opposite sides* have erred in equal *amount* and *degree,* truth will be in the *middle.*

Doubt is a counter-reason or a mere hindrance to holding-to-be-true that may be considered either *subjectively* or *objectively.* *Subjectively,* namely, doubt is sometimes taken to be the state of an undecided mind, and *objectively,* as the cognition of the insufficiency of the grounds of holding something to be true. In the latter regard it is called an *objection,* that is, an objective ground of holding a cognition held to be true, to be false.

A merely subjectively valid counter-reason against a holding-to-be-true is a *scruple.* With a scruple one does not know whether the hindrance to holding something to be true is objective or only subjective, e.g., grounded only on inclination, habit, and the like. One doubts without being able to explain oneself distinctly and definitely about the ground of doubt, whether it lies in the object itself or in the subject. If then we shall be able to remove such scruples, they must be raised to the distinctness and determinateness of an objection. For by objections certainty is raised to distinctness and completeness, and no one can be certain of a matter unless counter-reasons have been activated by which it can be determined how far apart from certainty one still is, or how close to it. Nor is it enough that every doubt merely be answered; one must also *resolve* it, that is, make comprehensible how the scruple originated. If this is not done the doubt is merely *turned away* but not *lifted;* the seed of doubt still remains. In many cases, of course, we cannot know whether the hindrance to holding something to be true has subjective or objective grounds, and we are thus unable to lift the scruple by disclosure of the illusion, since we cannot always compare our cognitions with the object but often only with one another. It is therefore modesty to put forward one's objections as doubts.

There is a principle of doubting which consists in the maxim of treating cognitions by making them uncertain and showing the impossibility of attaining certainty. This method of philosophizing is the *skeptical* manner of thinking, or *skepticism.* It is opposed to the *dogmatic* manner of thinking, or *dogmatism,* which is a blind trust in the ability of reason to expand a priori through mere concepts without critique, simply because of the seeming success of this expansion.

Both methods, if they become universal, are faulty. For there are many cognitions in respect of which we cannot proceed dogmatically; and on the other side, skepticism, by renouncing all affirmative cognition, exterminates all endeavors to attain possession of a cognition of what is *certain.*

Harmful, however, as this skepticism is, the *skeptical* method is yet useful and suitable, if one understands by it merely the manner of treating something as uncertain, and bringing it to the highest uncertainty in the hope of getting on the track of truth. This method therefore is actually a mere suspension of judgment. It is very useful to *critical* procedure, by which is to be understood that method of philosophizing which makes one examine the *sources* of one's affirmations or objections and the grounds on which they rest—a method that gives hope of attaining certainty.

In mathematics and physics skepticism has no place. Only that cognition has been able to occasion it which is neither mathematical nor empirical: the purely *philosophical.* Absolute skepticism passes off everything as illusion. It thus distinguishes illusion from truth and therefore must yet have a characteristic of the difference, and consequently presuppose a cognition of truth; thus it contradicts itself.

Of probability we noted above that it is a mere approximation to certainty. This is particularly the case with *hypotheses,* through which we can never attain apodeictic certainty in our cognition, but only a degree of probability, sometimes greater, sometimes lesser.

A hypothesis is a holding-to-be-true of a judgment of the truth of a ground, for the sake of its sufficiency for consequences;[92] or, in short: *The holding-to-be-true of a presupposition as a ground.*

All holding-to-be-true in hypotheses is based on a presupposition which, as a ground, is sufficient to explain other cognitions as consequences. For here we conclude from the truth of the consequence to the truth of the ground. But since this manner of conclusion, as noted above, gives a sufficient criterion of the truth and can lead to apodeictic certainty only when *all possible* consequences of an assumed ground are true, and since all possible consequences can never be determined by us, it becomes clear that hypotheses always remain hypotheses, that is, presuppositions whose complete certainty we can never attain. The probability of a hypothesis nevertheless can increase and rise to an *analogon* of certainty, if, namely, all consequences *that have occurred to us* can be explained out of the presupposed ground. For in such a case there is no reason why we should not assume that all possible consequences will be susceptible of being explained by it. We thus commit ourselves to

92. *um der Zulänglichkeit der Folgen willen,* "for the sake of the sufficiency of the consequences." We have clarified the meaning as expressed in the translation, in line with Akad. XVI, 2678, 2690, 2694.

the hypothesis as if it were perfectly certain, although it is so only *through induction*.

And yet, something must be apodeictically certain in every hypothesis, namely:

1) The *possibility of the presupposition itself*. For instance, when we assume a subterranean fire for the explanation of earthquakes and volcanoes, such a fire must be possible, if not as a flaming, yet as a heated body. But for the sake of certain other appearances, to make the earth an animal in which the circulation of inner fluids causes heat, is to put forward a mere piece of fiction and not a hypothesis. For actualities may be imagined, but not possibilities; these must be certain.

2) The *consequence*. From the assumed ground the consequences must follow correctly, otherwise the hypothesis becomes a mere chimera.

3) *Unity*. It is an essential requirement of a hypothesis that it be only one and need no subsidiary hypotheses for its support. If in the case of a hypothesis we have to adopt several others in support of it, it thereby loses much of its probability. For the more consequences can be derived from a hypothesis, the more probable it is; the fewer, the more improbable. Tycho de Brahe's hypothesis, for example, was not sufficient to explain a number of appearances; he therefore assumed several new hypotheses to supplement it. Here we may already guess that the adopted hypothesis is not the true ground. The Copernican system, on the contrary, is a hypothesis from which everything to be explained by it—*so far as it has yet occurred to us*—can be explained. Here we need no *subsidiary hypotheses*.

There are sciences that do not permit of hypotheses, e.g., mathematics and metaphysics. But in physics they are useful and indispensable.

Appendix: Of the Difference Between Theoretical and Practical Cognition

A cognition is called *practical* as opposed to *theoretical,* but also as opposed to *speculative* cognition.

Practical cognitions, namely, are either

     1) *imperatives,* and in so far are opposed to *theoretical* cognitions; or they contain

     2) the *grounds for possible imperatives,* and in so far are opposed to *speculative* cognitions.

By *imperative,* in general, is to be understood every statement that expresses a possible free action by which a certain end is to be made actual. Every cognition which contains imperatives must thus be called *practical,* that is, practical in opposition to *theoretical.* For theoretical cognitions are those which express not what ought to be, but what is, and thus have as their object *not an acting* but a *being.*

If, however, we oppose practical cognitions to *speculative* ones, they can also be *theoretical in so far as imperatives can be derived from them.* Viewed in this regard, they are practical as to *content (in potentia),* or *objectively* so. By speculative cognitions, on the other hand, we understand those from which no rules of behavior can be derived or which contain no grounds for possible imperatives. Such merely speculative propositions are very numerous, e.g. in *theology.* Speculative cognitions of this kind are always theoretical, but conversely, not every theoretical cognition is speculative; viewed in another regard, it can at the same time also be practical.

Everything gravitates ultimately toward the *practical;* and in this tendency of everything theoretical and everything speculative in respect of its use, consists the practical value of our cognition. This value, however, is an *unconditioned* value only if the *end* to which the practical use of cognition is directed is an *unconditioned* end. The only unconditioned and final end (ultimate end) to which all practical use of our cognition must lastly refer is *morality,* which for that reason we also call the *plainly* or *absolutely practical.* And that part of philosophy which has morality as its object would accordingly have to be called *practical* philosophy κατ'ἐξοχήν, although every other philosophical science may also contain its practical part, that is, a direction concerning the practical use of the theories set forth, for the purpose of realizing certain ends.

I. General Doctrine of Elements

First Section: Of Concepts

§ 1. Concept as Such and Its Difference from Intuition

All cognitions, that is, all presentations consciously referred to an object, are either *intuitions* or *concepts*.[1] Intuition is a *singular* presentation (*repraesentatio singularis*), the concept is a *general* (*repraesentatio per notas communes*) or *reflected* presentation (*repraesentatio discursiva*).

Cognition through concepts is called thinking (*cognitio discursiva*).

Note 1. Concept is opposed to intuition, for it is a general presentation or a presentation of what is common to several objects, a presentation, therefore, *so far as it may be contained in different objects*.[2]

Note 2. It is mere tautology to speak of general or common concepts, a mistake based on a wrong division of concepts into *general, particular,* and *singular.* Not the concepts themselves, only *their use* can be divided in this way.

§ 2. Matter and Form of Concepts

In every concept there is to be distinguished *matter* and *form.* The matter of concepts is the *object;* their form is *generality.*

---

1. See B 33, 74.

2. *in verschiedenen*, "in different ones" (as in Akad. XVI, 2877), which leaves the reference of the adjective open. It may refer either to objects or presentations. We have inserted "objects," also in line with 2661. It is equally true, however, that the concept is contained in different presentations, which are our only access to the object.

§ 3. Empirical and Pure Concept

The concept is either an *empirical* or a *pure* one (*vel empiricus vel intellectualis*). A pure concept is one that is not abstracted[3] from experience but springs from the understanding even *as to content.*

The *idea*[4] is a concept of reason, whose object can be met with nowhere in experience.

Note 1. The empirical concept springs from the senses through comparison of the objects of experience and receives, through the understanding, merely the form of generality. The reality of these concepts rests on actual experience, from which they have been extracted as to their content. Whether there are *pure concepts of the understanding* (*conceptus puri*) which, as such, spring solely from the understanding, independent of any experience, must be investigated by metaphysics.[5]

Note 2. Concepts of reason or ideas can in no way relate to actual objects, because these must all be contained in a possible experience. But ideas nevertheless serve to guide the understanding through reason in respect of experience and use of the latter's rules to the greatest perfection, or they serve to show that not all possible things are objects of experience and that the principles of the possibility of the latter [of objects of experience] are not valid for things in themselves, neither for objects of experience as things in themselves.

The idea contains the *archetype* of the use of the understanding, e.g., the idea of the *universe,* which must be neces-

---

3. *abgezogen,* drawn from, which had become a German substitute for the foreign word *abstrahiert.* Cf. the important Note 3, § 6.

4. This is the narrower systematic meaning of "idea," for which Kant asks to reserve the word, protecting it against its indiscriminate use as a name for all kinds of presentations (B 368 ff., B 376). In colloquial German, even recipes may call for adding to a soup "an idea" of salt.

5. As Kant has done in the *Critique of Pure Reason.* The concepts here in question, both empirical and pure, are analytic concepts. See above, Sec. VIII, p. 70, and below, § 4, §§100 ff. Pure concepts of the understanding, in this sense, are the unschematized categories of the *Critique of Pure Reason.*

sary, not as a *constitutive* principle of the empirical use of the understanding, but only as a *regulative* principle for the sake of the all-pervasive coherence of the empirical use of our understanding. The idea is also to be regarded as a necessary fundamental concept in order either to *complete* the subordinating acts of the understanding objectively or to regard them as *unlimited. Nor* can the idea be obtained by *composition;* for the whole is here prior to the part. Nevertheless there are ideas to which an approximation takes place. This is the case with *mathematical* ideas, or with the ideas of the *mathematical generation of a whole,* these being essentially different from *dynamic* ideas which are totally *heterogeneous* to all concrete concepts, because the [dynamic] whole differs from concrete concepts not in quantity (as does the mathematical [whole]) but in *kind.*

One cannot provide nor prove objective reality for any idea but for the idea of freedom; and this is the case because freedom is the condition of the *moral law,* whose reality is an axiom. The reality of the idea of God can be proved only through the moral law and therefore only with practical intent, i.e. the intent *so to act as if* there be a God—and this idea thus can be proved only *for* this intent.

In all sciences, especially those of reason, the idea of the science is the general *delineation* or *outline* of it, thus the extension of all cognitions belonging to it. Such an idea of the whole—the first thing one has to look to and to seek in a science—is *architectonic,* as, for example, the idea of the science of law.[6]

Most men lack the idea of humanity, the idea of a perfect republic, of a life in felicity, and the like. Many men have no idea of what they want, proceeding therefore by instinct or authority.

§ 4. Given (a priori or a posteriori) and Made Concepts

All concepts, as to their *matter,* are either *given (conceptus*

6. See B 860 ff.

dati) or *made* (*conceptus factitii*).[7] The former are given either a priori or a posteriori.

All *empirical* or a posteriori given concepts are called *experiential concepts;* a priori given concepts are called *notions.*[8]

Note. The form of a concept, as of a discursive presentation, is always made.

§ 5. Logical Origin of Concepts

The origin of concepts as to *mere form* rests on reflection and abstraction from the difference of things that are designated by a certain presentation. And here the question arises: *Which acts of the understanding make up a concept,* or—which is the same —*which do belong to the generation of a concept from given presentations?*

Note 1. Since general logic abstracts from all content of the cognition through concepts or from all matter of thinking, it can ponder the concept only in regard to *its form,* that is, subjectively only:[9] not how, through a characteristic, it determines an object, but only how it can be referred to several objects. Thus it is not for general logic to investigate the *source* of concepts, not how concepts *as* presentations arise, but solely how *given presentations become concepts in thinking*—whatever these concepts may contain, something taken from experience, or something thought out, or something gathered from the nature of the understanding. This *logical* origin of concepts—the origin as to their mere form—

7. Cf. below §§ 100–103.

8. Examples of these in the *Critique of Pure Reason* are the categories. The idea is a concept formed from notions. See B 377.

9. Ordinarily, as Kant himself mentions in the second part of this sentence, the form of a concept is regarded as its objective rather than subjective aspect. However, here, as in other parts of the *Logic*, Kant implies his treatment in the *Critique of Pure Reason*, where the form of concepts is situated in the understanding, which is subjectively seen in reflection. Cf. B 316 ff., 325, 367. In the last resort, the categories that are the source of concepts have their own source in transcendental apperception: "This pure, original, immutable consciousness. . . .," A 107. (See below, § 6, Note 1). For the objective nature of transcendental apperception, see below, § 60, and B 140–142.

consists in reflection, whereby arises a presentation common to several objects (*conceptus communis*) as the form required for the power of judgment. In logic, *merely the difference of reflection* in the concept is considered.

Note 2. The origin of concepts in respect of their *matter,* which makes a concept either *empirical,* or *constructed,* or intellectual,[10] is pondered in metaphysics.

§ 6. Logical Acts of Comparison, Reflection, and Abstraction

The logical acts of the understanding by which concepts are generated as to their form are:

1) *comparison,* i.e. the likening of presentations to one another in relation to the unity of consciousness;

2) *reflection,* i.e. the going back over[11] different presentations, how they can be comprehended in one consciousness; and finally

3) *abstraction* or the segregation of everything else by which given presentations differ.

Note 1. In order to make our presentations into concepts, one must thus be able to *compare, reflect,* and *abstract,* for these three logical operations of the understanding are the essential and general conditions of generating any concept whatever. For example, I see a fir, a willow, and a linden. In firstly comparing these objects, I notice that they are different from one another in respect of trunk, branches, leaves, and the like; further, however, I reflect only on what they have in common, the trunk, the branches, the leaves themselves, and abstract from their size, shape, and so forth; thus I gain a concept of a tree.

Note 2. The expression *abstraction* is not always used correctly in logic. We must not say, to abstract *something* (*abstrahere aliquid*), but to abstract *from something* (*abstrahere*

10. Akad. XVI, 2852: "... *dati vel a priori vel a posteriori*
                               intellectual   empirical concepts."
11. *Überlegung,* "reflection," here translated by "going back over" in order to avoid repetition of the preceding "reflection," which renders the original *Reflexion* (a foreign word in German). Cf. Akad. XVI, 2878.

ab aliquo). If, for example, by scarlet cloth I think only the red color, then I abstract from the cloth; if I further abstract from the scarlet, and think it as a material substratum[12] generally, I abstract from still more determinations, and my concept has thereby become even more abstract. For the more numerous the differentia of things omitted from a concept or the greater the number of determinations from which abstraction has been made, the more abstract is the concept. Abstract concepts should therefore properly be called *abstracting* concepts (*conceptus abstrahentes*), that is, concepts in which several abstractions occur. Thus, for example, the concept of *body* is, properly speaking, not an abstract concept, for from the body itself I cannot abstract, otherwise I would not have the concept of it. But I do have to abstract from size, color, hardness or liquidity; in short, from all special determinations of special bodies. The *most abstract* concept is that which has nothing in common with any concept differing from it. This is the concept of *something;* for what is different from it is *nothing,* which has nothing in common with something.

   Note 3. Abstraction is only the *negative* condition under which generally valid presentations may be generated; the *positive* is comparison and reflection. For by abstraction no concept comes into being; abstraction only completes and encloses the concept within its definite limits.[13]

§ 7. Intension and Extension of Concepts

   Every concept, *as a partial concept,* is contained *in* the presentation of things; as a *ground of cognition,* i.e. *as a characteristic,* it has these things contained *under it.* In the former regard, every concept has an *intension* [content]; in the latter, it has an *extension.*

   Intension and extension of a concept have an inverse rela-

---

12. *Stoff,* "matter." In order to avoid "material matter" for *materiellen Stoff,* we translated *Stoff* by "substratum."
   13. See below, § 21, Note 3, § 99; and B 755.

tion to each other. The more a concept contains under it, the less it contains in it.

Note. The generality or general validity of the concept does not rest on the concept being a *partial concept* but on its being a *ground of cognition.*

§ 8. Magnitude of the Extension of Concepts

The more things stand under a concept and can be thought through it, the larger its extension or *sphere.*

Note. Just as one says of a *ground* generally that it contains the *consequence* under it, so one may also say of a concept that *as a ground of cognition* it contains all those things under it from which it has been abstracted, e.g., the concept of metal: gold, silver, copper, and so forth. For since every concept, as a generally valid presentation, contains what is common to several presentations of different things, all these things which in so far are contained under it, may be presented through it. And this is what makes up the *utility* of a concept. The more things there are that can be presented by a concept, the greater is its sphere. The concept of *body,* for example, has a greater extension than the concept of *metal.*

§ 9. Higher and Lower Concepts

Concepts are called *higher* (*conceptus superiores*) so far as they have other concepts under them, which in relation to them are called *lower* concepts. A characteristic of a characteristic—a *distant* characteristic—is a higher concept; the concept in reference to a distant characteristic is a lower concept.

Note. Since higher and lower concepts carry these designations only *respectively,* one and the same concept, in different relations, can be at once a higher and a lower concept. The concept *mammal,*[14] for example, is in reference to the

---

14. There is a clear mistake in the original version of this example which has *Mensch,* "man," where we chose "mammal" to have terms that stand in the required relation of subordination. The Akademie edition retains *Mensch,* but changes the second term to *Neger,* "negro," in line with an example found in a transcript of Kant's lectures on logic by Benno Erdmann (cf. *Göttingische*

concept *horse* a higher one, in reference to the concept *animal* a lower one.

§ 10. Genus and Species

The higher concept in regard to its lower concept is called *genus,* the lower in respect of its higher, *species.*

Just as higher and lower concepts, so the concepts of *genus* and *species* are also not different by their nature but only in respect of their relation to one another in logical subordination (termini a quo or ad quod).

§ 11. Highest Genus and Lowest Species

The *highest* genus is that which is no species (*genus summum non est species*), just as the *lowest* species is that which is no genus (*species quae non est genus est infima*). According to the law of continuity, however, there can be neither a *lowest* nor a *nearest* species.

> **Note.** When we think a series of several concepts subordinated to one another, e.g., iron, metal, body, substance, thing, we can here obtain ever higher genera, for every *species* is always to be considered as a *genus* in respect of a lower concept, e.g., the concept *learned man* in respect of the concept *philosopher*—until we lastly come to a *genus* that cannot again be a *species.* And to such a one we must at last be able to come, because there must be in the end a highest concept (*conceptus summus*) from which as such no further abstraction can be made without making the entire concept disappear. But there is no lowest concept (*conceptus infimus*) or lowest species in the series of species and genera under which not yet another would be contained, because it is impossible to determine such a concept. For even if we have a concept that we apply *immediately* to individuals, there may still be present in respect of it specific differences

gelehrte Anzeigen, 1880, Vol. II, p. 616, which we were unable to inspect). Since a change was necessary if the faulty example was to be corrected, we felt free to make an emendation in the first term rather than in the second, thus eliminating the subordination of man to animal, a quite un-Kantian example, notwithstanding this is logic, and not metaphysics.

which we either do not notice or disregard. Only *relative to use* are there lowest concepts which have received this meaning, as it were, by convention, to the extent that one has agreed to go no further down.

In respect to the determination of the concepts of genera and species, the following general law is valid: *There is a genus that can no longer be a species; but there is no species that can no longer be genus.*

§ 12. Wider and Narrower Concept/Reciprocal Concepts

The higher concept is also called a *wider* concept, the lower a *narrower* concept.

Concepts that have the same sphere are called *reciprocal concepts (conceptus reciproci).*

§ 13. Relation of the Lower to the Higher— of the Wider to the Narrower Concept

The lower concept is not contained *in* the higher, for it contains *more* in itself than the higher; but it is yet contained *under* the latter, because the higher contains the cognitive ground of the lower.

Further, a concept is not *wider* than another because it contains *more* under it—for one cannot know that—but so far as it contains under it the *other concept* and *beside it still more.*

§ 14. General Rules with Respect to the Subordination of Concepts

In respect of the logical extension of concepts, the following general rules are valid:

    1) What appertains to or contradicts the higher concepts, that appertains to or contradicts also all lower concepts contained under those higher ones.

    2) Conversely: What appertains to or contradicts *all* lower concepts, that appertains to or contradicts also their higher concept.

    Note. Because that in which things agree derives from their *general* properties and that in which they differ from their *particular* properties, one cannot conclude: What appertains to or contradicts *one* lower concept, appertains to or contradicts also *other* lower concepts belonging with the former to one higher concept. Thus, one cannot conclude, for example: *What does not appertain to man, does not appertain to angels either.*

§ 15. Conditions of the Origin of Higher and Lower Concepts: Logical Abstraction and Logical Determination

By continued logical abstraction originate ever higher concepts, just as on the other hand ever lower concepts originate by continued logical determination.[15] The greatest possible abstraction gives the highest or most abstract concept—that from which thinking can remove no further determination. The highest complete determination would give the *all-sided determination* of a concept (*conceptum omnimode determinatum*), i.e. one to which thinking can add no further determination.

Note. Since only single things or individuals are of an all-sided determination, there can be cognitions of an all-sided determination only as intuitions, not, however, as concepts; in respect of the latter, logical determination can never be considered as complete (§ 11, Note).[16]

§ 16. Use of Concepts in Abstracto and in Concreto

Every concept can be used *generally* and *particularly* (*in abstracto* and *in concreto*). The lower concept is being used *in abstracto* in respect of its higher; the higher concept is being used *in concreto* in respect of its lower.

Note 1. The expressions of the *abstract* and the *concrete* thus refer not so much to the concepts in themselves—for every concept is an abstract concept—as rather to their use only. And this use again can have varying degrees, according as one treats a concept now in a more, now in a less abstract or concrete way, that is, either omits or adds a greater or smaller number of determinations. Through abstract use a

15. Cf. just above, n.13.
16. See B 599 ff., 751 f., 755, note.

concept gets nearer to the highest genus; through concrete use, however, nearer to the individual.

Note 2. Which use of concepts, the abstract or the concrete, is to be given preference over the other? On this nothing can be decided. Neither use is to be deemed less valuable than the other. By very abstract concepts we cognize *little* in *many* things, by very concrete concepts *much* in *few* things; what we therefore gain on the one hand, we lose on the other. A concept that has a large sphere is very useful in so far as one can apply it to many things; but on account of this there is the less contained *in* it. In the concept *substance,* for example, I do not think as much as in the concept *chalk.*

Note 3. The art of popularity consists in bringing about, in the same cognition, that proportion between presentation *in abstracto* and *in concreto,* of concepts and their exhibition [in intuition], by which the maximum of cognition is achieved both as to extension and intension.

Second Section: Of Judgments

§ 17. Explanation of a Judgment as Such

A judgment is the presentation of the unity of the consciousness of several presentations, or the presentation of their relation so far as they make up one concept.[17]

§ 18. Matter and Form of Judgments

To every judgment belong, as its essential components, *matter* and *form.* The *matter* of judgment consists in given cogni-

17. Here we have a definition of Relation (as unity of consciousness of several presentations), something logic textbooks in Kant's time—as again in ours—have shied away from. See below, §§ 23, 30 n.3, 60, and B 140 ff.

tions that are joined in judgment into unity of consciousness; in the determination of the manner in which various presentations as such belong to one consciousness consists the *form* of judgment.

§ 19. Object of Logical Reflection:
The mere Form of Judgments

Since logic abstracts from all real or objective differences of cognition, it can deal with the matter of judgments as little as with the content of concepts. It therefore has to ponder solely the difference of judgments in respect of their mere form.

§ 20. Logical Forms of Judgments: Quantity,
Quality, Relation, and Modality

The differences of judgments in regard to their form may be reduced to the four chief moments[18] of *quantity, quality, relation,* and *modality,* in respect of which as many different kinds of judgments are determined.[19]

§ 21. Quantity: Universal, Particular, Singular Judgments

As to quantity, judgments are either *universal, particular,* or *singular,* according as the subject in the judgment is either *completely included* in or *completely excluded* from the predicate concept,[20] or is only *partly included* in or *partly excluded* from it. In the *universal* judgment the sphere of one concept is completely enclosed within the sphere of the other; in the *particular* judgment part of the former is enclosed in the sphere of another; in the *singular* judgment, finally, a concept that has no sphere at all is enclosed, merely as a part, in the sphere of another.

Note 1. As to logical form, singular judgments are to be ranked equal in use with universal judgments, for in both the

---

18. Or functions of the understanding. Cf. above, p. 23, n. 18 and below, n. 25.

19. See B 95 ff.

20. *Notion,* which is here used not in the technical meaning of § 4, yet draws attention to the categorial nature of concept.

predicate holds good of the subject without exception. In the singular sentence, e.g. *Cajus is mortal,* an exception can take place no more than in the universal, *All men are mortal.* For there is only one Cajus.

Note 2. In respect to the generality of a cognition, a real difference takes place between comparatively *general* propositions and *universal* propositions, which, however, does not concern logic. Comparatively *general* propositions, namely, are such as contain merely something of the general of certain objects and consequently do not contain sufficient conditions of subsumption, e.g. the proposition, *Proofs must be made thoroughly. Universal* propositions are those which assert something of an object universally.

Note 3. Universal rules are either *analytically* or *synthetically* universal. The *former* abstract from differences; the *latter* attend to the differences and consequently are determinative also in respect of them. The simpler an object is thought, the more possible is analytic universality according to a concept.

Note 4. When insight is not possible into general propositions in their generality without knowing them *in concreto,* they cannot serve as a norm and therefore cannot be valid *heuristically* in application, but are tasks only to investigate the general grounds of what in special cases has first become known. The proposition, for example, *He who has no interest in lying and knows the truth speaks the truth,* is not susceptible of insight into its generality because we know the restriction to the condition of disinterestedness only through experience, namely, that men lie out of an interest, which comes from their not adhering firmly to morality. An observation that teaches us the weakness of human nature.

Note 5. Of the *particular* judgments it is to be noted that if they shall be susceptible of insight by reason and thus have a rational, not merely an intellectual (abstracted) form, the subject must be a wider concept (*conceptus latior*) than the predicate. Let the predicate always be $\bigcirc$, the subject $\square$, then is a particular judgment; for some things belonging under *a* are *b*, some not *b*—that follows from reason. But suppose

then, at least if it is smaller, all *a* can be contained under *b*, but not if it is larger; it is therefore only contingently particular.

§ 22. Quality of Judgments: Affirmative, Negative, Infinite

As to quality, judgments are either *affirmative, negative,* or *infinite.* In the *affirmative* judgment, the subject is thought under the sphere of the predicate; in the *negative* it is posited *outside* the sphere of the latter; and in the *infinite* it is posited in the sphere of a concept which lies outside the sphere of another.

Note 1. The infinite judgment does not merely indicate that a subject is not contained under the sphere of the predicate but that it lies outside its sphere somewhere in the infinite sphere; this judgment consequently presents the sphere of the predicate *as bounded.*

Everything possible is either *A* or *non-A.* To say: Something is *non-A,* e.g. *The human soul is non-mortal, Some men are non-scholars,* and the like is an infinite judgment. For beyond the finite sphere of *A* this judgment does not determine under which *concept* the object belongs, but solely that it belongs in the sphere outside *A,* which is actually no sphere at all but only the *bordering of a sphere on the infinite,* or *limitation itself.* Although this exclusion is a negation, the act by which a concept is bounded is a positive act. Limits are therefore positive concepts of bounded objects.

Note 2. According to the principle of the excluded middle (*exclusi tertii*), the sphere of a concept, relative to another, is either exclusive or inclusive. Since logic has to do only with the form of judgment, not with concepts as to their content, the distinction between infinite judgments and negative judgments does not belong to this science.[21]

Note 3. In negative judgments the negation always affects the copula; in infinite judgments, not the copula but the predicate is affected by the negation, which can best be expressed in *Latin.*

§ 23. Relation of Judgments: Categorical, Hypothetical, Disjunctive

As to relation, judgments are either *categorical, hypothetical,* or *disjunctive.* Namely, the given presentations in judgments are subordinated, one to another, for the sake of the unity of consciousness, either as *predicate* to the *subject,*[22] or as *consequence* to the *ground,* or as *member of the division to the divided concept.* By the first relation are determined *categorical,* by the second, *hypothetical,* and by the third, *disjunctive* judgments.[23]

§ 24. Categorical Judgments

In *categorical* judgments, subject and predicate make up their

21. For an elaboration see B 97 f.
22. In the sense of § 21, Note 5 above. Cf. Akad. XVI, 3053, 3060: "The judgment is the presentation of the unity of given concepts, so far as one is subordinated to the other: (1) as under the sphere of the other; (2) as consequence to the ground; (3) as member of the division to the divided concept."
23. Cf. below, § 60.

matter; the form through which the relation (of agreement or disagreement) between subject and predicate is determined and expressed is called *copula*.

Note. Categorical judgments indeed make up the matter of the other judgments; but for that reason one must not believe, as some logicians do, that both hypothetical and disjunctive judgments are nothing but different clothings of categorical judgments and therefore may be altogether reduced to the latter. All three kinds of judgments rest on essentially different logical functions of the understanding and must therefore be pondered according to their specific differences.

§ 25. Hypothetical Judgments

The matter of *hypothetical* judgments consists of two judgments that are connected with each other as ground and consequent. The first of these judgments, containing the ground, is the *antecedent proposition* (*antecedens, prius*); the second, which is related as the consequent to it, the *consequent proposition* (*consequens, posterius*); and the presentation of this kind of connection of the two judgments with each other in behalf of the unity of consciousness is called *consequence,* which makes up the *form* of hypothetical judgments.

Note 1. What the copula is to categorical judgments, the consequence is to the hypothetical—their form.

Note 2. Some believe that it is easy to convert a hypothetical proposition into a categorical one. However, it cannot be done, because the two are quite different as to their nature. In categorical judgments nothing is problematic but everything is assertoric; in hypothetical, however, only the consequent is assertoric. In the latter, I may therefore connect two false judgments with each other; for what matters here is only the correctness of the connection—the *form of the consequence* on which rests the logical truth of these judgments. There is an essential difference between the two sentences: *All bodies are divisible,* and *If all bodies are composite then they are divisible.* In the former sentence I assert the matter straightway; in the latter, only under a problematically expressed condition.

§ 26. Kinds of Connection in Hypothetical Judgments: modus ponens and modus tollens

The form of connection in hypothetical judgments is twofold: the *positing* (*modus ponens*) or the *deposing* (*modus tollens*) form.

1) If the ground (*antecedens*) is true, the consequent (*consequens*) determined by it is also true—*modus ponens*.

2) If the consequent (*consequens*) is false, the ground (*antecedens*) is also false—*modus tollens*.

§ 27. Disjunctive Judgments

A judgment is *disjunctive* if the parts of the sphere of a given concept determine one another in the whole of the divided cognition or as complements within a whole.[24]

§ 28. Matter and Form of Disjunctive Judgments

The several given judgments of which the disjunctive judgment is composed make up its *matter* and are called the *members of the disjunction or opposition*. In the *disjunction* itself, that is, in the determination of the relation of the various judgments as mutually exclusive and complementary members of the whole sphere of the divided cognition, consists the *form* of these judgments.

Note. All disjunctive judgments therefore present various judgments *as in the community* of one sphere and bring about each judgment only by a limitation of the other [judgments] in respect of the whole sphere; they thus determine the relation of each judgment to the whole sphere and thereby at the same time the relation which these various separate members (*membra disjuncta*) have to one another. Thus one member here determines any other only so far as they altogether share in a community as parts of a whole

24. See B 99

sphere of cognition, *outside which nothing can be thought in a definite relation.*

§ 29. Peculiar Character of Disjunctive Judgments

The peculiar character of disjunctive judgments, which determines their specific difference from other judgments as to the moment[25] of relation, consists in this: The members of the disjunction are altogether problematic judgments of which nothing else is thought but that they, taken together, are equal to the sphere of the whole as parts of the sphere of a cognition, each being the complement of the other (*complementum ad totum*). And from this follows: In one of these problematic judgments must be contained the truth or—which is the same—one of them must be *assertorically* valid, because outside of these judgments the sphere of cognition under the given conditions comprises nothing else, and one is opposed to the other; consequently, there can be true *neither* anything else *outside* them, *nor* more than one among them.

Note. In a categorical judgment, the thing whose presentation is considered as part of the sphere of another subordinated presentation is considered as contained under the higher concept; hence here, in the subordination of the spheres, the part of the part is compared with the whole. But in disjunctive judgments I go from the whole to all parts taken together. What is contained under the sphere of a concept is also contained under a part of that sphere. Accordingly, the sphere must first be divided. When, for example, I pronounce the disjunctive judgment: *A scholar is either a historian or a rationalist,* I determine that these concepts, as to sphere, are parts of the sphere of scholar, but not at all parts of each other, and that all taken together are complete.

The following schema of comparing categorical with disjunctive judgments may illustrate that in disjunctive judgments the sphere of the divided concept is not considered as contained in the sphere of the divisions, but that what is con-

25. See B 95: The function of thinking in the form of judgments "can be brought under four titles, each of which contains three moments under it."

tained under the divided concept is regarded as contained under one of the members of the division.

In categorical judgments, x that is contained under b is also contained under a.

In disjunctive judgments, x that is contained under a is contained either under b or c, etc.

The division in disjunctive judgments thus indicates the coordination not of the parts of the whole concept, but all the parts of its sphere. There I think *many things* through *one concept*; here *one thing through many concepts,* e.g., the definitum through all characteristics of coordination.[26]

§ 30. Modality of Judgments: Problematic, Assertoric, Apodeictic

As to modality, by which moment is determined the relation of the entire judgment to the faculty of cognition, judgments are either *problematic, assertoric,* or *apodeictic.* Problematic

---

26. E.g. the world in general through the characteristics of "either by blind chance, or . . . inner necessity, or . . . an external cause," B 99. Also B 112. Cf. B 600.

judgments are accompanied with the consciousness of the mere possibility, assertoric judgments with the consciousness of the actuality, apodeictic judgments, lastly, with the consciousness of the necessity of judging.

Note 1. This moment of modality indicates the manner in which something is asserted or negated in judgment: Whether one does not make out anything about the truth or untruth of a judgment, as in the problematic judgment, *The soul of man may be immortal;* or whether one determines something about its truth or untruth, as in the assertoric judgment, *The human soul is immortal;* or lastly, whether one expresses the truth of a judgment even with the dignity of necessity, as in the apodeictic judgment, *The soul of man must be immortal.* This determination of the merely possible, actual, or necessary truth, thus, concerns only *the judgment itself,* not at all *the matter* that is judged.

Note 2. In problematic judgments, which one may also explain as judgments whose matter is given with the possible relation between predicate and subject, the subject must always have a smaller sphere than the predicate.[27]

---

27. Kant seems to mean that in problematic judgments the belonging of the subject to the predicate is not certain, or that the subject may belong to any number of predicates. A problem consists precisely in the fact that *no* concept is given to a set of items, or that an aggregate is not a class, that is, defined by a certain predicate. (See below, § 95, and B 201, 212, 441, 673, 862.) This means that the subject must be a member of the class sought or a class included in the class sought, e.g. *Horses on Jupiter may be tailless animals* (as against *Tailless animals may be horses on Jupiter*). As judgments with optional predicates, problematic judgments are to be classed with aesthetic judgments; see *Critique of Judgment,* Introduction, VII, §§ 4, 40, 49, and below, § 81. It may be said that in this sense, a problematic judgment has an optional predicate only and that its predicate is really a variable rather than a constant. Note that problematic judgments cannot be either analytic or synthetic *a priori.* One can say neither that *Bachelors may be unmarried men,* nor that *7 + 5 may be 12.* For Kant, a problem is seen as practical (see below, § 38), though he also deals with theoretical problems, as states of affairs lacking (synthetic) concepts, for example, see *Metaphysical Foundations of Natural Science,* Preface, Akad. IV, 470 f (trans. James Ellington, Indianapolis: Bobbs-Merrill, 1970).

Note 3. On the difference between problematic and assertoric judgments rests the true difference between judgments
and *propositions*,[28] which otherwise one is used to placing
falsely in the mere expression by words—without which one
could not judge anyway. In a judgment the relation of different presentations to the unity of consciousness is thought as
merely problematic, in a proposition, however, as assertoric.
A problematic proposition is a *contradictio in adjecto*. Before
I have a proposition, I must indeed first judge, and I judge of
much that I do not make out; the latter, however, I do have
to do as soon as I determine a judgment *as a proposition*. It
is, by the way, advisable first to judge problematically, before
one adopts the judgment as assertoric, in order to test it.
Moreover, it is not always necessary for our purpose to have
assertoric judgments.

§ 31. Exponible Judgments

Judgments in which at the same time an affirmation and a
negation are contained—but in a covert way, so that the affirmation takes place distinctly, the negation, however, covertly—are
exponible propositions.

Note. In the exponible judgment, e.g., *Few men are
learned,* lies 1) though covertly, the negative judgment: *Many
men are not learned,* and 2) the affirmative: *Some men are
learned*. Since the nature of exponible propositions depends
solely on conditions of language, under which one can express with brevity two judgments at once, the remark that in
our language there may be judgments that require to be ex-
posed, belongs not to logic but to grammar.

§ 32. Theoretical and Practical Propositions

Theoretical propositions are those which refer to the object
and determine what appertains to it or does not appertain to it;
practical propositions, however, are those which state the action
that is the necessary condition for an object to become possible.

Note. Logic has to treat of practical propositions only in so

28. See B 100 f.

far as their *form* is opposed to *theoretical* propositions. Practical propositions *as to content,* and thus as distinguished from speculative ones,[29] belong to morality.

§ 33. Indemonstrable and Demonstrable Propositions

Demonstrable propositions are those which are capable of proof; those not capable of proof are called *indemonstrable.*

Immediately certain judgments are indemonstrable and thus are to be regarded as elementary propositions.[30]

§ 34. Fundamental Propositions

Immediately certain judgments *a priori* may be called fundamental propositions, so far as other judgments can be proved from them, while they themselves cannot be subordinated to any other judgment. For that reason they are also called *principles* (beginnings).

§ 35. Intuitive and Discursive Fundamental Propositions: Axioms and Akroamata

Fundamental propositions are either *intuitive* or *discursive.* The former can be exhibited in *intuition* and are called axioms (*axiomata*); the latter can only be expressed by concepts and may be called *akroamata.*[31]

§ 36. Analytic and Synthetic Propositions

Analytic propositions one calls those propositions whose certainty rests on *identity* of concepts (of the predicate with the notion of the subject). Propositions whose truth is not grounded on identity of concepts must be called *synthetic.*

Note 1. *To every x to which appertains the concept of body*

---

29. Cf. Appendix of the Introduction, above, p. 94. Akad. XVI, 3118, which Jäsche apparently used, runs: "Practical propositions as to form: of these treats logic and distinguishes them from what is theoretical.

"Practical propositions as to content: of these treats morality and distinguishes them from what is speculative."

30. *Elementar-Sätze.* Cf. § 34, "fundamental propositions": *Grundsätze.* Cf. *Prolegomena* § 35.

31. See B 761. Also above, p. 33, n. 35, and Translators' Introduction, n. 140.

(a + b) *appertains also* extension (b)—is an example of an *analytic* proposition.

To every x *to which appertains the concept of body* (a + b) *appertains also attraction* (c)—is an example of a *synthetic* proposition. Synthetic propositions augment cognition *materialiter, analytic* propositions merely *formaliter*. The former contain *determinations*, the latter only *logical predicates*.

Note 2. Analytic principles are not axioms, for they are *discursive*. And synthetic principles are axioms only if they are *intuitive*.[32]

§ 37. Tautological Propositions

The identity of concepts in analytic judgments can be either *explicit* (*explicita*) or *non-explicit* (*implicita*). In the former case analytic propositions are *tautological*.

Note 1. Tautological propositions are *virtualiter* empty or *void of consequences,* for they are of no avail or use. Such is, for example, the tautological proposition, *Man is man.* For if I know nothing else of man than that he is man, I know nothing else of him at all.

Implicitly identical propositions, on the contrary, are not void of consequences or fruitless, for they clarify the predicate which lay undeveloped (*implicite*) in the concept of the subject through *development* (*explicatio*).

Note 2. Propositions void of consequences must be distinguished from propositions *void of sense,* which are void of understanding for the reason that they concern the determination of so-called *hidden properties* (*qualitates occultae*).[33]

§ 38. Postulate and Problem

A *postulate* is a practical, immediately certain proposition or a fundamental proposition which determines a possible action of which it is presupposed that the manner of executing it is immediately certain.

Problems (*problemata*) are demonstrable propositions in

---

32. Above, Sec. IX, no. 3, *Knowledge,* pp. 78 ff.
33. This was a technical term of alchemy.

need of an instruction, or such as express an action whose manner of execution is not immediately certain.

Note 1. There can also be *theoretical* postulates for the purpose of practical reason. These are theoretical hypotheses, necessary in reason's practical respect, such as God's existence, freedom, and another world.

Note 2. To a problem belongs (1) the *question,* which contains what shall be accomplished, (2) the *resolution,* containing the manner in which may be carried out what is to be accomplished, and (3) the *demonstration* that when I shall have proceeded that way, the required result will take place.

§ 39. Theorems, Corollaries, Lemmata, and Scholia

Theorems are theoretical propositions capable and in need of proof. *Corollaries* are immediate consequences from one of the preceding propositions. *Lemmata* are called propositions which are not immanent in the science that presupposes them as proven, but borrowed from other sciences. *Scholia,* lastly, are *explanatory propositions,* which do not belong as members to the whole of the system.

Note. Essential and general moments of every theorem are *thesis* and *demonstration.* The difference between theorems and corollaries, by the way, may also be stated by saying that the *former* are immediately concluded, the *latter,* however, drawn from immediately certain propositions through a series of consequents.

§ 40. Perceptional and Experiential Judgments

A *perceptional judgment* is merely subjective; an objective judgment from perceptions is an *experiential judgment.*

Note. A judgment from mere perceptions is not possible except by stating my presentation *as a perception:* I who perceive a tower, perceive on it red color. I can, however, not say: *It is red.* For this would not merely be an empirical but also an *experiential judgment,* i.e. an empirical judgment by which I gain a concept of the object. For example, *When touching the stone I sense warmth* is a perceptional judgment; *The stone is warm,* however, an experiential judgment.

To the latter belongs that I do not reckon to the object what
is merely in me, the subject; for an experiential judgment is
the perception from which springs a concept of the object,
e.g. whether lighted points move in the *moon,* in the *air,* or
in my *eye.*[34]

Third Section: Of Inferences[35]

§ 41. Conclusion in General
By *concluding* is to be understood that function of thought in
which one judgment is deduced from another. A conclusion in
general is thus the deduction of one judgment from another.

§ 42. Immediate and Mediate Conclusions
All conclusions are either *immediate* or *mediate.* An *immediate conclusion* (*consequentia immediata*) is the deduction of
one judgment from another without an intermediate judgment
(*judicium intermedium*). A conclusion is *mediate* if beside the
concept contained in a judgment one needs others to deduce a
cognition from it.

§ 43. Conclusions of the Understanding, Conclusions of Reason, and Conclusions of Judgment
The immediate conclusions are also called *conclusions of the
understanding;* all *mediate conclusions,* however, are either
conclusions of *reason* or conclusions of *judgment.* We treat
here first of immediate conclusions or conclusions of the understanding.[36]

34. See B 142; *Prolegomena,* § 20, note.
35. Cf. above, p. 6, n. 1.
36. Cf. *The Mistaken Subtlety of the Four Syllogistic Figures,* 1762 (*Die
falsche Spitzfindigkeil der vier syllogistischen Figuren,* Akad. II, 45 ff.)

I. Conclusions of the Understanding

§ 44. Peculiar Nature of Conclusions of the Understanding

The essential character of all immediate conclusions and the principle of their possibility consists solely in a change of the *mere form* of judgments, while their *matter,* subject and predicate, remains *the same, unchanged.*

Note 1. Because in immediate conclusions only the form of judgment is changed and by no means the matter, they distinguish themselves essentially from all mediate conclusions in which judgments differ also *as to matter,* in that a new concept as mediating judgment, or as middle concept (*terminus medius*), must supervene in order to deduce one judgment from another. When I conclude, for example, *All men are mortal, therefore also Cajus is mortal,* this is no immediate conclusion. For here, for the consequence, I still need the mediating judgment: *Cajus is a man;* through this new concept, however, the matter of the judgment is changed.

Note 2. One can also make a *judicium intermedium* in conclusions of the understanding, but then this mediating judgment is merely tautological, e.g. in the immediate conclusion *All men are mortal; some men are men; therefore some men are mortal,* the middle concept is a tautological proposition.

§ 45. Modi of the Conclusions of the Understanding

The conclusions of the understanding go through all the classes of logical functions of judging and are consequently determined, in their main kinds, by the moments of quantity, quality, relation, and modality. On this rests the following division of these conclusions.

§ 46. 1. Conclusions of the Understanding (with Reference to the Quantity of Judgment) per judicia subalternata

In the conclusions of the understanding per *judicia subalternata* the two judgments differ as to quantity, and the special judgment is deduced from the universal according to the fundamental proposition: *From the universal the conclusion is valid to the particular* (*ab universali ad particulare valet consequentia*).

Note. A *judicium* is called *subalternatum* so far as it is contained under another, e.g. *particular* judgments under *universal.*

§ 47. 2. Conclusions of the Understanding (with Reference to the Quality of Judgments) per judicia opposita

In conclusions of the understanding of this kind the change concerns the *quality* of judgments, that is, considered in reference to opposition. Since this opposition now can be threefold, the following special division of immediate conclusions results: through judgments that are *contradictorily opposed;* through *contrary* judgments; and through *subcontrary* judgments.

Note. Conclusions through *equivalent* judgments (*judicia aequipollentia*) cannot be called conclusions, for here no consequence takes place; they are to be regarded rather as mere substitution of words signifying one and the same concept where the judgments remain unchanged also as to form. For example, *Not all men are virtuous,* and *Some men are virtuous.* Both judgments tell the same.

§ 48. a. Conclusions of the Understanding per judicia contradictorie opposita

In conclusions of the understanding through judgments that are contradictorily opposed and as such make up the genuine and pure opposition, the truth of the one of the contradictorily opposed judgments is deduced from the falsity of the other and *vice versa.* For the genuine opposing that here takes place contains neither more nor less than what belongs to opposition. According to the *principle of the excluded middle* not both contradictory judgments can therefore be true; as little, however, can they both be false. If therefore one is true, the other is false, and *vice versa.*

§ 49. b. Conclusions of the Understanding per judicia contrarie opposita

Contrary or conflicting judgments (*judicia contrarie opposita*) are judgments of which one is universally affirmative, the other universally negative. Since one of them states more than the other and since in the superfluous that it states beside the mere negation of the other may lie the falsity, they cannot both be true, but they can both be false. In regard to these judgments therefore only the conclusion is valid *from the truth of the one to the falsity of the other,* but not *vice versa.*

§ 50. c. Conclusions of the Understanding per judicia subcontrarie opposita

Subcontrary judgments are those of which the one particularly (*particulariter*) affirms or negates what the other particularly negates or affirms.

Since they can both be true but not both be false, only the following conclusion is valid in respect of them: *If one of these propositions is false, the other is true, but not vice versa.*

Note. In subcontrary judgments no pure, strict opposition takes place, for in the one of them we are not negating or affirming of the *same* objects what was affirmed or negated in the other. For example, in the conclusion *Some men are learned, therefore some men are not learned,* there is not asserted, in the first judgment, of the *same* men what is negated in the second.

§ 51. 3. Conclusions of the Understanding (in Regard to the Relation of Judgments) per judicia conversa s. per conversionem

The immediate conclusions through conversion concern the relation of judgments and consist in the transposition of the subjects and predicates in the two judgments, so that the subject of the one is made the predicate of the other and *vice versa.*

§ 52. Pure and Changed Conversion

In conversion, the quantity of judgment is either being changed or it remains unchanged. In the former case, the converted (*conversum*) differs from the converting (*convertente*) as to quantity, and the conversion is called *changed* (*conversio per accidens*); in the latter case the conversion is called *pure* (*conversio simpliciter talis*).

§ 53. General Rules of Conversion

In respect to conclusions of the understanding through conversion the following rules are valid:

1) Universally affirmative judgments can be converted only *per accidens,* for the predicate in these judgments is a wider concept and thus only some of it is contained in the subject.

2) All universally negative judgments can be converted *simpliciter,* for here the subject is lifted out of the sphere of the predicate. Likewise, lastly,

3) all particular-affirmative propositions can be converted *simpliciter,* for in these judgments part of the sphere of the subject is subsumed under the predicate, therefore part of the sphere of the predicate can also be subsumed under the subject.

Note 1. In universally affirmative judgments the subject is considered as a *contentum* of the predicate, since it is contained under its sphere. I am therefore only permitted to conclude: *All men are mortal, thus some of those contained under the concept "mortals" are men.* The cause for the fact that universally negative judgments may be converted *simpliciter* is that two concepts contradicting each other universally contradict each other *to the same extent.*

Note 2. Some universally affirmative judgments may be converted *simpliciter.* But the reason thereof lies not in their form but in the special quality of their matter, as, for example, in the two judgments *Everything unchangeable is necessary,* and *Everything necessary is unchangeable.*

§ 54. 4. Conclusions of the Understanding (with Reference to the Modality of Judgments) per judicia contraposita

The immediate manner of concluding through contraposition consists in that transposition (*metathesis*) of judgments in which the quantity remains the same, the *quality,* however, is changed.[37] They concern only the modality of judgments, in changing an assertoric into an apodeictic judgment.[38]

---

37. E.g., All *S* are *P* ≡ All non-*P* are non-*S*.
38. See above § 30 and below §§ 55 and 60, Note 1.

§ 55. General Rule of Contraposition

In respect to contraposition the general rule holds: *All universally affirmative judgments may be contraposited simpliciter.* For if the predicate as that which contains the subject under it, hence the entire sphere, is negated, then also a part of it must be negated, i.e. the subject.

Note 1. The metathesis of judgments by conversion and that by contraposition thus are opposed in so far as the former changes merely quantity, the latter merely quality.

Note 2. The said kinds of immediate conclusions refer to *categorical* judgments only.

II. Conclusions of Reason[39]

§ 56. Syllogism in General

A syllogism is the cognition of the necessity of a proposition by subsumption of its condition under a given general rule.

§ 57. General Principle of All Syllogisms

The general principle on which rests the validity of all conclusions through reason, may be expressed in the following formula:

What stands under the condition of a rule stands also under the rule itself.

Note. The syllogism premises [presupposes] a *general rule* and a *subsumption* under its *condition*. One thereby cognizes the conclusion a priori not by itself but as contained in the general and as necessary under a certain condition. The fact that everything stands under the general and may be determined by general rules, is the very principle of *rationality* or of *necessity* (*principium rationalitatis s. necessitatis*).

§ 58. Essential Components of the Syllogism

The following three essential pieces[40] belong to every syllogism:

---

39. In the following paragraphs we are translating *Vernunftschluss*, "conclusion of reason," or simply *Schluss*, always by "syllogism."

40. Against such piecemeal presentation of the syllogism Kant himself protests in *The Mistaken Subtlety of the Four Syllogistic Figures.*

1) a general rule, which is called *major proposition* (*propositio major*);

2) the proposition that subsumes a cognition under the condition of the general rule and is called minor proposition (*propositio minor*); and lastly,

3) the proposition that affirms or negates the predicate of the rule as valid of the subsumed cognition, the *concluding proposition* (*conclusio*).

The first two propositions in their conjunction with each other are called *antecedent propositions* or *premises*.

Note. A rule is an assertion under a general condition.[41] The relation of the condition to the assertion, how, namely, the latter stands under the former, is the *exponent* of the rule.

The cognition that the condition (somewhere) takes place is the *subsumption*.

The conjunction of what has been subsumed under the condition with the assertion of the rule is the *conclusion*.

§ 59. Matter and Form of Syllogisms

In the antecedent propositions or premises consists the *matter,* and in the conclusion, so far as it contains the consequence, the *form* of syllogisms.

Note 1. Thus, first the truth of the premises must be examined in every syllogism, and then the correctness of the consequence. In rejecting a syllogism, one must never reject the conclusion first but always either the premises or the consequence first.

Note 2. In every syllogism the conclusion is given at once when the premises and the consequence are given.

§ 60. Division of Syllogisms (as to Relation) into Categorical, Hypothetical, and Disjunctive

All rules (judgments) contain objective unity of consciousness of the manifold of cognition, hence a condition under which a cognition belongs with another to one consciousness. Now, only three conditions of this unity can be thought,

41. See A 105, 113, B 387.

namely: as subject of the inherence of characteristics; or as ground of the dependence of a cognition on another; or, lastly, as connection of the parts in a whole (logical division).[42] Consequently there can be only that many kinds of general rules (*propositiones majores*) through which the consequence of a judgment from another is mediated.

On this is founded the division of all syllogisms into categorical, hypothetical, and disjunctive.

Note 1. Syllogisms can be divided neither as to *quantity*, for every *major* is a rule, thus something general; nor in respect of *quality*, for it is equally valid whether the conclusion is affirmative or negative; nor, finally, in regard to *modality*, for the conclusion is always accompanied by the consciousness of necessity and consequently has the dignity of an apodeictic proposition. It is solely *relation* which thus remains as the only possible ground of dividing syllogisms.

Note 2. Many logicians take only the categorical syllogisms for *ordinary*, the others, however, for *extra-ordinary* syllogisms. Yet, this is groundless and false. For these three kinds are all products of equally correct functions of reason that are in essence equally different from one another.[43]

§ 61. Peculiar Difference Between Categorical, Hypothetical, and Disjunctive Syllogisms

The difference among the three kinds of syllogism lies in the *major*. In *categorical* syllogisms the *major* is a *categorical*, in *hypothetical* it is a hypothetical or problematical, in *disjunctive*, a disjunctive proposition.

§ 62. Categorical Syllogisms

In every categorical syllogism there are three main concepts (*termini*), namely:

1) the predicate in the conclusion, which concept is called the *major term* (*terminus major*) because it has a sphere larger than the subject;

---

42. Cf. above, § 23.
43. This is the thesis of *The Mistaken Subtlety of the Four Syllogistic Figures.*

2) the subject (in the conclusion), whose concept is called the *minor term* (*terminus minor*); and

3) a mediating characteristic (*nota intermedia*) which is called *middle term* (*terminus medius*) because a cognition is subsumed through it under the condition of the rule.

Note. This difference in the said *termini* takes place only in categorical syllogisms, because these alone conclude through a *terminum medium;* the others conclude through the subsumption of a proposition that is presented in the *major* problematically and in the *minor* assertorically.

§ 63. Principle of Categorical Syllogisms

The principle on which the possibility and validity of all categorical syllogisms rests is this:

What appertains to the characteristic of a thing, that appertains also to the thing itself; and what contradicts the characteristic of a thing, that contradicts also the thing itself (nota notae est nota rei ipsius; repugnans notae, repugnat rei ipsi).

Note. From the principle just set up the so-called *dictum de omni et nullo* is readily deduced, and it can therefore not pass for the highest principle, either of syllogisms in general or of categorical syllogisms in particular.

The concepts of *genera* and *species,* namely, are general characteristics of all things standing under these concepts. Accordingly, here the rule is valid: *What appertains to or contradicts the genus or species, appertains to or contradicts also the objects contained under that genus or species.* And it is this very rule which is called the *dictum de omni et nullo.*

§ 64. Rules for Categorical Syllogisms

From the nature and the principle of categorical syllogisms derive the following rules:

1) In every categorical syllogism there can be no more and no less than three main concepts (*termini*), for I shall join here two concepts (subject and predicate) through a mediating characteristic.

2) The antecedent propositions or premises must not be all negative (*ex puris negativis nihil sequitur*), for the subsumption in the minor must be affirmative, as it states that a cognition stands under the condition of the rule.

3) The premises must not be all *particular* propositions (ex *puris particularibus nihil sequitur*), for then there would be no rule, that is, no general proposition from which a particular cognition could be concluded.

4) *The conclusion follows always the weaker part of the syllogism,* that is, the negative or particular proposition in the premises, which is called the weaker part of the categorical syllogism (*conclusio sequitur partem debiliorem*). Therefore,

5) if one of the antecedent propositions is a negative proposition, the conclusion must also be negative. And

6) if an antecedent proposition is a particular proposition, the conclusion must also be particular.

7) In all categorical syllogisms the *major* must be a universal, the *minor,* however, an affirmative proposition, and from this follows, finally, that

8) the conclusion in regard to *quality* conforms with the *major;* in regard to *quantity,* however, with the *minor.*

Note. That the conclusion always conforms to the negative and to the particular proposition, is a matter of ready insight. If I make the minor particular only and say: Something is contained under the rule, I can, in the conclusion, also only say that the predicate of the rule appertains to something, because I have subsumed *not more than this* under the rule. And if I have a negative proposition for a rule (*major*), I must make the conclusion also negative. For if the major says: Of everything standing under the condition of the rule this or that predicate must be negated, then the conclusion must also negate the predicate of that (subject) which has been subsumed under the condition of the rule.

§ 65. Pure and Mixed Categorical Syllogisms

A categorical syllogism is pure if no immediate conclusion is mixed into it, nor the lawful order of the premises changed; otherwise it is called an impure or mixed syllogism (*ratiocinium impurum* or *hybridum*).

§ 66. Mixed Syllogisms through Conversion of Propositions/Figures

Among mixed syllogisms are to be reckoned those which originate by conversion of propositions and in which thus the position[44] of these propositions is not the lawful one. This takes place in the three latter so-called figures of the categorical syllogism.

§ 67. Four Figures of Syllogisms

By figures is to be understood those four kinds of syllogisms whose difference is determined by the special position of the premises and their terms.

§ 68. Determining Ground of Their Difference By Different Position of the Middle Term

The middle term, namely, whose position is what actually counts here, can occupy either (1) in the major, the place of the subject, and in the minor, the place of the predicate; or (2) in both premises, the place of the predicate; or (3) in both, the place of the subject; or, lastly, (4) in the major, the place of the predicate, and in the minor, the place of the subject. By these four cases the differences of the four figures are determined. Let S denote the subject of the conclusion, P its predicate, and M the *terminum medium,* then the schema for the said four figures may be exhibited in the following table:

$M \quad P$	$P \quad M$	$M \quad P$	$P \quad M$
$\underline{S \quad M}$	$\underline{S \quad M}$	$\underline{M \quad S}$	$\underline{M \quad S}$
$\underline{S \quad P}$	$\underline{S \quad P}$	$\underline{S \quad P}$	$\underline{S \quad P}$

44. *Stellung,* position, in this context applies to both propositions considered as units and to their terms. Similarly, the word *metathesis* in these paragraphs is also used in reference to both propositions considered as units and to their terms. Cf. §§ 54, 55, 69, 73.

§ 69. Rule of the First Figure as the Only Lawful One

The rule of the *first* figure is that the major is a *universal,* the *minor* an affirmative proposition. And since this must be the general rule of all categorical syllogisms in general, it follows from this that the first figure is the only lawful one which underlies all others and to which all others, so far as they are to have validity, must be reduced by conversion of the premises (*metathesin praemissorum*).

Note. The first figure may have a conclusion of any quantity and quality. In the other figures there are only conclusions of a certain kind; some of their *modi* are here excluded. This already indicates that these figures are not perfect but have certain restrictions that prevent the conclusion from taking place in all *modi* as in the first figure.

§ 70. Condition of Reducing the Three Last Figures to the First

The condition of the validity of the three last figures under which a correct *modus* of concluding in each of them is possible amounts to this, that the *middle term,* in these propositions, assume a place from which, through immediate conclusions (*consequentias immediates*), can arise their place according to the rules of the first figure. From this the following rules result for the last three figures.

§ 71. Rule of the Second Figure

In the second figure the *minor* is regular, thus the *major* must be *converted,* and, moreover, in such a way that it remains universal. This is possible only if it is *universally negative;* if it is affirmative, it must be contraposited. In both cases, the conclusion becomes negative (*sequitur partem debiliorem*).

Note. The rule of the second figure is: What is contradicted by the characteristic of a thing, that contradicts the matter itself. Here I must first convert and say: What is contradicted by a characteristic, that contradicts this characteristic; or I must convert the conclusion: What is contradicted by the characteristic of a thing, that is contradicted by the matter itself; consequently it contradicts the matter.

§ 72. Rule of the Third Figure

In the third figure the *major* is regular, hence the *minor* must be converted, but in such a way that an affirmative proposition arises. This, however, is possible only if the affirmative proposition is a *particular* one; consequently the conclusion is *particular*.

Note. The rule of the third figure is: What appertains to or contradicts a characteristic, that appertains to or contradicts some of those which have this characteristic. Here I must first say: It appertains to or contradicts all those which have this characteristic.

§ 73. Rule of the Fourth Figure

If in the fourth figure the *major* is universally negative, it can be converted pure (*simpliciter*); likewise the minor as particular; thus the conclusion is negative. If, however, the *major* is universally affirmative, it can either be converted *per accidens* only or contraposited; thus the conclusion is either particular or negative. If the conclusion shall not be converted (*P S* changed into *S P*), a transposition of the premises (*metathesis praemissorum*) or a conversion of both (*conversio*) must take place.

Note. In the fourth figure it is concluded: The *predicate* is connected with the *medium terminum,* the *medius terminus* with the *subject* (of the conclusion), hence the *subject* with the *predicate;* which, however, does not follow at all, but at the utmost, its converse. To make this possible, the *major* must be made the *minor* and *vice versa* and the conclusion must be converted, because in the first transformation *terminus minor* is changed into *majorem*.

§ 74. General Results Concerning the Three Latter Figures

From the rules given for the last three figures it becomes clear that

1) in none of them there is a universally affirmative conclusion, but the conclusion is always either negative or particular;

2) in each there is mixed in an *immediate conclusion* (*consequ. immediata*) which is not expressly designated but

must yet be tacitly understood to be implied; hence, that on this account

    3) all three latter *modi* of concluding must be called not pure but impure syllogisms (*ratiocinia hybrida*), since every pure syllogism can have no more than three main propositions (*termini*).

§ 75. 2. Hypothetical Syllogisms[45]

    A hypothetical conclusion is one that has as its *major* a hypothetical proposition. It consists therefore of two propositions, (1) an *antecedent* and (2) a *consequent;* and the conclusion takes place either according to *modus ponens* or *modus tollens.*

    Note 1. Hypothetical syllogisms have no *medium terminum,* but the consequence of one proposition out of another is only indicated in them. In their *major* is expressed the consequence of two propositions out of one another, of which the first is a premise, the second a conclusion. The *minor* is a commutation of the problematic condition into a categorical proposition.

    Note 2. It can be seen from the fact that the hypothetical syllogism consists of two propositions only, without having a middle term, that it actually is no syllogism at all but rather an immediate conclusion to be proved from an antecedent proposition and a consequent according to matter or form (*consequentia immediata demonstrabilis ex antecedente et consequente vel quoad materiam vel quoad formam*).

    Every syllogism shall be a proof. But the hypothetical syllogism carries only the *ground* of proof with it. It follows from this also that it cannot be a syllogism.

---

45. By this name, *Hypothetische Vernunftschlüsse,* "hypothetical conclusions of reason" or "syllogisms," such conclusions were commonly known in Meier's textbook. Jäsche retained this name in the heading of this paragraph and its two notes, which are negative. "Hypothetical syllogisms" are shown not to be real syllogisms or conclusions of reason. Reich (*Die Vollständigkeit der Kantischen Urteilstafel*) objects to this kind of presentation, even though it is the same as that of the three last figures of the syllogism which also, according to Kant, are no real syllogisms.

§ 76. Principle of Hypothetical Syllogisms

The principle of hypothetical conclusions is that of *sufficient reason: A ratione ad rationatum, a negatione rationati ad negationem rationis valet consequentia.*

§ 77. 3. Disjunctive Syllogisms

In disjunctive syllogisms the *major* is a disjunctive proposition and as such must have members of the division or disjunction.

Here the conclusion goes either (1) from the truth of one member of the disjunction to the falsity of the others, or (2) from the falsity of all members bar one to the truth of this one. The former takes place through *modus ponens* (or *ponendo tollens*), the latter through *modus tollens* (*tollendo ponens*).

Note 1. All members of the disjunction taken together bar one make up the contradictory of that one. Thus a dichotomy takes place according to which, if either is true, the other must be false and *vice versa.*

Note 2. All disjunctive syllogisms of more than two members of the disjunction are thus actually polysyllogistic. For all true disjunction can only be *bimembris,* and the logical division is also *bimembris;* but the *membra subdividentia* are, for the sake of brevity, counted as *membra dividentia.*[46]

§ 78. Principle of Disjunctive Syllogisms

The principle of disjunctive syllogisms is the *principle of the excluded middle: A contradictorie oppositorum negatione unius ad affirmationem alterius; a positione unius ad negationem alterius, valet consequentia.*

§ 79. Dilemma

A dilemma is a hypothetical-disjunctive syllogism, or a hypothetical conclusion, whose *consequens* is a disjunctive judgment. The hypothetical proposition whose *consequens* is disjunctive, is the *major;* the *minor* affirms that the *consequens* (*per omnia membra*) is false, and the conclusion affirms that the *antecedens* is false. (*A remotione consequentis ad negationem antecedentis valet consequentia.*)

46. See below, § 110 and above § 28.

Note. The ancients made much of the dilemma and called this conclusion *cornutus*. They knew how to corner an adversary by citing everything to which he could turn, and then refuting everything. They showed him many difficulties in any opinion he might assume. But it is a sophist's trick, not to refute propositions straightway but to show only difficulties; as can be done with many things, indeed most.

If anything in which difficulties appear is at once declared false by us, it is an easy game to reject everything. Certainly it is good to demonstrate the impossibility of the opposite; but something deceptive lies herein, if one takes the *incomprehensibility* of the object for its *impossibility*. The *dilemmata* therefore have much in them that is precarious, even though they conclude correctly. They may be used to defend true propositions, but also to attack true propositions by raising difficulties against them.

§ 80. Formal and Cryptic Syllogisms (Ratiocinia formalia et cryptica)

A formal syllogism is one that contains not only everything required as to matter but is correctly and completely expressed as to form. Opposed to formal are *cryptic* syllogisms, among which may be reckoned all those in which either the premises are transposed, or one of the premises is omitted, or lastly, the middle term alone is connected with the conclusion. A cryptic syllogism of the second kind, in which a premise is not expressed but only thought, is called a *mutilated* syllogism or an *enthymeme*. Those of the third kind are called *contracted* syllogisms.

III. Conclusions of Judgment[47]

§ 81. Determinative and Reflective Judgment

The power of judgment is twofold, either *determinative* or *reflective*. The former proceeds from the *universal* to the *particular,* the latter from the *particular* to the *general*. The latter

---

47. *Urteilskraft,* "power of judgment."

has only *subjective* validity, for the general to which it proceeds is *empirical* generality only—a mere analogon of the *logical*.

§ 82. Conclusions of (Reflective) Judgment

The conclusions of judgment are certain kinds of conclusions to reach general concepts from particular ones. They thus are not functions of *determinative* but of *reflective* judgment; hence they do not determine the *object* but only the *manner of reflecting* on it in order to attain its cognition.

§ 83. Principle of These Conclusions

The principle underlying the conclusions of judgment is this: *It is impossible for many to conform in one without a common ground; rather, what appertains to many in this manner will be necessary out of a common ground.*[48]

Note. Since such a principle is underlying the conclusions of judgment, they can on that account not be taken for *immediate* conclusions.

§ 84. Induction and Analogy—the Two Manners of Conclusions of Judgment

In proceeding from the particular to the general in order to draw general judgments from experience—hence not a *priori* ([but] *empirically*) general judgments—the power of judgment concludes *either* from *many* to *all* things of a kind or from *many* determinations and properties in which things of the same kind agree, to *the others so far as they belong to the same principle.* The first manner of concluding is called conclusion through *induction,* the second, conclusion by *analogy.*

Note 1. *Induction* thus concludes from the particular to the universal (*a particulari ad universale*) according to the principle of *generalization: What appertains to many things of a genus, that appertains also to the remainder. Analogy* concludes from *partial*[49] similarity of two things to *total* similarity according to the principle of *specification:* Things of one genus which we know to agree in much, also agree in the remainder as we know it in some of the genus but do not

48. The conclusion is from many to all.
49. *partikularer.*

perceive it in others. Induction expands the empirically given from the particular to the general in respect of *many objects;* analogy, however, expands the *given properties* of one thing to further properties of *the same thing.* One in many, hence in all: *induction;* much in one (that is also in others), thus also the remainder in the one: *analogy.* Thus, for example, the ground of proof for immortality from the complete development of natural dispositions of every creature, is a conclusion by analogy.

In the conclusion by analogy, however, only *identity of the ground (par ratio)* is required.[50] By analogy our conclusion only goes to rational inhabitants of the moon, not to men. Also one cannot conclude by analogy beyond the *tertium comparationis.*

Note 2. Every syllogism must yield necessity. *Induction* and *analogy* are therefore no syllogisms but only *logical presumptions* or empirical conclusions; and through induction one does get general, but not universal propositions.

Note 3. The said conclusions of judgment are useful and indispensable to the expansion of our experiential cognition. Since, however, they give only empirical certainty, we must avail ourselves of them with care and caution.

§ 85. Simple and Composite Syllogisms

A syllogism is called *simple* if it consists of one, *composite* if it consists of several syllogisms.

---

50. The original, as reprinted by the Akademie edition (without further annotation), obviously is defective, as it has *nicht,* "not," where we have translated "only" for a German *nur.* Without our emendation, the original would express the very opposite of Kant's view and of the logical relations under discussion. The change to "only" is confirmed by Akad. XVI, 3292, which gives the same example of inhabitants of the moon and continues: ". . . thus, in the case of analogy only [*nur*] *identity of the ground, par ratio,* is required." Cf. also *Critique of Judgment,* § 90, no. 2: "The principle of concluding in this manner lies in the identity of the ground. . . . There is *par ratio.* Likewise, I can think the causality of the supreme cause of the world according to the analogy of an understanding, when comparing its purposive products in the world with man's art products, but I cannot conclude these properties through analogy, because here the principle of such kind of conclusion is lacking, namely *paritas rationis. . . .*"

§ 86. Ratiocinatio polysyllogistica

A composite syllogism in which several syllogisms are connected not by mere coordination but by *subordination,* that is as grounds and consequents, is called a chain of syllogisms (*ratiocinatio polysyllogistica*).

§ 87. Prosyllogisms and Episyllogisms

In the series of composite syllogisms one can conclude in a twofold manner, either down from the grounds to the consequents, or up from the consequents to the grounds. The first takes place through *episyllogisms,* the second through *prosyllogisms.*

An episyllogism is that syllogism in the series of syllogisms whose premise becomes the conclusion of a *prosyllogism*—thus of a syllogism that has the premise of the episyllogism as its conclusion.[51]

§ 88. Sorites or Chain of Syllogisms

A syllogism consisting of several abridged syllogisms joined with one another in one conclusion is called a *sorites* or *chain of conclusions,* which may be either progressive or regressive, according as one moves up from proximate grounds to more distant ones, or down from more distant grounds to proximate ones.

§ 89. Categorical and Hypothetical Sorites

The progressive as well as regressive sorites again can be *categorical* or *hypothetical.* The former consists of *categorical propositions* as a series of predicates; the latter of *hypothetical propositions* as a series of consequents.

§ 90. Fallacious Syllogism/Paralogism/Sophism

A syllogism that is false as to form, though it has the semblance of a correct one, is called a fallacious syllogism (*fallacia*). Such a syllogism is a *paralogism,* in so far as one deludes oneself by it; a *sophism,* in so far as one deliberately tries to delude others by it.

51. Cf. B 387f.

Note. The ancients busied themselves with the art of contriving sophisms. Therefore many of this kind have appeared, e.g. the *sophisma figurae dictionis,* in which the *medius terminus* is taken in different meanings; *fallacia a dicto secundum quid ad dictum simpliciter; sophisma heterozeteseos, elenchi, ignorationis,* and the like.

§ 91. Saltus in Concluding

A saltus in concluding or proving is the connection of one premise with the conclusion, so that the other premise is omitted. Such a jump to a conclusion is *legitimate,* when everybody can readily add the missing premise in thought; *illegitimate,* however, if the subsumption is not clear. Here a distant characteristic is connected with a thing without any intermediate characteristic (*nota intermedia*).

§ 92. Petitio principii/circulus in probando

By petitio principii one understands the assumption of a proposition as an immediately certain proposition for serving as a ground of proof, although it is in need of a proof. One commits a circle in proving, when the proposition one wanted to prove is underlying one's *own* proof.

Note. The circle in proving is often difficult to discover, and this mistake is committed most frequently where proofs are difficult.

§ 93. Probatio plus et minus probans

A proof can prove *too much* but also *too little.* In the *latter* case it proves only part of what shall be proved; in the *former* it appertains also to what is false.

Note. A proof that proves too little can be true and is thus unobjectionable. If, however, it proves too much, it proves more than is true, and this then is false. The proof against suicide, for example, that he who has not given himself his life is not allowed to take it, proves too much, since for that reason we would not be allowed to kill animals either. It is therefore false.

II. General Doctrine of Method

§ 94. Mode and Method

All cognition, and any whole of cognition, must conform to a rule. (Lack of rules is irrationalism.) The rule, however, is either that of *mode*[52] (free) or of *method* (constraint).

§ 95. Form of Science—Method

Cognition as a science must be organized after a method. For science is a whole of cognition as a system and not merely an aggregate. It therefore requires a systematic cognition drawn up according to deliberate rules.

§ 96. Doctrine of Method—Its Object and End

Just as the doctrine of elements in logic has the elements and conditions of the perfection of a cognition as its content, so on the other hand the general doctrine of method, as the second part of logic, has to deal with the form of a science as such, or with the manner of connecting the manifold of cognition into a science.[53]

§ 97. Means of Developing the Logical Perfection of Cognition

The doctrine of method is to put forward the manner of attaining perfection of cognition. Now, one of the most essential logical perfections of cognition consists in distinctness, in

---

52. *Manier.* Cf. Akad. xvi, 3326: "*Modus,* mode [*die manier*], is distinguished from *methodo* in that the latter is a modus out of principles, the former out of empirical grounds."

53. The General Doctrine of Method of the *Logic* has the same fundamental content, namely the structure of a science, as the Transcendental Doctrine of Method of the *Critique of Pure Reason.*

thoroughness, and in its systematic arrangement into the whole of a science. Accordingly, the doctrine of method will primarily have to state the means of furthering these perfections of cognition.

§ 98. Conditions of the Distinctness of Cognition

Distinctness of cognitions and joining them into a systematic whole depends on distinctness of concepts both in respect of what is contained *in* them and in regard to what is contained *under* them.

The distinct consciousness of the *intension* of concepts is furthered by their *exposition* and *definition;* the distinct consciousness, however, of their *extension,* by their *logical division.* First, then, more about the means of furthering distinctness of concepts *in respect of their intension.*

I. Development of Logical Perfection in Cognition by Definition, Exposition, and Description of Concepts

§ 99. Definition

A definition is a sufficiently distinct and delimited [precise] concept (*conceptus rei adaequatus in minimis terminis; complete determinatus*).

Note. The definition alone is to be considered as a logically complete and perfect concept, for in it the two most essential perfections of a concept are united: distinctness, and, with distinctness, completeness and precision (quantity of distinctness).

§ 100. Analytic and Synthetic Definition

All definitions are either analytic or synthetic. The former are definitions of a *given,* the latter of a *made* concept.

§ 101. Given and Made Concepts, a priori and a posteriori

The given concepts of an analytic definition are given either a priori or a posteriori just as the made concepts of a synthetic definition are made either a priori or a posteriori.

§ 102. Synthetic Definitions Through Exposition or Construction

The synthesis of made concepts from which spring synthetic definitions is either that of *exposition* (of the appearances) or that of *construction*. The latter is the synthesis of *arbitrarily* [freely] made concepts, the former the synthesis of empirically made concepts, that is, of concepts made out of given appearances as their matter (*conceptus factitii vel a priori vel per synthesin empiricam*). Arbitrarily made concepts are the *mathematical*.

Note. All definitions of mathematical and also of experiential concepts—provided that, for empirical concepts, definitions could take place at all—must thus be made synthetically. For even with concepts of the latter kind, e.g. the empirical concepts "water," "fire," "air," and the like, I shall not analyze what lies *in* them but learn through experience what belongs *to* them. All empirical concepts must thus be considered as made concepts, whose synthesis, however, is not arbitrary but empirical.[54]

§ 103. Impossibility of Empirically Synthetic Definitions

Since the synthesis of empirical concepts is not arbitrary but empirical and as such can never be complete (for in experience ever new characteristics of the concept can be discovered), empirical concepts cannot be defined.

Note. Thus only arbitrarily made concepts can be defined synthetically. Such definitions of arbitrarily made concepts, which are not only always possible but also necessary and must precede anything said by means of an arbitrarily made concept, could also be called *declarations,* since in them one declares one's thoughts or renders account of what one understands by a word. This is the case with *mathematicians*.

---

54. Not construction but (empirical) exposition. See below, § 105.

§ 104. Analytic Definitions by Analysis of a priori or a posteriori Given Concepts

All *given* concepts, be they given a priori or a posteriori, can only be defined through *analysis*. For given concepts can only be made distinct by making their characteristics successively clear. If *all* characteristics of a given concept are made clear, the concept becomes *completely* distinct; and if it does not contain too many characteristics, it is at the same time precise, and from this springs a definition of the concept.

Note. Since one cannot become certain by any proof whether all characteristics of a given concept have been exhausted by complete analysis, all analytic definitions must be held to be uncertain.

§ 105. Expositions and Descriptions

Not all concepts *can*, but also not all *need* to be defined. There are approximations to the definition of certain concepts; these are partly *expositions* (*expositiones*), partly *descriptions* (*descriptiones*).

The *exposition* of a concept consists in the connecting (successive) presentation of its characteristics so far as these have been found by analysis.

The *description* is the exposition of a concept so far as it is not precise.

Note 1. We can expound either a *concept* or *experience*. The first takes place through analysis, the second through synthesis.[55]

Note 2. Exposition thus takes place only with *given* concepts, which are made distinct by it;[56] it thereby differs from the *declaration*, which is a distinct presentation of *made* concepts.

As it is not always possible to make an analysis complete,

---

55. See above, § 102.

56. This is analytic exposition *of concepts,* as against the synthetic exposition of appearances in § 102 above.

and since, generatim, an analysis must be incomplete before it becomes complete, also an incomplete exposition as part of a definition is a true and useful exhibition of a concept. Here the definition always remains only the idea of a logical perfection that we must seek to attain.

Note 3. Description can take place only with empirically given concepts. It has no definite rules and contains only materials for definition.

§ 106. Nominal and Real Definitions

By mere *explanations of the name* or *nominal definitions* are to be understood those which contain the meaning arbitrarily assigned to a certain name, and which therefore designate only the logical essence of their object, or merely serve to distinguish it from other objects. *Material explanations*[57] or real definitions, on the other hand, are those which are sufficient for a cognition of the object as to its inner determinations by setting forth the possibility of the object out of inner characteristics.

Note 1. If a concept is internally sufficient to distinguish the thing, it is certainly also externally so; if, however, it is not internally sufficient, it can be externally sufficient only in a *certain relation,* namely in comparing the definitum with others. However, the *unlimited* external sufficiency is not possible without the inner.

Note 2. Objects of experience admit of nominal definitions only. Logical nominal definitions of given concepts of the understanding are taken from an attribute; real definitions, however, from the essence of the thing, the first ground of possibility. The latter therefore contain what always appertains to the thing—its real essence. Merely *negative* definitions cannot be called real definitions, because negative characteristics may serve to distinguish a thing from another just as well as affirmative characteristics, but not to cognize the thing as to its inner possibility.

In matters of morality it is always real definitions that must be sought; all our striving must be directed to this.—There

---

57. *Sach-Erklärungen.*

are real definitions in mathematics, for the definition of an arbitrarily made concept is always *real*.[58]

Note 3. A definition is *genetic* if it gives a concept through which the object can be exhibited *a priori in concreto;* such are all mathematical definitions.[59]

§ 107. Main Requirements of Definitions

The essential and general requirements belonging to the perfection of a definition may be considered under the four chief moments of quantity, quality, relation, and modality.

1) As to *quantity*—concerning the sphere of the definition—the definition and the definitum must be *reciprocal concepts* (*conceptus reciproci*) and thus the definition must be neither *wider* nor *narrower* than its definitum;

2) as to *quality,* the definition must be a *complete* and at the same time *precise* concept;

3) as to *relation,* it must not be *tautological;* i.e. the characteristics of the definitum, as *grounds of its cognition,* must be different from the definitum itself; and, lastly,

4) as to *modality,* the characteristics must be *necessary* and thus not be such as accede through experience.

Note. The condition that the concept of the genus and the concept of the specific difference (*genus* and *differentia specifica*) shall make up the definition is valid only in respect of nominal definitions in a *comparison,* but not for real definitions in *derivation.*

§ 108. Rules for Testing of Definitions

In testing definitions, four acts are to be carried out: It is to be investigated whether the definition, considered

1) as a proposition, is *true;*

2) as a concept, is *distinct;*

3) as a distinct concept, is *complete,* and, lastly,

4) as a complete concept, is at the same time *determinate,* i.e. adequate to the thing itself.

---

58. Because here the (a priori) object arises together with the (synthetic) concept. See B ix f., 743 f., 757 f.

59. "Genetic" here refers to the genesis of a construction.

§ 109. Rules for Preparing Definitions

The very same acts that belong to the testing of definitions are to be carried out also in their making. To that end, therefore, seek (1) true propositions, (2) such propositions as do not already presuppose the concept of the thing in their predicate, (3) collect several of them and compare each of them with the concept of the matter itself to see whether it is adequate, and, lastly, (4) see whether one characteristic does not lie in another or is not subordinate to it.

Note 1. As is probably understood without a reminder, these rules are valid only of analytic definitions. Since here one can never be certain whether the analysis has been complete, one may set up the definition on trial only and avail oneself of it only as if it were not a definition. Under this restriction one may yet use it as a distinct and true concept and draw corollaries from the characteristics of this concept. I am permitted to say: If the concept of the definitum appertains to something, the definition also appertains to it; but not conversely, since the definition does not exhaust the entire definitum.

Note 2. To avail oneself of the concept of the definitum in the explanation or to presuppose the definitum in the definition is called explaining through a *circle* (*circulus in definiendo*).

II. Development of Perfection in Cognition Through Logical Division of Concepts

§ 110. Concept of Logical Division

Every concept contains a manifold *under* it in so far as the manifold agrees, but also in so far as it is different. The determination of a concept in respect of everything possible contained under it, so far as the elements are opposed to one another, i.e. differ from one another, is called the *logical division of the* concept. The higher concept is called the *divided concept* (*divisum*), and the lower concepts are called the *members of the division* (*membra dividentia*).

Note 1. To dissect a concept and *to divide* it are two very different things. In dissecting the concept I see what is contained *in* it (through analysis); in dividing it I consider what is contained *under* it. Here I divide the sphere of the concept, not the concept itself. The division, far from dissecting the concept, rather adds to it through its members, for they contain more within them than does the concept.

Note 2. We move up from lower to higher concepts, and afterwards can again move down from higher to lower ones —by division.

§ 111. General Rules of Logical Division

In every division of a concept it is to be heeded that

    1) the members of the division exclude or are opposed to one another; further,

    2) they belong under a higher concept (*conceptum communem*) and, lastly,

    3) they all together make up the sphere of the divided concept or are equal to it.

Note. The members of the division must be separated from one another by *contradiction,* not by mere contrariness.

§ 112. Co-division and Subdivision

Different divisions of a concept made in different respects are called co-divisions; and the division of the members of a division is called *subdivision* (*subdivisio*).

Note 1. Subdivision may be continued to infinity; comparatively, however, it may be finite. Co-division, particularly with experiential concepts, also goes to infinity, for who can exhaust all relations of concepts?

Note 2. As one may call *co-division* also a division according to difference of concepts of the same object (viewpoints), so one may call *subdivision* a division of the viewpoints themselves.

§ 113. Dichotomy and Polytomy

A division into two members is called *dichotomy;* if, however, it has more than two members, it is called *polytomy.*

Note 1. All polytomy is empirical; dichotomy is the only division out of principles *a priori*—thus the only *primary* division. For the members of the division shall be opposed to one another, and the opposite of every *A* is indeed nothing more than a *non A.*

Note 2. Polytomy cannot be taught in logic, for *cognition of the object* belongs to it. Dichotomy needs only the *proposition of contradiction,* without knowing the concept one wants to divide as to content. Polytomy needs *intuition,* either *a priori,* as in mathematics (e.g. the division of conic sections), or *empirical* intuition, in describing nature. Yet, the division out of the *principle of synthesis a priori* has [the characteristics of] *trichotomy,* namely (1) the concept as the condition, (2) the conditioned, and (3) the deduction of the latter from the former.[60]

§ 114. Various Divisions of Method

Concerning the *method* itself in treating of, and working at, scientific cognitions, we can state several main methods according to the following division.

§ 115. 1. Scientific and Popular Method

The *scientific* or *scholastic* method is distinguished from the *popular* method by starting from fundamental or elementary propositions, whereas the latter starts from the *ordinary* or *interesting.* The former is directed to *thoroughness* and therefore eliminates anything foreign; the latter aims at *entertainment.*

Note. These two methods thus are distinguished as to *kind,* and not only as to manner of presentation; and popularity in method is thus something different from popularity in presentation.[61]

---

60. See *Critique of Judgment,* Introduction, last note.
61. See above, Introduction, V, p. 42; VI, p. 52.

§ 116. 2. Systematic or Fragmentary Method

The systematic method is opposed to the *fragmentary* or *rhapsodic* method. When one has thought according to a method and then expressed this method and distinctly stated the transition from one proposition to the next, then one has treated a cognition systematically. When one has thought, however, according to a method, but not organized the presentation methodically, then such a method is to be called *rhapsodic*.[62]

Note. As the *systematic* presentation is opposed to the *fragmentary,* so is the *methodical* presentation to the *tumultuary.* He who thinks methodically, can be systematic or fragmentary in his presentation. The externally fragmentary, though in itself methodical presentation, is *aphoristic*.

§ 117. 3. Analytic and Synthetic Method

The *analytic* method is opposed to the *synthetic* method. The former begins with the conditioned and with what is grounded and goes on to principles (*a principiatis ad principia*); the latter goes from principles to consequents, or from the simple to the composite. As the first could be called the *regressive* method, so the latter could be called the *progressive* method.

Note. The analytic method is also called the method of *discovery*.[63] For the purpose of popularity the analytic method is more suitable, for the purpose of scientific and systematic elaboration of cognition, however, the synthetic method.[64]

§ 118. 4. Syllogistic—Tabular Method

The syllogistic method is that method by which a science is presented in a chain of syllogisms.

Tabular is called that method by which an already finished doctrinal edifice is presented in its entire context.

§ 119. 5. Akroamatic and Erotematic Method

Akroamatic is the method in so far as one merely teaches;

---

62. See B 106, 860.
63. *Erfindung.*
64. See B 395, 758; *Prolegomena,* Preface, last paragraph, and § 5, note.

erotematic, in so far as one also questions. The latter method again may be divided into the *dialogic* or *Socratic* and the *catechetic,* according as questions are directed either at the *understanding* or merely at *memory.*

Note. Erotematically one cannot teach otherwise than by *Socratic Dialogue,* in which both teacher and pupil ask and must mutually answer, so that it seems as if the disciple were also the teacher. For the Socratic dialogue teaches through questions, making the apprentice cognizant of his own principles of reason and sharpening his attention to them. Through common *catechizing,* however, one cannot teach but only examine what one has taught akroamatically. The catechetic method therefore is valid only for empirical and historical cognitions, the dialogic method, however, for rational cognitions.

§ 120. Meditating

By meditating is to be understood deliberating or *methodical thinking.* Meditating must accompany all reading and learning; and that requires *first* making preliminary investigations and *then* ordering one's thoughts or connecting them by a method.

Index of Passages in Kant's Writings to which Reference is Made in the Notes

A Roman numeral following the title refers to the volume of the Academy edition, whose page number for the passage is given in the left-hand column, except for passages from the *Prolegomena* and *The Critique of Judgment* which are listed by paragraph number, and the *Reflections,* in which each Reflection is listed by its individual number. Reference to passages from the *Critique of Pure Reason* is to A (first edition) and B (second edition) followed by original page numbers, which are given in most editions and translations of the work. The right-hand column gives the page number in the present book.

The Mistaken Subtlety of the Four Syllogistic Figures—II (1762)

	45 ff.	120
	57	xliii, xliv

Inquiry on the Distinctness of the Principles of Natural Theology and Morality—II (1764)

Second Consideration

		xvi
	276	xxxiv
	277	xxxiv, cviii
	278 f.	cii
	284	cii
	291	cii, cx
	292	cxiv
	310 f.	xxii

Critique of Pure Reason (1781, 2d ed. 1786)

A	10	37
	105	126
	107	99
	113	126
	122	cii
	241	xxxv

Index of Names

Abbott, T. K., ix
d'Alembert, J. le Rond, 48
Ancients, the, 51, 87
Antonius, 35
Arcesilaus, 35
Aristotle, 8, 23, 31, 34, 36

Bacon, Francis, 36
Bardili, Ch. G., 11, 12
Baumgarten, A. G., 17, 24
Beck, I. J., lxivn, lxvn
Beck, L. W., xlvin
Bolyai, J., xcix
de Brahe, T., 93
Buchdahl, G., lxxxii, lxxxiii, lxxxivn
Burtt, E. A., lviin

Cantor, G., cxvn
Carneades, 35
Cassirer, E., xxn, lixn, lxn, cxivn
Chrysippus, 34
Cicero, 35, 52
Cleanthes, 34
Cohen, H., cv
Copernicus, N., 93
Crusius, Chr. A., 24

Descartes, René, xx, xxii, lix, lx–lxvii,
    lxviii, lxix, xciii, xcvi, xcviii, cv, cvii,
    cxiv, cxv, 36
Duhem, P., cix

Eberhard, J. A., lxx
Epictetus, 35
Epicurus, 34
Ewing, A. C., xxxiv, xxxviin

Faraday, M., lvn
Fichte, J. G., 9n
Fischer, K., xlvn
Frank, Ph., lviii

Galileo, lvii ff, xcvi, cvii, cxv
Gauss, F., 21n

Gewirth, A., xxxixn

Hartman, Robert S., xxin, xcixn, cvin
Heinze, M., vii
Hertz, M., xxxvi
Hilbert, D., cxvn
Home, H., 17
Horace, 52
Hume, D., lviii, 52
Husserl, E., 46n

Jacob, L. H., 8
Jasche, Gottlob Benjamin, viii, ix
Jørgensen, J., xxxixn, xlin

Körner, St., xxn, xcvi

Lambert, J. H., lxvi, lxxiin, cxiv, 23
Laplace, P. S., lvii
Lavoisier, A. L., lviii
Leibniz, G., xx, lix, lxvii–lxxvii, xciii,
    xcvi, xcviii, cv, cviii, cxv, 24, 36
Leonard, H. S., xxin
Lobachevski, N. I., xcix
Locke, J., 24, 36
Lucas, P. G., xiii
Luria, A. R., cxii, cxiii

Mach, E., lvi, xcixn
Mahnke, D., lxix
Malebranche, N., 24
Marc-Wogau, K., xxiv, xlviiin, lin
Martin, G., lxx, cii, ciii, civn, cviin,
    cixn, cxivn, cxvn
Meier, G. F., 5, 24, 55n

Newton, I., xvi, lv–lx, xciv, xcvi, ciii,
    cxv, 37

Paton, H. J., xln, xlvin, xlvii, xlviiin,
    lxviin, lxxivn, ciin
Pherecydes, 32
Plato, lxi, 34, 35
Plinius the Elder, 35
Port Royal, logic of, xx

157

Index of Subjects

The German expression for the following principal concepts is in many instances the same as the English word, except for ending or orthography. Occasionally there is complete identity. Only where the corresponding German word has a different root, it is given in parentheses.

29-103